Design, Implementation, and Analysis of Next Generation Optical Networks:

Emerging Research and Opportunities

Waqas Ahmed Imtiaz
University of Engineering and Technology Peshawar – Jalozai, Pakistan

Rastislav Róka
Slovak University of Technology in Bratislava, Slovakia

A volume in the Advances in
Wireless Technologies and
Telecommunication (AWTT) Book
Series

Published in the United States of America by
    IGI Global
    Information Science Reference (an imprint of IGI Global)
    701 E. Chocolate Avenue
    Hershey PA, USA 17033
    Tel: 717-533-8845
    Fax: 717-533-8661
    E-mail: cust@igi-global.com
    Web site: http://www.igi-global.com

Library of Congress Cataloging-in-Publication Data

Names: Imtiaz, Waqas Ahmed, 1985- editor. | Roka, Rastislav, 1972- editor.
Title: Design, implementation, and analysis of next generation optical
  networks : emerging research and opportunities / Waqas Ahmed Imtiaz and
  Rastislav Roka, editors.
Description: Hershey, PA : Information Science Reference, an imprint of IGI
  Global, [2020] | Includes bibliographical references and index.
Identifiers: LCCN 2019009419| ISBN 9781522597674 (hardcover) | ISBN
  9781522597681 (softcover) | ISBN 9781522597698 (ebook)
Subjects: LCSH: Optical fiber communication.
Classification: LCC TK5103.592.F52 D47 2020 | DDC 621.39/81--dc23 LC record available at
https://lccn.loc.gov/2019009419

This book is published in the IGI Global book series Advances in Wireless Technologies and Telecommunication (AWTT) (ISSN: 2327-3305; eISSN: 2327-3313)

British Cataloguing in Publication Data
A Cataloguing in Publication record for this book is available from the British Library.

For electronic access to this publication, please contact: eresources@igi-global.com.

Advances in Wireless Technologies and Telecommunication (AWTT) Book Series

ISSN:2327-3305
EISSN:2327-3313

Editor-in-Chief: Xiaoge Xu, University of Nottingham Ningbo China, China

MISSION

The wireless computing industry is constantly evolving, redesigning the ways in which individuals share information. Wireless technology and telecommunication remain one of the most important technologies in business organizations. The utilization of these technologies has enhanced business efficiency by enabling dynamic resources in all aspects of society.

The **Advances in Wireless Technologies and Telecommunication Book Series** aims to provide researchers and academic communities with quality research on the concepts and developments in the wireless technology fields. Developers, engineers, students, research strategists, and IT managers will find this series useful to gain insight into next generation wireless technologies and telecommunication.

COVERAGE

- Digital Communication
- Grid Communications
- Broadcasting
- Wireless Sensor Networks
- Virtual Network Operations
- Wireless Technologies
- Cellular Networks
- Network Management
- Mobile Communications
- Radio Communication

IGI Global is currently accepting manuscripts for publication within this series. To submit a proposal for a volume in this series, please contact our Acquisition Editors at Acquisitions@igi-global.com or visit: http://www.igi-global.com/publish/.

Titles in this Series

For a list of additional titles in this series, please visit:
https://www.igi-global.com/book-series/advances-wireless-technologies-telecommunication/73684

Handbook of Research on the IoT, Cloud Computing, and Wireless Network Optimization
Surjit Singh (National Institute of Technology Kurukshetra, India) and Rajeev Mohan Sharma
(National Institute of Technology Kurukshetra, India)
Engineering Science Reference • ©2019 • 563pp • H/C (ISBN: 9781522573357) • US $425.00

Recent Advances in Satellite Aeronautical Communications Modeling
Andrii Mikhailovich Grekhov (National Aviation University, Ukraine)
Engineering Science Reference • ©2019 • 313pp • H/C (ISBN: 9781522582144) • US $225.00

Strategic Innovations and Interdisciplinary Perspectives in Telecommunications and ...
Natarajan Meghanathan (Jackson State University, USA)
Information Science Reference • ©2019 • 348pp • H/C (ISBN: 9781522581888) • US $195.00

Next-Generation Wireless Networks Meet Advanced Machine Learning Applications
Ioan-Sorin Comşa (Brunel University London, UK) and Ramona Trestian (Middlesex
University, UK)
Information Science Reference • ©2019 • 356pp • H/C (ISBN: 9781522574583) • US $195.00

Paving the Way for 5G Through the Convergence of Wireless Systems
Ramona Trestian (Middlesex University, UK) and Gabriel-Miro Muntean (Dublin City
University, Ireland)
Information Science Reference • ©2019 • 350pp • H/C (ISBN: 9781522575702) • US $195.00

Enabling Technologies and Architectures for Next-Generation Networking Capabilities
Mahmoud Elkhodr (Central Queensland University, Australia)
Information Science Reference • ©2019 • 384pp • H/C (ISBN: 9781522560234) • US $195.00

Mobile Devices and Smart Gadgets in Human Rights
Sajid Umair (National University of Sciences and Technology (NUST), Pakistan) and
Muhammad Yousaf Shah (Ministry of Human Rights, Pakistan)
Information Science Reference • ©2019 • 304pp • H/C (ISBN: 9781522569398) • US $195.00

For an entire list of titles in this series, please visit:
https://www.igi-global.com/book-series/advances-wireless-technologies-telecommunication/73684

701 East Chocolate Avenue, Hershey, PA 17033, USA
Tel: 717-533-8845 x100 • Fax: 717-533-8661
E-Mail: cust@igi-global.com • www.igi-global.com

Table of Contents

Chapter 5

*Muhammad Ishaq, Pakistan Institute of Research and Development,
    Pakistan*
Mohammad Kaleem, COMSATS University – Islamabad, Pakistan
Numan Kifayat, KAIST, South Korea

Preface

With the ever-growing applications of Internet, the associated data traffic demand in both fixed and mobile networks is increasing dramatically. Consequently, the network operators need to migrate the existing optical networks towards next generation solutions. However, an optical network migration requires enormous investment in equipment and infrastructure at a cost sensitive domain. Therefore, one of the main challenges for network operators is to find out a proper cost-effective next generation optical network solution that can match future high capacity demands in terms of data, reach and a number of subscribers, and flexibly support multiple network services on a common network infrastructure. The passive optical network is anticipated as the most promising low-cost solution for the implementation of next generation solutions. The adaptability of passive optical networks requires a suitable network architecture employing low cost equipment, flexibility of implementation, suitable access and multiplexing techniques, etc., along with the support for the migration and emerging applications at both wired and wireless media. This book provides a platform to discuss the next generation of high capacity optical networks in terms of design, implementation and analysis, and offers a reference of technology solutions for next generation optical networks.

For next generation optical networks, the key factor is providing a seamless, ultra-high bandwidth at extended reach. However, an adaptability of such networks requires a complete architecture that uses cost-effective solutions. This book aims to provide a comprehensive insight about requirements for high capacity next generation optical networks and address different technologies along with passive optical networks. This book helps in understanding the basic requirements, techniques and methods for designing, implementing and analyzing feasible next generation optical networks. The book is a

useful resource for researchers, engineers, scientists and students interested in emerging research and opportunities related to next generation optical networks.

The target audiences of the book *Design, Implementation, and Analysis of Next Generation Optical Networks: Emerging Research and Opportunities* are professionals, researchers, students and scientists interested in working on optical networks in terms of their design, implementation, analysis and applications.

The book will cover important aspects of the emerging research and opportunities in this multi-technology multi-user environment with the main focus on the design, implementation and analysis problems in next generation optical networks. It presents various approaches and adaptive techniques identifying the main research issues and challenges and presents a survey of the proposed solutions in the literature.

The manuscript is structured in one section. This section describes the current environment which leads towards the next generation of optical networks. It includes important chapters written by researchers from prestigious laboratories from Slovakia, Canada, Pakistan, India and South Korea which present the current state of the art in the heterogeneous optical and wireless communication environment including resource allocation of wavelengths, multi-access edge computing, integrated circuit and hardware prototypes, performance analysis and intra data center challenges, ensuring optical power budget optimization, best experience of applications, smart cities and data center networks, interference mitigation, wireless and fiber optics convergence, etc. The section consists of five chapters. A brief description of each of the chapters in this section is given below:

Chapter 1 identifies wavelength allocation and scheduling methods in wavelength division multiplexing-passive optical networks with securing of the traffic protection. First, principles of wavelength allocation and scheduling methods are summarized. Specifically, the static wavelength allocations without and with constraints are characterized. Then, the dynamic wavelength allocations including the offline, online and hybrid wavelength scheduling are presented together with groups of allocated wavelengths. Subsequently, different designs of wavelength division multiplexing-passive optical networks with traffic protection securing are analyzed and compared. Mentioned network designs are considered with different passive optical components. For presented network designs, possible capabilities related to utilized technologies and their abilities are considered. Moreover, protection

possibilities for various network parts and elements are characterized and optical power budgets for a considered network design are evaluated and optimized. Finally, a deployment of dynamic wavelength allocation algorithms for the selected wavelength division multiplexing-passive optical network design is introduced and functionalities of the offline and online wavelength scheduling are considered.

Chapter 2 highlights the performance gains obtained by the decentralization of computation resources using a proposed hierarchical cooperative computation offloading in multi-access edge computing enabled fiber-wireless enhanced heterogeneous networks, which relies not only on the computational capabilities of edge/cloud servers but also on the limited local computing resources at the device side. More specifically, a two-tier architecture, where the mobile devices as well as the edge servers cooperatively offload their computation tasks towards achieving a reduced average response time, is designed. Limitations stemming from both communications and computation via accurate modeling of the fronthaul/backhaul as well as edge/cloud servers, while paying particular attention to the offloading decision, are taking into account in a design approach. Next, fiber-wireless access networks in the context of conventional clouds and emerging cloudlets, thereby highlighting the limitations of centralized cloud radio access network in light of future 5G networks moving toward decentralization based on cloudlets and multi-access edge computing, are revisited. A proposed hierarchical cooperative computing scheme for fiber-wireless enhanced heterogeneous networks, which leverages on a two-level non-local computing hierarchy as well as local computing to obtain a reduced response time in a cooperative manner, is presented. Finally, an analytical framework for estimating the energy-delay performance of our proposed cooperative task offloading scheme and numerical results are presented.

Chapter 3 introduces the light fidelity as a relatively new subclass under the larger umbrella of visible light communication that presents one of the possible solutions suggested to problems providing infrastructure to each cell and increased power consumptions in wireless communication networks. Most of the related research available is simulation based. However, some prototypes have been developed on various platforms that shall be discussed later in this chapter. Designers have implemented prototype transceivers on microcontrollers, integrated circuits, Raspberry Pi and Arduino using a range of physical layer devices from expensive light-emitting diode packages including drive circuits to cheap off the shelf devices. A visible light

communication mostly deals with the physical implementation of optical wireless communications. However, for such system capable of complimenting the existing wireless networks and providing significant spectrum relief, a full network solution is required. This is what we call the light fidelity. The idea is to use the existing light-emitting diode lights available for illumination, for the purpose of data transfer.

Chapter 4 analyzes a free space optical or optical wireless communication as an emerging technology that transmits data wirelessly under free space using the laser beam in the line of sight connectivity. Free-space optical links can serve as a promising alternative to the conventional fiber optic cables used for backhaul links. Recent developments of optical technology have advanced a free space optical communication to make it an alternative to a radio-frequency wireless communication. First, advantages and disadvantages of the free space optical communication are in detail introduced. Next, atmospheric turbulences induced free space optical channels are analyzed from a viewpoint of the channel characterization. Also, statistical models for turbulence induced fading channel are analyzed and modulation techniques for optical wireless are presented. Subsequently, a spatial diversity in fading channels is characterized for mitigating the turbulence effects. Finally, various forms of the cooperative transmission are considered for improving the free space optical link performance.

Chapter 5 explores challenges in intra data center networks. A function of intra data center networks is allowing resilient, high bit-rate and low-latency communications between the data center computing and storage resources. This is a critical task since a failure (or congestion) in the network would degrade the performance of the connections or directly block them. If this happens, the outcome (from the user's point of view) is the same as if the computing or storage resources were down since his request cannot be attended. Therefore, the currently deployed intra data center network architecture is analyzed in order to determine if it will be able to meet the requirements for future intra data center networks. For solving drawbacks of the current architecture, several optical architectures including transparent optical networks, optical circuit switching and optical packet switching are discussed for intra data center networks. In order to achieve goals of future intra data center networks, several optical architectures have been proposed and technical details of such architectures and their scalability drawbacks are introduced. Finally, features and characteristics for existing solutions of intra data center architectures are summarized.

The prospective audience of this book is mainly the undergraduate students, postgraduate students, and researchers who are interested in learning more about emerging research and opportunities in the area of next generation optical network communications. It also targets industry professionals who are working or are interested in this area, providing them with a reference of the latest efforts which bring the research further by addressing some of the shortcomings of the existing solutions.

Design, Implementation, and Analysis of Next Generation Optical Networks: Emerging Research and Opportunities is published by the IGI Global. For additional information regarding the publisher, please visit www.igi-global. com.

The editors hope that beginners and professionals in the field would benefit by going through the details given in the chapters of this book. We wish you a pleasant reading.

Rastislav Róka
Slovak University of Technology in Bratislava, Slovakia

Waqas Ahmed Imtiaz
University of Engineering and Technology Peshawar – Jalozai, Pakistan

Chapter 1
Wavelength Allocation and Scheduling Methods for Various WDM–PON Network Designs With Traffic Protection Securing

Rastislav Róka

(iD) https://orcid.org/0000-0001-9767-9547

Slovak University of Technology in Bratislava, Slovakia

ABSTRACT

The wavelength division multiplexing passive optical network (WDM-PON) is a natural path forward to satisfy demands of optical network operators to develop valuable converged optical metropolitan and access networks. For effective utilization of possible transmission capacities, available wavelengths must be carefully designed for their utilization. Therefore, some principles of wavelength allocation and scheduling methods are characterized and specified. For ensuring the network reliability, efficient traffic protection mechanisms must be implemented. Simultaneously, different equipment in remote nodes can be installed. Therefore, different WDM-PON network designs with traffic protection securing are analyzed and compared. Protection possibilities for various network parts and elements are characterized and optical power budgets are evaluated and optimized. Finally, a research of the DWA algorithms can be realized using functionalities of selected wavelength scheduling methods. Moreover, the wavelength transmission capacity characterizing can be simultaneously determined.

DOI: 10.4018/978-1-5225-9767-4.ch001

INTRODUCTION

In the design of optical telecommunication networks, it is necessary to take into account various parameters and characteristics, for example network type, utilized technology, distance for the signal transmission, network traffic protection, mutual interconnection between network components, network control and many others (Róka, 2014), (Róka, 2019). The idea for utilizing multiple wavelength channels in metropolitan and access optical networks is well known (Róka, 2003). This chapter is focusing on the realistic design of the Wavelength Division Multiplexing - Passive Optical Network (WDM-PON) from a viewpoint of its interconnecting scheme. First, an in-depth survey of existing methods and algorithms is presented. Subsequently, basics of the main protocol are introduced and main wavelength allocation categories - static and dynamic - are particularly presented. Next, various WDM-PON network designs are analyzed with regard to the traffic protection securing. For this aim, passive optical components are mainly considered and a protection of another control element and access part is characterized. Finally, optical power budget possibilities for various WDM-PON network designs are optimized. Simultaneously, a deployment environment for dynamic wavelength algorithms is introduced and main functionalities of wavelength scheduling techniques are summarized.

There are certain basic variants of WDM-PON architectures (Grobe, 2008), (Róka, 2015) varying in utilization of the wavelength routing - Broadcast-and-Select (B&S), Arrayed Waveguide Grating (AWG), Spectrum Slicing (SS). Except fundamental changes in the Optical Line Terminal (OLT) equipment (WDM transmitters, circulators), real WDM-PON network implementations could include several stages of splitting points, allowing the topology to be scalable with a number of users connected using the Optical Network Terminal (ONT) equipment. There are various approaches that have been proposed for implementing in WDM-PON networks (Abbas, 2016), also different architectural options (Mahloo, 2014) varying in the Remote Node (RN) equipment (power splitter, array wavelength grating) are defined. In presented WDM-PON network designs, an attention is paid to only passive components in the RN location based on extensive utilization.

For current Time Division Multiplexing - Passive Optical Network (TDM-PON) networks, one of main tasks is increasing the effective utilization of the determined transmission capacity on the available wavelength used in the upstream direction of data transmitting. This can be achieved using advanced

dynamic bandwidth allocation algorithms compared to a unified Time Division Multiple Access (TDMA) approach. For near-future WDM-PON networks, a corresponding task is increasing the effective utilization of the transmission capacity on available wavelengths used in both downstream and upstream directions for data transmitting. Investigating appropriate dynamic wavelength allocation algorithms is very difficult and complex process. As its integrated part, a wavelength scheduling process must be carefully designated and analyzed. Therefore, wavelength allocation and scheduling methods must be considered for various WDM-PON network designs before their real implementations. It must be stressed that first and foremost passive optical components are focused. However, a task of active optical components is likewise important. For example, optical sources (light-emitting diodes and lasers) in WDM-PON networks and their resulting performance analysis in terms of improvements as well as limitations is very interesting topic.

The evolution of WDM-PON networks moves toward larger coverage of access areas, higher numbers of users and higher bandwidth per user. Advanced users request a reliable connectivity and network operators expect to provide an uninterrupted access to network services. A substantial requirement is ensuring the network reliability by implementing traffic protection mechanisms. Therefore, it is essential to provide efficient fault management in order to meet network reliability requirements. The benefit of deploying traffic protection mechanisms - significant reduction of the total costs of ownership compared to the unprotected access in all of considered (rural, urban, dense urban) scenarios - at very low increase of infrastructure expenses and large reduction of operational expenditures can be obtained as a consequence of the network reliability performance improvement and the service interruption decrement experienced by users. It can be beneficial either provide traffic protection functionalities at the time of network deployment or at least install a sufficient amount of optical fibers in advance. It can be recommended to provide traffic protection securing as early as possible (Mas Machuca, 2014). Various types of security threats can be appeared in the optical network layer, so several protection procedures and monitoring techniques are used to improve a network attach survivability (Dahan, 2017). For implementing of survivability and recovery techniques in elastic optical networks, many fault recovery events are challenging - a multiple failures recovery, reliability mechanisms in multi-provider multilevel networks and others (Papadimitriou, 2014). Proposed survivable architectures can also be applied to passive optical networks with more than one stage of remote

nodes based on power splitters or other passive optical components (Abbas, 2016). Optical fiber' paths require more attention as compared to other network components in order to ensure a failure-free data transmission. Another approaches for survivability can be more easily install later, even over the network working activity (Róka, 2014), (Róka, 2015), (Róka, 2016), (Róka, 2018). For aims of the application-aware protection in DWDM optical networks, criteria for determining the quality of survivability mechanism can be established and utilized. Two protections - link-based and path-based - can be considered according to a short recovery time and/or a reduced use of resources (Drid, 2011).

It can be shown a clear benefit when a network planning is done with possible traffic protection securing, which leads to a decrease in investment costs. If the protection deployment time is longer, then total capital expenditures are higher. This confirms an importance of the right deployment plan for future passive optical networks (Mahloo, 2014). The impact of optical fiber duplication in different protection architectures is analyzed with regard to its feasibility in passive optical networks (Imtiaz, 2017). The optimization of traffic protection schemes in PON networks is analyzed and traffic protection types with advanced implemented specifications for selected Hybrid Passive Optical Networks (HPON) architectures are evaluated (Róka, 2016). In considered WDM-PON network designs, traffic protection securing is realized above all by optical fiber duplications in both - metropolitan and access - parts of the Optical Distribution Network (ODN) and by a protection of the OLT control element. The OLT control element protection is depending on a location of the backup OLT element. The ODN metropolitan part protection is the most important task because the ring topology is utilized for data traffic from/to all ONT terminals. The traffic protection in the ring topology can be realized by interconnecting various optical fibers into the double-ring or the four-ring in 1+1 or 1:1 operation modes. For the ODN access part protection, a key factor is the tree topology and a number of ONT terminals. In most of cases, this protection type is not very effective and significant.

Amongst other challenges for future next-generation passive optical networks, power saving plays an important role (Abbas, 2016). Further, an optimization of the optical power budget is very important for the accurate functionality of traffic protection schemes. For investigating, the optical power budget analysis in nonlinear optical communication systems utilizing various multi-channel digital techniques for compensation nonlinear impairments (Liga, 2014), (Maher, 2015), (Semrau, 2017) can be very interesting.

Moreover, potential physical-layer security scenarios for current Wavelength Division Multiplexing (WDM) and future Elastic Optical Network (EON) networks are presented (Kapov, 2016). Elastic optical networks present a promising approach for future optical transmission networks. With regard to a protection, various EON architectures and their survivability mechanisms are analyzed (Goscien, 2016). By comparing, a traditional WDM fixed-grid may result in lower efficiency from both spectral occupation and power consumption perspectives and higher flexibility with the EON paradigm is expected. The power consumption is substantially increased in a traditional approach with dedicated resources compared to the unprotected case. An important power reduction can be acquired by adapting transmission link rates to the current required bandwidth and/or wavelength (Lopez, 2012).

This chapter is focused on wavelength allocation and scheduling methods in WDM-PON networks with securing of the traffic protection. First, principles of wavelength allocation and scheduling methods in WDM-PON networks are summarized. Subsequently, different WDM-PON network designs with traffic protection securing are analyzed and compared. For presented network designs, possible capabilities related to utilized technologies and their abilities are considered. Moreover, protection possibilities for various network parts and elements are characterized and optical power budgets for a considered WDM-PON network design are evaluated and optimized.

WAVELENGTH ALLOCATION AND SCHEDULING METHODS IN WDM-PON NETWORKS

In this subchapter, an in-depth survey of various existing bandwidth and wavelength allocation algorithms and schemes for evolved passive optical networks are presented. For a Next-Generation Passive Optical Network (NG-PON), a new Dynamic Wavelength and Bandwidth Allocation (DWBA) scheme that meets the QoS requirements of tactile services via dedicating it upstream wavelengths, and also enables inter-channel statistical multiplexing so as to maximize the network throughput without impairing the QoS requirements for all types of services is presented using OMNET++ (Neaime, 2018). In previous periods, three architectures for the NG-PON were classified. They are called Single-Scheduling Domain (SSD) PON, Multi-Scheduling Domain (MSD) PON, and Wavelength-Agile (WA) PON, and they differ based on how a group of optical network terminals share wavelengths. Existing DWBA schemes for

conventional PON networks can be applied to MSD-PON and SSD-PON, but not WA-PON. This is because the WA-PON is a new architecture with full flexibility where a flexible number of wavelengths can be assigned to one ONT and multiple ONT terminals can transmit at the same time. Therefore, novel DWBA schemes for transmission scheduling in WA-PON networks are developed. Multiple optical network terminals are interconnected through a tree- or ring-based optical distribution network (Wang, 2017). Besides, a DWBA algorithm for the NG-PON to schedule upstream wavelength channels while providing a low average packet delay and catering frame resequencing problem is proposed. An online scheduling framework with gated service grant sizing policy has been demonstrated (Hussain, 2017). Also, an online gated service Dynamic Bandwidth Allocation (DBA) algorithm for NG-PON to assign a flexible number of wavelengths and a dynamic grant size on each upstream wavelength is proposed. The proposed DBA algorithm's performance is evaluated in comparison to the modified-IPACT, the proposed First- Fit DBA and the water-filling-algorithm-based DBA algorithms on networks consisting of the generic tree topology (Hussain, 2018).

Impacts of DWBA algorithms on frame reordering in the NG-PON network is investigated and a DWBA algorithm for mitigating frame reordering without affecting bandwidth utilization is proposed. The theoretical upper bound of a frame-reordered ONU number with the proposed algorithm is analyzed, when ONU units are capable of working on multiple wavelength channels simultaneously (Wang, 2018).

New wavelength allocation and scheduling methods can be realized also for EON networks. The elastic optical network is a novel idea that is targeted at realizing flexible bandwidth allocation according to diverse traffic needs and requirements. A kind of elastic optical access network based on the WDM-PON and the Orthogonal Frequency-Division Multiplexing (OFDM) technology, in which finer bandwidth allocation granularity and a flexible wavelength switch are realized, is proposed. For this case, ONU units and the reconfigurable optical switch module in the optical distributed network are considered (Huang, 2015). Population distribution and migration have increasing influence on traffic distribution in metro elastic optical networks. Based on the traditional routing and spectrum allocation algorithm, which provides end-to-end connection by allocating frequency slot resources in the EON network, algorithms to enhance bandwidth efficiency based on the onion tidal traffic model in EON networks are proposed (Yan, 2018). A novel ring-based WDM-PON network that can efficiently mitigate the optical beat interference noise induced by Rayleigh backscattering is demonstrated.

Only one wavelength is required for each ONU unit by using orthogonal and correlation techniques (Yao, 2017).

Another wavelength allocation and scheduling methods can be considered for other possible future optical networks. Basic dynamic wavelength allocation scenarios for a hybrid wavelength division multiplexing-time division multiple access PON network are presented and analyzed. In this case, optical network terminals are assumed to be color-free, i.e., any wavelength can be assigned to an ONT (Vardakas, 2011). Moreover, a hybrid optical architecture combining path (circuit) and packet switching can be a good candidate for future optical networks because it exploits the best of both worlds. A control dynamic optical wavelength and flow allocation framework, which can dynamically change the ratio of path and packet wavelengths, is presented. A feedback control for estimating the wavelength allocation ratio for varying traffic is proposed. Path/packet integrated network is modeled with as a mesh network (Alparslan, 2017). In an orthogonal frequency-division multiple access passive optical network, a two-dimensional (i.e., subcarriers and time) upstream bandwidth allocation method based on interleaved polling with adaptive cycle time is proposed to guarantee delay performances for time-sensitive services. The OFDMA-PON architecture is considered to be built in a point-to-multipoint topology (Bang, 2013).

For correct operation of the upstream signal transmission in passive optical networks, the main OLT terminal must evaluate requests from all appropriate ONT terminals and manage data traffic using certain control mechanisms. Except correct network design, a traffic management is one of key elements for operation, effectiveness and costs of passive optical networks. For solving of wavelength allocation issues, it is necessary to focus on distribution of control information and on algorithms for evaluating signal transmission from connected ONT terminals (Gutierrez, 2010).

The MPCP Protocol

The Multipoint Control Protocol (MPCP) according to the IEEE 802.3ah standard is utilized for distribution of control information. It means that it doesn't specify any concrete Dynamic Wavelength Allocation (DWA) and/ or Dynamic Bandwidth Allocation (DBA) algorithm, just it transmits control messages between the OLT terminal and appropriate ONT terminals. The MPCP transmission is realized as in Ethernet-based networks by transmitting IP packets, i.e. there are included basic information related to addresses,

packet lengths, applied protocols, check sums and other. For utilizing in WDM networks, the MPCP protocol is extended with some fields in the overhead determined for wavelength management. Transmitted packets from ONT terminals contain information about their readiness for operation and data transmitting, supported wavelengths, a retuning time for other wavelengths, a buffer size for data transmitting and other parameters. Transmitted packets from the OLT terminal contain information evaluated by some algorithm for wavelength allocation, a starting time of data transmitting, a transmission duration, allowable wavelength and other parameters (Kim, 2007), (Gutierrez, 2010).

The MPCP protocol consists of five control messages divided into two detection and operation modes with ONT terminals:

- The automatic detection mode contains three control messages - Register_Req, Register and Register_Ack. Using these control messages, newly connected ONT terminals are detected. First, the OLT terminal determines a time slot where new ONT terminal can be registered and subsequently sends this information to the ONT. Next, an unregistered ONT terminal answers this message with its parameters in the assigned time slot and the OLT terminal adds it into the registration table. Simultaneously, the OLT assigns particular parameters for data transmitting to the ONT.
- The normal mode contains two 64 kB messages - Report and Gate. The Report message includes requests for data transmitting from ONT terminals where a data size is included. The Gate message represents an answer from the OLT terminal where assigned parameters for data transmitting in the closest cycle are transmitted to appropriate ONT terminals.

Transmitted messages with assigned parameters for ONT terminals present results of processing realized by wavelength allocation algorithms in the OLT terminal. There exist two main categories of the wavelength allocation - static and dynamic.

The Static Wavelength Allocation

The Static Wavelength Allocation (SWA) presents a group of algorithms that are very simple and undemanding from a viewpoint of creating and operation,

however they are ineffective from a viewpoint of wavelength utilization. In a principle, assigned parameters for data transmitting are tightly (static) defined for particular ONT terminals and they stay unchanged over all the network traffic. It this case, a transmission capacity of allocated wavelengths for the upstream direction is utilized with less efficiency. Algorithms for the static wavelength allocation can be defined without and/or with constraints (Rafiq, 2007).

The Static Wavelength Allocation Without Constraints

At the static wavelength allocation without constraints, a proper/own wavelength is allocated for each ONT terminal for data transmitting in any time and any data size. This wavelength allocation is the most ineffective wavelength utilization and increases traffic and equipment costs simultaneously (Rafiq, 2007). An example for the SWA without constraints is displayed in Figure 1, where each ONT-i terminal is transmitting on its own wavelength TX λ_i.

Figure 1. Example of the static wavelength allocation without constraints

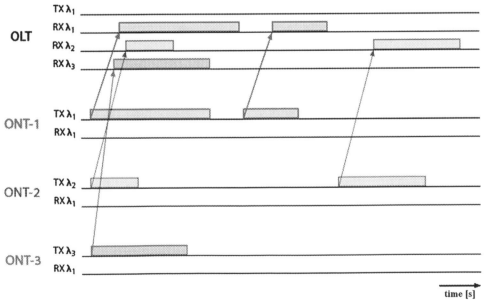

The Static Wavelength Allocation With Constraints

At the static wavelength allocation with constraints, more ONT terminals share the same allocated wavelengths. In this case, each ONT terminal has its own assigned time slot for data transmitting. It means that ONT terminals share the wavelength transmission capacity. This wavelength allocation provides also ineffective wavelength utilization and increases traffic and equipment costs simultaneously, however it is more effective comparing to previous one (Dhaini, 2007). An example for the SWA with constraints is displayed in Figure 2, where ONT-1 and ONT-2 terminals are transmitting on the same wavelength TX λ_1.

The Dynamic Wavelength Allocation

The Dynamic Wavelength Allocation (DWA) presents a group of algorithms that are more complex and demanding from a viewpoint of designing and operation, but they are very effective from a viewpoint of the wavelength utilization. In a principle, assigned parameters for data transmitting accommodate to actual requests from particular ONT terminals. By this way, wavelengths (according to DWA algorithms) and also timeslots (according to

Figure 2. Example of the static wavelength allocation with constraints

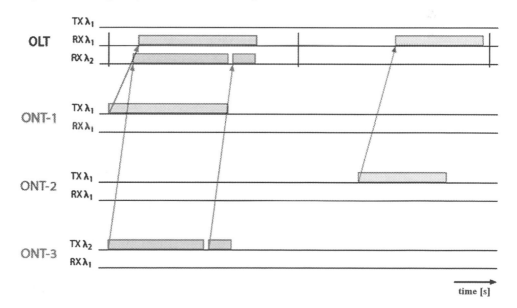

DBA algorithms) are dynamically assigned for particular ONT terminals. In this case, a transmission capacity of allocated wavelengths is utilized in the most efficient way. A hybrid mode for access to the transmission medium combines Wavelength Division Multiplexing (WDM) and Time Division Multiplexing (TDM), respectively Optical TDM (OTDM) techniques. Algorithms for the dynamic wavelength allocation can be integrated using various approaches designed for wavelength scheduling processes (Rafiq, 2007), (Gutierrez, 2010).

The Offline Wavelength Scheduling

- The first step of each DWA algorithm is the initialization state when the OLT termination collects requests for data transmitting from ONT terminals using MPCP messages with information about their readiness for operation and other parameters.
- The next step is the evaluation of the access to the transmission medium for ONT terminals according to defined criteria. For each ONT terminal, the assigned wavelength, the starting time for data transmitting and the broadcasting period are determined. Criteria for preferring ONT terminals are dependent on the data size, different times and delays, priority and importance, eventually on other features characterizing transmitted data or ONT terminals.
- Subsequently, parameters for data transmitting in the first cycle are reported to each ONT terminal and then ONT terminals start data transmitting according to assigned transmission parameters. At the end of each cycle of data transmitting, requests for the next cycle are reported to the OLT terminal.

The offline scheduling consists in a fact that the OLT terminal waits for finish data transmitting in all ONT terminals whereby it determines the overall network state and ONT terminal requests. Subsequently, a decision making about wavelength allocation is executed based on parameters from ONT terminals and a selected strategy, whereby this scheduling makes efforts to ensure the fairest access to the transmission medium and simultaneously the most effective utilization of available wavelengths from a viewpoint of the transmission capacity (Rafiq, 2007), (Gutierrez, 2010). An interval for decision making is called the Inter-Scheduling Cycle Gap (ISCG), it means that a scheduling process is executed in the time period when all ONT terminals are inactive. An example for the DWA with the offline wavelength

Figure 3. Example of the offline wavelength scheduling

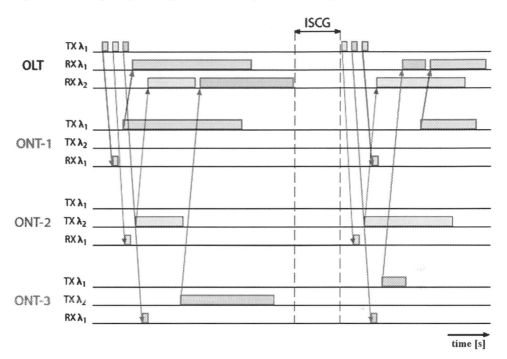

scheduling is displayed in Figure 3, where the ONT-3 terminal is transmitting on different wavelengths TX λ_1 or λ_2.

The Online Wavelength Scheduling

- As in a case of the offline wavelength scheduling, the first step of the online wavelength scheduling is also the initialization state.
- Based on this step, initial parameters are assigned to ONT terminals for data transmitting according to selected strategy. The online scheduling consists in a fact that the OLT terminal makes effort to find the nearest available wavelength possible for allocating to given ONT terminal for data transmitting without collisions. This process is executing immediately after finishing data transmitting of some given ONT terminal and reporting requests for data transmitting in the next cycle. After wards, the nearest available wavelength, the starting time for data transmitting and the broadcasting period are reporting to the ONT

terminal without waiting for finish data transmitting from remaining ONT terminals.

The evaluation process of the data transmitting in the online scheduling works individually with each ONT terminal, i.e. independently on other ONT terminals (Rafiq, 2007), (Gutierrez, 2010). This scheduling is executed in a real time and presents the Next Available Supported Channel (NASC), it means a strategy with supporting the nearest available wavelength. An example for the DWA with the online wavelength scheduling is displayed in Figure 4, where all ONT-i terminals are transmitting on different wavelengths TX λ_1 or λ_2.

The Hybrid Wavelength Scheduling

Except common wavelength scheduling methods, there exists also the hybrid scheduling combining their advantages. At the offline wavelength scheduling, a priority is a fair access to the transmission medium for ONT terminals. At the online wavelength scheduling, priorities are a decision rate and a securing of the fastest data transmitting for ONT terminals. Any

Figure 4. Example of the online wavelength scheduling

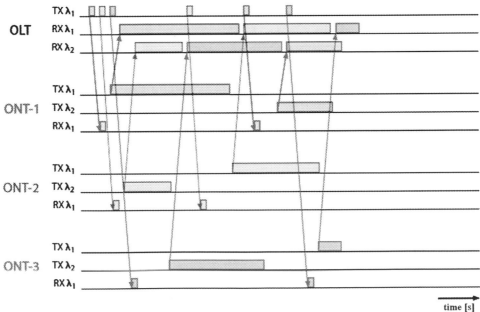

hybrid wavelength scheduling can evaluate a situation by various ways and can assign transmission parameters for ONT terminals according different rules (Rafiq, 2007), (Gutierrez, 2010).

- One of hybrid scheduling techniques is the Just-In-Time (JIT) approach. At this scheduling, the first step is the same as in offline and/or online wavelength scheduling.
- After that, a time period when the OLT terminal collects a certain number of requests from ONT terminals for the next cycle is determined. This collecting period of requests is determined in a way that a decision process for the next cycle is closed before finish data transmitting from the last ONT terminal in the actual cycle. Or, it allows data transmitting of extra size for processing requests from other ONT terminals, whereby the inactive period specific for the offline wavelength scheduling is eliminated.
- After the collecting period, requests are processed and evaluated according to one of strategies from the offline wavelength scheduling for securing a fair access to the transmission medium. Subsequently, assigned transmission parameters are reported to ONT terminals and the collecting period of requests is again determined by subsequent requests.

Groups of Allocated Wavelengths

The ODN network can present either a uniform system with optical elements valid for the complete network or a system consisting of smaller groups of optical elements with particular rules designed for given scheduling approaches. Groups of allocated wavelengths in a distribution part can be created either with the intention of transmission directions and Grouped Wavelength Paths (GWP) in more complex and extensive networks or with the intention of more simple control and management of terminal equipment devices in simpler access networks. A creating of allocated wavelength groups can lead to optimizing a computing performance with decreasing of the calculating time and costs and to allowing better scalability and network expandability with individual approaches. In WDM networks, either groups can be created within one wavelength framework or several wavelengths can create one group depending on provided services or on custom locations, whereby a number of possible collisions is reduced. Wavelengths groups can be created as the Static Wavelength Grouping (SWG) or as the Dynamic Wavelength Grouping

(DWG) (Kanonakis, 2010), (Taniguchi, 2013), (Srivinas, 2014), (Takano, 2015). In SWG static groups, wavelengths are fixed defined and unchanged through all around the network. Therefore, they are easy implemented and less effective in more complex and extensive networks. In DWG dynamic groups, wavelengths can be changed at transition through different network nodes depending on wavelength scheduling approaches and on realized optical elements. By this way, a wavelength utilization is more effective, especially in long-haul networks with a large number of wavelengths. An example of the wavelength group creating is displayed in Figure 5, where all wavelength groups are designed with the same number of wavelengths.

In a case that the ODN network consists from AWG or OADM optical components working with individual wavelengths or with specified wavelength spectrum, wavelength groups must be allocated to ONT terminals depending on supported wavelengths in a given ODN access part. Therefore, considered WDM-PON network designs will be prepared by means of the static wavelength grouping.

THE ANALYSIS OF WDM-PON NETWORK DESIGNS WITH TRAFFIC PROTECTION SECURING

In this subchapter, an analysis of various WDM-PON network designs with the traffic protection securing is evaluated and presented. Comparing to (Róka, 2018), protection possibilities for further parts and elements in passive optical networks are characterized.

At the network designing, a possibility for traffic protection solution must be included for consideration. From this reason, a number of connected ONT terminals, amount of the data transmission, a network size, a traffic with higher priority, optical power budgets for higher number of optical elements,

Figure 5. Example of the wavelength group creating

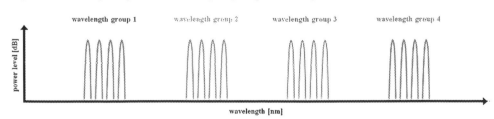

network costs must be considered. A protection of the ODN metropolitan part is the most important task because its ring topology is utilized for data transmitting from/to all ONT terminals. A traffic protection securing in the ring topology can be realized by interconnecting various optical fibers into double-ring or four-ring configurations in 1+1 or 1:1 operation modes. The double-ring presents a configuration of two optical fibers and the four-ring presents a configuration of four optical fibers. We can suppose that a traffic communication in the protection fiber is directed in an opposite direction related to the working fiber. If more optical fibers are used, than a number of utilized optical network elements is also increased and a complexity of interconnections and a coordination between different network parts is more exacting. Therefore, the ODN metropolitan part utilizing a ring topology with the double-ring configuration in the 1:1 protection mode for considered WDM-PON network designs is selected. This solution of the ODN metropolitan part protection is capable dealing with failures caused by a fiber interruption and/or a fiber bundle interruption. For presented network designs, a network design consists from one OLT line terminal, one ring topology network presenting the ODN metropolitan part with the traffic protection securing and some tree topology networks corresponding to the ODN access part without traffic protection securing.

In the creating process of WDM-PON networks where dynamic wavelength allocation algorithms will be implemented, the first step is focused on network design. Each network is prepared with only one dominated passive optical element used for the ODN network interconnecting. Each passive optical component has specific features and applications; therefore, it isn't suitable for utilization in any topology or in any part of the ODN network. The Power Splitter (PS) is flexible based on a number of ports; so it is suitable for utilization in both ODN - metropolitan and access - parts. The Arrayed Waveguide Gratings (AWG) element disposes higher number of ports with isolated wavelengths or a spectrum of wavelengths; hereby it is suitable more likely for utilization in the ODN access network. However, because of relatively small number of Optical Network Terminals (ONT) per each access network, the utilization of the AWG element is not worth having. The circulator as a self-employed element is inapplicable in any PON topology. Its practical utilization consists in conjunction with other optical element to ensure a signal distribution for correct output ports, as in a case of the Optical Add-Drop Multiplexor (OADM) element. The OADM element disposes smaller number of ports and it is flexible from a viewpoint of wavelength processing,

therefore it is suitable for using in the ODN metropolitan network. Resume, it is appropriate apply either the symmetrical/asymmetrical power splitter or the OADM element in the ODN metropolitan part (the ring topology). In the ODN access part (the tree topology), it is appropriate utilized just the symmetrical power splitter. Therefore, considered WDM-PON network designs will be prepared by means of these passive optical elements.

The WDM-PON Network Design With Symmetrical Power Splitters

In Figure 6, a scheme of the possible WDM-PON network design using symmetrical power splitters is presented.

This network design contains the 1:1 double-ring traffic protection in the ODN metropolitan part. From the OLT termination, two optical fibers are piped; the first is dedicated to the working fiber connection and the second one to the protection fiber connection (Mahloo, 2014). At this network design, both optical fibers are fully controlled and the traffic management with more sophisticated network control can be realized. All network elements are linked in a bidirectional mode. In the ONT-OLT direction, a signal is transmitted in

Figure 6. The possible WDM-PON network design scheme using symmetrical power splitters

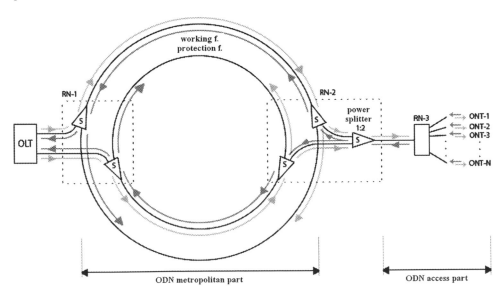

both optical fibers and the OLT terminal can select a signal version for further processing. In the OLT-ONT direction, a signal can be transmitted only in one optical fiber on all available wavelengths or in both optical fibers with diverse wavelength allocations for avoiding collisions in a particular ONT terminal. In a case of the ODN access part, a network traffic protection is not tasked together with the network control.

Optical power splitters (S) located in the ODN metropolitan part are the main factor for determining the maximum number of ONT terminals in this network design. These power splitters used with the symmetrical splitting ratio 1:2 (50%:50%) are as well cheap and working with the full wavelength spectrum, but they ineffective distribute the optical power on their particular outputs. If more optical access parts are joined to the ODN metropolitan part, then 50% transmitted power budget for each of them is just waste of optical power decreasing the network potential.

The WDM-PON Network Design With OADM Elements

In Figure 7, a scheme of the possible WDM-PON network design using a majority of OADM elements is presented, other elements are determined only for the appropriate OADM connection and for optical signal delivering at the corresponding port.

Figure 7. The possible WDM-PON network design scheme using OADM elements

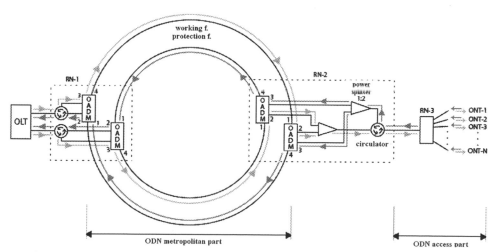

Also, as in a previous case, this network design contains the 1:1 double-ring traffic protection only in its ODN metropolitan part again. At this network design, both optical fibers are fully controlled and the traffic management with more sophisticated network control can be also realized. All network elements are linked in a bidirectional mode. For the ODN access part, a protection together with a network control is not tasked.

OADM elements located in the ODN metropolitan part are the main factor for determining the maximum number of ONT terminals in this network design. For connecting the ODN access part, cheap and simple OADM elements can be used because they are able to work with only a few (e.g. four) wavelengths. For interconnecting the OLT terminal and the ODN metropolitan part, the more complicated OADM element must be used because it works with all wavelengths utilized in each access network. By this approach, working wavelengths in particular access networks are fully controlled. Moreover, specific wavelength groups can be created and a possibility for a self-employed work with the considered wavelength group without others is provided. With higher number of working wavelengths in the OADM element, than higher attenuation is imbedded at the signal transmission between particular input and output ports. Therefore, this network design is adequate for utilizing in areas with less intensive data transmission with less number of wavelengths or for deployment less numbers of ONT terminals in access networks.

The WDM-PON Network Design With Asymmetrical Power Splitters And Wavelengths Groups

In Figure 8, a scheme of the possible WDM-PON network design using asymmetrical power splitters is presented.

This network design presents a hybrid approach where advantages from previous network designs with symmetrical power splitters and with OADM elements are utilized.

This network design is appearing from the WDM-PON network design with symmetrical power splitters. However, main elements are asymmetrical power splitters (A1, A2) located in the ODN metropolitan part intended for interconnecting access networks. By this exchange of passive optical elements, interconnecting the highest number of ONT terminals can be guaranteed. Using asymmetrical power splitters with specific splitting ratios, just avoidable optical power budget for operating each access network can be

Figure 8. The possible WDM-PON network design scheme using asymmetrical power splitters

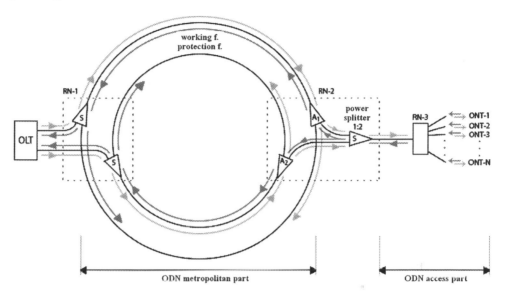

provided without waste of the optical power and a remaining optical power is distributed through the ODN metropolitan part to other access networks.

Based on analyzing demands for transmitted data in the area of passive optical network deployment, it is important to determine an available number of utilized wavelengths. Each ONT terminal keeps at disposal just specific limited number of working wavelengths for communication with the OLT terminal. For ensuring the requested Quality of Service (QoS) level, each ONT terminal is assigned to a group with specific working wavelengths. By this way, an individual approach and self-employed work with wavelength groups can be provided for better evaluation of statistical data and effectiveness of exploited dynamic wavelength allocation algorithms.

The OLT Control Element Protection

A protection of the OLT control element consists of a backup optical line terminal located in a network that can take all control functions in a case of the main OLT failure. A location of this backup OLT element plays also an important role. For this explanation, various locations of the backup OLT control element are introduced in Figure 9 (Abbas, 2013).

Figure 9. The location of the backup OLT control element; a) in the main OLT, b) in the same network outside the main OLT, c) in the other network

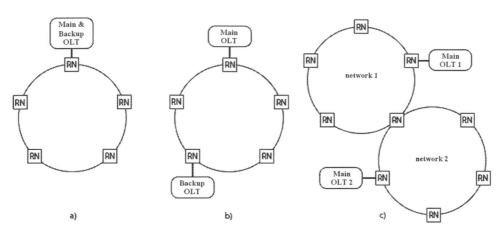

In Figure 9a, the backup OLT terminal is located together with the main OLT terminal. However, a main disadvantage of this location is a fact that in a case of the optical fiber's failure, both optical line terminals can't communicate and execute their tasks and functions.

In Figure 9b, the backup OLT terminal is located in the same network infrastructure as the main OLT terminal, but outside the main OLT structure, e.g. at the opposite side in a ring topology.

In Figure 9c, the backup OLT terminal is simultaneously the main OLT terminal in the other network, e.g. when an interconnection of two networks with ring topologies is created where various main OLT terminals control its own network. In a case of the first OLT failure, the second OLT takes control functions for both passive optical networks.

For passive optical networks with backup OLT locations according the first or the second cases, the backup OLT terminal is working in an idle mode and is monitoring entire network traffic at the same time. In a case of detecting un-running communications from the main OLT terminal, the backup OLT takes control functions and continues in network traffic.

The ODN Access Part Protection

In the ODN access part with a tree topology, a utilization of two optical fibers for connecting one common subscriber is non-effective and worthless. At least, a small importance can be found by adding the protection optical fiber

Figure 10. The realization of the ODN access part traffic protection

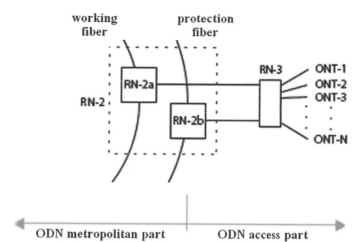

between the OLT terminal and appropriate RN equipment. This protection optical fiber can be shared by all ONT terminals in a given access network. Figure 10 presents a realization of the traffic protection in the remote node using the protection optical fiber in the ODN access part (Jin, 2007).

When a number of ONT terminals in the access network is small (less than eight), then the traffic protection has no large significance. Except a situation if very important subscriber is located in given access network. In this case, the protection optical fiber terminates directly to a relevant ONT terminal.

THE OPTIMIZATION OF OPTICAL POWER BUDGET POSSIBILITIES FOR WDM-PON NETWORK DESIGNS

In this subchapter, an optimization of optical power budget possibilities for various WDM-PON network designs with the traffic protection securing is presented. Comparing to (Róka, 2018), functionalities of considered wavelength scheduling methods are in addition presented.

The simulation model for analyzing various WDM-PON network designs is created in the Matlab (Matrix Laboratory) programming environment and its additional parts are oriented on the optimization of optical power budget possibilities and on the transmission medium dedicated for communication in passive optical networks. In this environment, approaches for particular

dynamic wavelength allocation algorithms related to the WDM-PON network designs will be employed.

The Analysis of WDM-PON Network Designs From a Viewpoint of Connected ONT Terminals

WDM-PON network designs are created in the simulation model and subsequently they are verified for availability of utilization based on defined parameters of optical fibers and critical passive optical elements. In the first input step, common parameters (Table 1) are defined.

In the second input step, attenuation values for symmetric power splitters and for OADM elements (Table 2) are determined.

Based on these values of input parameters, various possibilities for connecting particular access networks with different number of ONT terminals to the ODN metropolitan part are created. Each possibility for the network connecting is subsequently verified and its availability for the network design

Table 1. Common parameters for creating WDM-PON network designs

	value
Maximum distance between ONT and OLT [km]	20
Detection ability [dB]	30
Specific attenuation of the optical fiber [dB/km]	0.5000
Minimum number of ONT per access network	8

Table 2. Attenuation values for symmetric power splitters and for OADM elements

Values for Power Splitters							
Splitting ratio	1:2	1:4	1:8	1:16	1:32	1:64	1:128
Max. att. [dB]	3.4	7.5	10.7	13.7	16.9	20.4	23.6
Values for OADM Elements							
Number of wavelengths	1		2		4		8
Attenuation: Input → Drop ch. [dB]	≤ 0.6		≤ 0.9		≤ 2.0		≤ 3.2
Attenuation: Add ch. → Output [dB]	≤ 0.6		≤ 0.9		≤ 2.0		≤ 3.2
Attenuation: Input → Output [dB]	≤ 0.8		≤ 1.2		≤ 2.5		≤ 4.0

Figure 11. Possibilities for WDM-PON network designs with various RN equipment

Symmetrical power splitters

	Number of ONT per access network
1. network design	8 8
2. network design	16

OADM elements

	Number of ONT per access network
1. network design	8 8 8 8
2. network design	16 8

Asymmetrical power splitters + wavelength groups

	Number of ONT per access network
1. network design	8 8 8 8 8 8 8
2. network design	16 8 8 8 8 8
3. network design	16 16 8 8 8 8
4. network design	16 16 16 8 8
5. network design	32 8 8 8 8
6. network design	32 16 8 8
7. network design	32 16 16

Select the network design

6 ▼	OK

with symmetric power splitters and OADM elements is determined. As an example, possibilities for WDM-PON network designs based on presented input parameters are presented in Figure 11.

The aim of network designs is achieving a status when no new access network with defined minimum number of ONT terminals can be added according to defined common input parameters presented in Table 1. This implies that particular ODN access networks can have different numbers of ONT terminals depending on their maximum available attenuation.

As it can be seen in Figure 11, network designs consisting from symmetrical power splitters and OADM elements are not suitable options from a viewpoint of the available total transmission capacity because they misspend a potential and possibilities of optical access networks resulting in lower number of connected ONT terminals comparing with network designs consisting from asymmetrical power splitters.

By changing defined and determined input parameters to achieve higher number of connected ONT terminals, the analysis can be executed. It proves that a network design consisting from symmetrical power splitters is more suitable option for lower number of access networks with larger splitting ratios and a network design consisting from OADM elements is a preferable option for higher number of access networks with smaller splitting ratios in particular access networks.

The Selection of WDM-PON Network Designs and Their Optimization of the Optical Power Budget

Based on the analysis of possibilities for WDM-PON network designs presented in a previous subsection, the most suitable option from a viewpoint of the available total transmission capacity is a network design consisting from asymmetrical power splitters. Therefore, it can be selected as the WDM-PON network architecture where dynamic wavelength allocation algorithms will be applicable. After selecting the specific WDM-PON network design, the simulation model calculates required splitting ratios of asymmetrical splitters for both working and protecting optical fibers for each access network. Splitting ratios for asymmetric power splitters related to the selected network design are presented in Table 3.

Because a production process of optical power splitters is not ideal and, at the same time, power losses due to material absorption are coming into the existence, values of required splitting ratios for particular access networks are rounded up to integer above to meet minimum optical power budget with a possible backup for supporting better quality at the signal transmission and for detecting optical signals at ONT terminals.

Table 3. Splitting ratios of asymmetrical power splitters for the selected WDM-PON network design No.6

Number of ONT terminals in particular access networks				
Access network No.	1	2	3	4
ONT terminals	32	16	8	8
Splitting ratios in the working path				
Asymmetrical splitter No.	1	2	3	4
Access part [%]	23	25	23	29
Metropolitan part [%]	77	75	77	71
Splitting ratios in the protection path				
Asymmetrical splitter No.	1	2	3	4
Access part [%]	93	31	11	6
Metropolitan part [%]	7	69	89	94

For the selected network design, optical power level diagrams can be calculated depending on the distance that both working and protecting optical fibers can reach in each ODN access part (Figure 12).

As it can be seen in Figure 12, only one ODN access network can reach the 20 km distance for both optical fibers, but not all. This is caused by positioning of the access network in the ODN metropolitan part. The optical power budget of each access network is characterized by the linear decreasing due to attenuation of the optical fiber and by the large jump at the determined distance. This jump is caused by positioning of asymmetrical power splitters and by allocating of the minimal power amount for the availability of access

Figure 12. Optical power level diagrams for working and protection optical fibers for the selected WDM-PON network design No.6

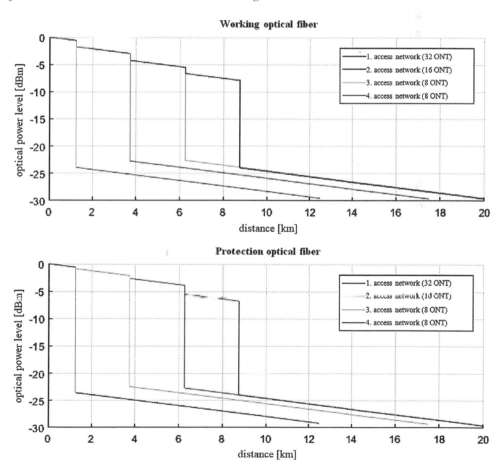

network. A remaining part of the optical power is transmitted through the ODN metropolitan part to subsequent access networks. Simultaneously, the attenuation caused by symmetrical power splitter serving for ONT terminal interconnecting into this access network is involved. From a viewpoint of subsequent access networks, a small decrement of the optical power level is occurring at point that is characterized by allocation of the determined optical power amount into previous positioned access network.

The Deployment of DWA Algorithms for Selected WDM-PON Network Design

After creating a transmission path in the ODN access part, ONT terminals are located into particular access networks. A deployment of dynamic wavelength allocation algorithms can be based on bandwidth scheduling methods for the upstream traffic in TDM-PON networks (Bosternák, 2017), (Bosternák, 2018) including possible wavelength extensions. For each ONT terminal, a distance characterizing its deployment is generated within its access network. Based on this distance, the Round-Trip Time (RTT) for each ONT terminal is determined for both working and protection optical fibers. The RTT value is a time characterizing a packet transmission through the considered optical fiber from the OLT terminal to the specific ONT and backwards (McGarry, 2006), (Dhaini, 2007). Simultaneously, each ONT terminal is incorporated into a specific wavelength group representing its actual possibilities. This incorporation can be realized by various ways. For the WDM-PON network design with OADM elements, wavelength groups can be created based on their geographic positioning depending on the access network where they are utilized.

Thereafter, the optical fiber (working or protection) for data transmitting between the OLT terminal and ONT terminals can be selected. The wavelength capacity characterizing the maximum transmission rate for particular wavelengths can be simultaneously determined for specifying the Guard Time (GT). The GT parameter is dedicated for ensuring a collision-less data transmission incoming from ONT terminals working on the same wavelength. The GT value is a time between the last transmitted bit destined for the actual ONT terminal and the first bit destined for the following ONT terminal. In the simulation model, default GT values are specified in the range $1 \div 5$ μs depending the wavelength transmission capacity. For presented examples,

the working optical fiber has the 1 Gbit/s transmission capacity per one wavelength and the 5 μs GT value (Dhaini, 2007), (Kanonakis, 2010).

Each ODN network part – metropolitan and access - has different requirements for DWA algorithms that must be satisfied. The WDM-PON network designs are characterized by utilizing various wavelengths. Moreover, wavelength groups can be created in some cases. Therefore, all these conditions must be incorporated at designing DWA algorithms. In a process of the deployment, two methods for wavelength scheduling are focused - offline and online. Their functionalities are presented from a viewpoint of the considered WDM-PON network design.

Functionalities of the Offline Wavelength Scheduling

At the offline wavelength scheduling, a demand for specific input values characterizing each ONT terminal is necessary for data processing - working wavelengths allocated for each ONT terminal, RTT and GT values and requests for data transmitting in the next cycle.

In the first step, an ideal number of wavelengths must be determined based on requests for data transmitting in each wavelength group. Also, an average traffic load is estimated for particular wavelengths. Next, each wavelength group is processing separately.

In the second step, each active wavelength in the wavelength group is processed and ONT terminals are assigned to it in descending order from the largest request up to estimated average traffic load. Consequently, time slots for data transmitting for all ONT terminals are assigned after the wavelength allocation. Time slots are assigned to ONT terminals in ascending order from the smallest request for particular wavelengths for the QoS assurance. For this allocation, RTT and GT values for particular ONT terminals must be known together with a data transmission time depending on the wavelength transmission capacity. As results, working wavelengths and time slots (the starting and finishing time) are allocated to each of ONT terminals in a given cycle of data transmitting.

These two steps repeat in each following cycle.

A possible enhancement of this wavelength scheduling method focuses on particular wavelength groups. When any wavelength group utilize some wavelengths not utilized in other wavelength groups, then processing can be executed separately in each wavelength group. ONT terminals assigned to these specific wavelengths in one wavelength group can access to the

transmission medium independently on other ONT terminals. At the same time, a computing performance will be decreased because a wavelength scheduling is working only with given ONT terminals at the moment, not with all active ones.

Functionalities of the Online Wavelength Scheduling

As well as in the offline method, the online wavelength scheduling needs to know specific input values characterizing each ONT terminal. Except parameter values mentioned in a previous case, time slots from the previous cycle of data transmitting must be added.

In the first step, the first cycle of data transmitting is processed using the offline wavelength scheduling because the primary initialization is in progress along with preparing ONT terminals for data transmitting.

In the second step, the primary decision process must be executed. If data transmitting in the fastest ONT terminal completes and requests for the next cycle are reported, then the online wavelength scheduling checks an availability and utilization of working wavelengths in the assigned wavelength group. The nearest available wavelength must be allocated in a way that its transmission capacity is not exceeded and simultaneously the smallest number of wavelengths will be used. Subsequently, a time slot is assigned to the ONT terminal for data transmitting. As results, working wavelengths and time slots (the starting and finishing time) are allocated are allocated to the concrete ONT terminal for the next cycle of data transmitting.

Finally, an availability of wavelengths is updated and a completing data transmitting in the fastest ONT terminal is expected. This process repeats in all cycles until all data from all ONT terminals are transmitted.

FUTURE RESEARCH DIRECTIONS

WDM-PON systems present optical fiber infrastructures to support various applications of many service providers. Technological improvements of broadband, broadcast and cellular technologies will require a reliable support in optical metropolitan and access networks. Therefore, appropriate advanced technologies utilizing the optical transmission medium and its available frequency spectrum and wavelength bands can be expected in a near future

and more reasons begin effect on utilization and implementation of WDM multiplexing techniques in converged passive optical networks.

On the other hand, the WDM-PON technology must be able to protect the investment of legacy passive optical networks. Therefore, a strong interest for utilization of traffic protection securing in different terminals and network parts of converged passive optical networks is present. Moreover, an area of research directions in converged WDM-PON networks is very wide and can include e.g. a mutual convergence of technologies between optical metropolitan and optical access networks, an expansion of dynamic wavelength and bandwidth allocation algorithms and scheduling methods, an optimization of the optical power budgets, a utilization of power saving methods for control and subscriber terminals, etc.

CHALLENGES AND OPEN ISSUES

In the near future, a convergence of optical network technologies will be continued. A concept of elastic optical networks with a flexible wavelength grid can be utilized in converged passive optical networks. Broadband WDM-PON networks can be deployed by various scenarios to address different cases with diverse degrees of consolidation. And therefore, also various converged WDM-PON deployments could be included into possible future implementations. A variety of users - residential, corporate/business and telco - must be considered. Therefore, more flexible hybrid passive optical network architectures should be considered as an evolutionary transition from the TDM-PON network utilizing few WDM components up to the full WDM-PON network with a fixed grid. Simultaneously, elastic optical networks based on the flexible grid will be evolved. From these reasons, much more effective utilization of available wavelength bands will play a very important role.

For practical implementation, there are some open issues. A high importance is dedicated to the power saving in long-reach broadband optical metropolitan and access networks and energy efficient efforts associated with the optimization of optical power budget on both terminal sides in converged optical fiber networks. From this viewpoint, WDM-PON possibilities with reliable traffic protection securing can also play an important role. For enhancing broadband WDM-PON networks, DSP-based approaches can be utilized for flexible per-wavelength rate upgrades and for extending reach of optical metropolitan and access network systems. The virtualization

of converged optical fiber networks with reconfigurable OLT and ONT elements is expected. Subsequently, ICT infrastructures can be mentioned for supporting wireless/metallic access and backhauling solutions of residential, corporate/business and telco installations. For this scenario, possible HPON deployments can be extended with prospective variations of future broadband WDM-PON networks.

CONCLUSION

The evolution of WDM-PON networks moves toward larger coverage of access areas, higher numbers of users and higher bandwidth per user. A substantial requirement is logically the network reliability ensured by implementing traffic protection mechanisms. Therefore, it can be beneficial either provide traffic protection functionalities at the time of network deployment or at least install a sufficient amount of optical fibers in advance. In considered WDM-PON network designs, traffic protection securing is realized above all by optical fiber duplications in both ODN network parts and by a protection of the OLT control element. The OLT element protection is dependent on a location of the backup OLT element. The most important task is to protect the ODN metropolitan part because its ring topology is utilized for data transmitting from/to all ONT terminals. For the ODN access part protection, a key factor is the tree topology and a number of ONT terminals. In most of cases, this protection is not very effective and less significant.

Considered WDM-PON network designs are created by means of only passive optical elements. For determining the maximum number of ONT terminals in each network design, main factors are just these optical elements located in the ODN metropolitan part and the utilization of wavelengths. In the first case, optical power splitters are used with the symmetrical splitting ratio and working with the full wavelength spectrum, but they ineffectively distribute the optical power on their particular outputs. In the second case, specific wavelength groups in the OADM element can be moreover created and a possibility for a self-employed work with the considered wavelength group without others is provided. If a number of working wavelengths is higher, then the attenuation imbedded at the signal transmission between particular input and output ports is higher. Therefore, this network design is adequate for utilizing in areas with less intensive data transmission with less number of wavelengths or for deployment less numbers of ONT terminals. In the third case, the highest number of ONT terminals can be interconnected by

exchange of power splitters with asymmetrical ones. Moreover, the avoidable optical power budget for operating each access network can be provided just using asymmetrical power splitters with specific splitting ratios without waste of the optical power and with remaining optical power distributed through the ODN metropolitan part to other access networks.

Each possibility for the WDM-PON network design is subsequently verified. Following conclusions based on the analysis created by changing defined input parameters to achieve higher number of connected ONT terminals can be considered:

• a network design consisting from symmetrical power splitters is more suitable option for lower number of access networks with larger splitting ratios,

• a network design consisting from OADM elements is a preferable option for higher number of access networks with smaller splitting ratios in particular access networks can be determined,

• mentioned network designs are not suitable options for practical implementations because they misspend a potential and possibilities of optical access networks resulting in lower number of connected ONT terminals comparing with network designs consisting from asymmetrical power splitters.

Subsequently, optical power level diagrams for these WDM-PON network designs can be calculated depending on the distance for both working and protecting optical fibers for each ODN access part. Of course, these expected optical power budgets of each access network can be optimized. Finally, WDM-PON network designs with asymmetrical power splitters can be selected as the network architecture where DWA algorithms will be deployed.

After creating a transmission path in the ODN access part, ONT terminals are located into particular access networks. Thereafter, the optical fiber (working or protection) for data transmitting between the OLT control element and ONT terminals can be selected. For each ONT terminal, a distance characterized its deployment is generated within its access network. Simultaneously, each ONT terminal is incorporated into a specific wavelength group representing its actual possibilities. This incorporation can be realized by various ways. Subsequently, a research of the DWA algorithms can be realized using selected offline and online wavelength scheduling methods. Moreover, the wavelength transmission capacity characterizing the maximum transmission rate for particular wavelengths can be simultaneously determined for specifying

the guard time for data transmitting between various ONT terminals in the ODN access part.

In future works, advanced protection procedures and monitoring techniques for improving network survivability can be invented. After determining the quality of survivability criteria, the application-aware protection in WDM optical networks can be established. Moreover, WDM-PON network designs with traffic protection securing utilizing also active optical elements can be analyzed in terms of optical power budget possibilities. Advanced wavelength allocation and scheduling methods should be considered for converged WDM-PON network designs with new survivability and recovery techniques.

For future elastic optical networks, potential physical-layer security scenarios and many fault recovery events are challenging and various EON architectures and their survivability mechanisms must be analyzed with regard to a traffic protection. From this viewpoint, the accommodation of wavelength allocation and scheduling methods can be expected.

ACKNOWLEDGMENT

This work is a part of research activities conducted at Slovak University of Technology Bratislava, Institute of MICT, within the VEGA agency project - 1/0462/17 "Modeling of qualitative parameters in IMS networks".

REFERENCES

Abbas, H. S., & Gregory, M. A. (2013). Feeder fiber and OLT protection for ring-and-spur long-reach passive optical network. In *Telecommunication Networks and Applications Conference*, (*vol. 23*, pp. 63-68). Melbourne, Australia: Academic Press. 10.1109/ATNAC.2013.6705358

Abbas, H. S., & Gregory, M. A. (2016). The next generation of passive optical networks: A review. *Journal of Network and Computer Applications*, *67*, 53–74. doi:10.1016/j.jnca.2016.02.015

Alparslan, O., Arakawa, S., & Murata, M. (2017). Dynamic wavelength allocation and analytical model for flow assignment in optical packet and path integrated networks. *Journal of Optical Communications and Networking*, *9*(4), 304–318. doi:10.1364/JOCN.9.000304

Bang, H., Doo, K.-H., Myong, S., Stea, G., & Park, C.-S. (2013). Design and analysis of IPACT-based bandwidth allocation for delay guarantee in OFDMA-PON. *Journal of Optical Communications and Networking*, 5(11), 1236–1249. doi:10.1364/JOCN.5.001236

Bosternák, Z., & Róka, R. (2017). Approach of the T-CONT allocation to increase the bandwidth in passive optical networks. *Radioengineering*, 26(4), 954–960. doi:10.13164/re.2017.0954

Bosternák, Z., & Róka, R. (2018). Bandwidth scheduling methods for the upstream traffic in passive optical networks. *Przeglad Elektrotechniczny*, 94(4), 9–12. doi:10.15199/48.2018.04.03

Dahan, D., & Mahlab, U. (2017). Security threats and protection procedures for optical networks. *IET Optoelectronics*, 11(5), 186–200. doi:10.1049/iet-opt.2016.0150

Dhaini, A. R., Assi, C. M., Maier, M., & Shami, A. (2007). Dynamic wavelength and bandwidth allocation in hybrid TDM/WDM EPON networks. *Journal of Lightwave Technology*, 25(1), 277–286. doi:10.1109/JLT.2006.886683

Drid, H. (2011). Application-aware protection in DWDM optical networks. *Annual Wireless and Optical Communications Conference*, 20.

Goscien, R., Walkowiak, K., Klinkowski, M., & Rak, J. (2016). Protection in elastic optical networks. *IEEE Network*, 29(6), 88–96. doi:10.1109/MNET.2015.7340430

Grobe, K., & Elbers, J. P. (2008). PON in adolescence: From TDMA to WDM-PON. *IEEE Communications Magazine*, 46(1), 26–34. doi:10.1109/MCOM.2008.4427227

Gutierrez, L. (2010). Next generation optical access networks: From TDM to WDM. In *Trends in Telecommunications Technologies*. Rijeka, Croatia: InTech. doi:10.5772/8473

Huang, K., Ji, W., Xue, X., & Li, X. (2015). Design and evaluation of elastic optical access network based on WDM-PON and OFDM technology. *Journal of Optical Communications and Networking*, 7(10), 987–994. doi:10.1364/JOCN.7.000987

Hussain, S. B., Hu, W., Xin, H., & Mikaeil, A. M. (2017). Low-latency dynamic wavelength and bandwidth allocation algorithm for NG-EPON. *Journal of Optical Communications and Networking, 9*(12), 1108–1115. doi:10.1364/JOCN.9.001108

Hussain, S. B., Hu, W., Xin, H., Mikaeil, A. M., & Sultan, A. (2018). Flexible wavelength and dynamic bandwidth allocation for NG-EPONs. *Journal of Optical Communications and Networking, 10*(6), 643–652. doi:10.1364/JOCN.10.000643

Imtiaz, W. A. (2017). Impact of fiber duplication on protection architectures feasibility for passive optical networks. In *Optical Fiber and Wireless Communications*. Rijeka, Croatia: InTech. doi:10.5772/intechopen.68237

ITU-T Telecommunication Standardization Sector. (2001a). *A broadband optical access system with increased service capability using dynamic bandwidth assignment*. Recommendation G.983.4.

ITU-T Telecommunication Standardization Sector. (2001b). *A broadband optical access system with increased service capability using wavelength allocation*. Recommendation G.983.3.

ITU-T Telecommunication Standardization Sector. (2005). *Broadband optical access systems based on Passive Optical Networks*. Recommendation G.983.1.

ITU-T Telecommunication Standardization Sector. (2016a). *Optical system design and engineering considerations*. Supplement 39, Series G.

ITU-T Telecommunication Standardization Sector. (2016b). *Passive optical network protection considerations*. Supplement 51, Series G.

Jin, S. (2007). Survivability characterization of PON *International Conference on Communications and Networking, 2*.

Kanonakis, K., & Tomkos, I. (2010). Improving the efficiency of online upstream scheduling and wavelength assignment in hybrid WDM/TDMA EPON networks. *IEEE Journal on Selected Areas in Communications, 28*(6), 838–848. doi:10.1109/JSAC.2010.100809

Kapov, N. (2016). Physical-layer security in evolving optical networks. *IEEE Communications Magazine, 54*(8), 110–117. doi:10.1109/MCOM.2016.7537185

Kim, H. (2007). A cost-efficient WDM-PON architecture supporting dynamic wavelength and time slot allocation. *International Conference on Advanced Communication Technology*, 9, 1564-1568. 10.1109/ICACT.2007.358666

Liga, G., Xu, T., Alvarado, A., Killey, R. I., & Bayvel, P. (2014). On the performance of multichannel digital back propagation in high-capacity long-haul optical transmission. *Optics Express*, 22(24), 53–62. doi:10.1364/OE.22.030053

Lopez, J. (2012). Traffic and power-aware protection scheme in elastic optical networks. *International Telecommunications Network Strategy and Planning Symposium*, 15. 10.1109/NETWKS.2012.6381659

Maher, R., Xu, T., Galdino, L., Sato, M., Alvarado, A., Shi, K., ... Bayvel, P. (2015). Spectrally shaped DP-16QAM super-channel transmission with multi-channel digital back-propagation. *Scientific Reports*, 5(1), 1–8. doi:10.1038rep08214

Mahloo, M., Chen, J., Wosinska, L., Dixit, A., Lannoo, B., Colle, D., & Mas Machuca, C. (2014). Toward reliable hybrid WDM/TDM passive optical networks. *IEEE Communications Magazine*, 52(2), S14–S23. doi:10.1109/MCOM.2014.6736740

Mas Machuca, C., Chen, J., & Wosinska, L. (2012). Cost-efficient protection in TDM PONs. *IEEE Communications Magazine*, 50(8), 110–117. doi:10.1109/MCOM.2012.6257535

McGarry, M. P., Reisslein, M., Maier, M., & Keha, A. (2006). Bandwidth management for WDM EPONs. *Journal of Optical Networking*, 5(9), 637–654. doi:10.1364/JON.5.000637

Neaime, J., & Dhaini, A. R. (2018). Resource management in cloud and tactile-capable next-generation optical access networks. *Journal of Optical Communications and Networking*, 10(11), 902–914. doi:10.1364/JOCN.10.000902

Papadimitriou, D. (2014). Practical issues for the implementation of survivability and recovery techniques in optical networks. *Optical Switching and Networking*, 14(part 2), 179–193.

Rafiq, A. (2007). Comparative analysis of scheduling frameworks for efficient wavelength utilization in WDM EPONs. In: *International Conference on Electrical Engineering*, 1. 10.1109/ICEE.2007.4287319

Róka, R. (2003). The utilization of the DWDM/CWDM combination in the metro/access networks, *Joint 1st Workshop on Mobile Future & Symposium on Trends in Communications, 1*, 160-162. doi:10.1109/TIC.2003.1249111

Róka, R. (2014). Broadband NG-PON networks and their designing using the HPON Network Configurator. In *Convergence of Broadband, Broadcast, and Cellular Network Technologies*. Hershey, PA: IGI Global. doi:10.4018/978-1-4666-5978-0.ch012

Róka, R. (2015). *Hybrid PON networks - features, architectures and configuration*. Saarbrücken, Germany: LAP Lambert Academic Publishing.

Róka, R. (2016). Optimization of traffic protection schemes for utilization in hybrid passive optical networks. *International Journal of Application or Innovation in Engineering & Management, 5*(9), 107–116.

Róka, R. (2018). Optimization of the optical power budget for various WDM-PON network designs with traffic protection securing. *International Conference on Software, Telecommunications and Computer Networks*, 26. 10.23919/SOFTCOM.2018.8555824

Róka, R. (2019). Converged Fi-Wi Passive Optical Networks and Their Designing using the HPON Network Configurator. In *Paving the Way for 5G Through the Convergence of Wireless Systems*. Hershey, PA: IGI Global. doi:10.4018/978-1-5225-7570-2.ch006

Semrau, D., Xu, T., Shevchenko, N. A., Paskov, M., Alvarado, A., Killey, R. I., & Bayvel, P. (2017). Achievable information rates estimated in optically amplified transmission systems using nonlinearity compensation and probabilistic shaping. *Optics Letters, 42*(1), 121–124. doi:10.1364/OL.42.000121

Srinivas, R. (2014). Virtual network embedding in hybrid datacenters with dynamic wavelength grouping. *International Conference on Cloud Computing Technology and Science, 6*, 905-910. 10.1109/CloudCom.2014.34

Takano, K., & Karube, R. (2015). Impact of wavelength grouping method on waveband switching size in Japan topology network. *International Broadband and Photonics Conference, 1*, 19-22. 10.1109/IBP.2015.7230758

Taniguchi, Y. (2013). Dynamic grouped routing optical networks for cost effective and agile wavelength services. *Optical Fiber Communication Conference and Exposition and the National Fiber Optic Engineers Conference*, 18. 10.1364/OFC.2013.OM3A.5

Vardakas, J. S., Moscholios, I. D., Logothetis, M. D., & Stylianakis, V. G. (2011). An analytical approach for dynamic wavelength allocation in WDM–TDMA PONs servicing ON–OFF traffic. *Journal of Optical Communications and Networking*, *3*(4), 347–358. doi:10.1364/JOCN.3.000347

Wang, L., Wang, X., Tornatore, M., Chung, H. S., Lee, H. H., Park, S., & Mukherjee, B. (2017). Dynamic bandwidth and wavelength allocation scheme for next-generation wavelength-agile EPON. *Journal of Optical Communications and Networking*, *9*(3), B33–B42. doi:10.1364/JOCN.9.000B33

Wang, W., Guo, W., & Hu, W. (2018). Dynamic wavelength and bandwidth allocation algorithms for mitigating frame reordering in NG-EPON. *Journal of Optical Communications and Networking*, *10*(3), 220–228. doi:10.1364/JOCN.10.000220

Yan, B., Zhao, Y., Yu, X., Wang, W., Wu, Y., Wang, Y., & Zhang, J. (2018). Tidal-traffic-aware routing and spectrum allocation in elastic optical networks. *Journal of Optical Communications and Networking*, *10*(11), 832–842. doi:10.1364/JOCN.10.000832

Yao, H., Li, W., Feng, Q., Han, J., Ye, Z., Hu, Q., ... Yu, S. (2017). Ring-based colorless WDM-PON with Rayleigh backscattering noise mitigation. *Journal of Optical Communications and Networking*, *9*(1), 27–35. doi:10.1364/JOCN.9.000027

KEY TERMS AND DEFINITIONS

Bandwidth Allocation: A process of assigning time slots to different ONU units for the upstream direction in common TDM-PON networks; the frequency bandwidth of the optical fiber is a finite resource with a need for the effective allocation process.

Network Design: An iterative process, encompassing topological design, network-synthesis, and network-realization, for creating new telecommunications networks satisfying needs of the operator and subscribers.

Optical Add-Drop Multiplexor: A device used in wavelength-division multiplexing systems for multiplexing, switching and routing different lightpath channels into or out of a single-mode optical fiber; a type of optical node generally used for the formation and the construction of optical telecommunications networks.

Optical Power Budget: An allocation of the available optical power (launched into a given optical fiber by a given source) among various loss-producing mechanisms in order to ensure adequate optical power levels available at the receiver side.

Power Splitter: A device used in the optical network for coupling optical signals from various input branches into one output optical signal to the common OLT terminal and for splitting an optical signal from one input into various output branches for distribution to different ONT terminals; one of the most important passive devices in the optical fiber link.

Traffic Protection: Any protection scheme used in different network architectures for protecting data traffic against inevitable failures on service providers' network/fibers/nodes; any failure occurred at any point along the path will cause nodes to move/pick the data traffic to/from a new route.

Wavelength Allocation: A process of assigning wavelengths to different OLT and ONT terminals for downstream and upstream directions in future WDM-PON networks; the wavelength band of the optical fiber is a finite resource with a need for the effective wavelength allocation process.

Wavelength Scheduling: A process of arranging, controlling and optimizing wavelengths used for data transmitting between for different OLT and ONT terminals in future WDM-PON networks; it is an important tool for creating and effective utilization of the wavelength transmission capacity.

WDM-PON: A passive optical network with utilization of the WDM principle on a physical layer with assigning different multiple wavelengths for separate ONU units.

Chapter 2

Next Generation Multi-Access Edge-Computing Fiber-Wireless-Enhanced HetNets for Low-Latency Immersive Applications

Amin Ebrahimzadeh
INRS, Canada

Martin Maier
INRS, Canada

ABSTRACT

Next generation optical access networks have to cope with the contradiction between the intense computation and ultra-low latency requirements of the immersive applications and limited resources of smart mobile devices. In this chapter, after presenting a brief overview of the related work on multi-access edge computing (MEC), the authors explore the potential of full and partial decentralization of computation by leveraging mobile end-user equipment in an MEC-enabled FiWi-enhanced LTE-A HetNet, by designing a two-tier hierarchical MEC-enabled FiWi-enhanced HetNet-based architecture for computation offloading, which leverages both local (i.e., on-device) and nonlocal (i.e., MEC/cloud-assisted) computing resources to achieve low response time and energy consumption for mobile users. They also propose a simple yet efficient task offloading mechanism to achieve an improved quality of experience (QoE) for mobile users.

DOI: 10.4018/978-1-5225-9767-4.ch002

INTRODUCTION

The Internet has constantly evolved from the mobile Internet dominated by human-to-human (H2H) traffic to the emerging Internet of Things (IoT) with its underlying machine-to-machine (M2M) communications. The advent of advanced robotics, along with the emerging ultra responsive networking infrastructures, will allow for transmitting the modality of touch (also known as haptic sensation) in addition to the traditional triple-play traffic (i.e., voice, video, and data) under the commonly known term *Tactile Internet*. The term Tactile Internet was first coined by G. P. Fettweis in 2014. In his seminal paper, Fettweis (2014) defined the Tactile Internet as a new breakthrough enabling unprecedented mobile applications for tactile steering and control of real and virtual objects by requiring a round-trip latency of 1-10 milliseconds. Later in 2014, ITU-T published a Technology Watch Report (2014) on the Tactile Internet, which emphasized that scaling up research in the area of wired and wireless access networks will be essential, ushering in new ideas and concepts to boost access networks' redundancy and diversity to meet the stringent latency as well as carrier-grade reliability requirements of Tactile Internet applications.

The IoT without any human involvement in its underlying M2M communications is useful for the automation of industrial and other machine-centric processes while keeping the human largely out of the loop. In contrast, according to Maier et al. (2016) and Maier et al. (2018), the Tactile Internet, which allows for the tactile steering and control of not only virtual but also real objects via teleoperated robots, will be centered around human-to-robot/machine (H2R/M) communications, thus calling for a human-centric design approach. To give it a more 5G-centric flavor, the Tactile Internet has been more recently also referred to as the 5G-enabled Tactile Internet (see Simsek et al. (2016) and Aijaz et al. (2017)). Andrews et al. (2014) have argued that unlike the previous four generations, future 5G networks will lead to an increasing integration of cellular and WiFi technologies and standards. Furthermore, the importance of the so-called *backhaul bottleneck* needs to be recognized as well, calling for an end-to-end design approach leveraging on both wireless front-end and wired backhaul technologies. Or as once eloquently put by J. G. Andrews et al. (2013), "placing base stations all over the place is great for providing the mobile stations high-speed access, but does this not just pass the buck to the base stations, which must now somehow get this data to and from the wired core network?".

This mandatory end-to-end design approach is fully reflected in the key principles of the reference architecture within the emerging IEEE P1918.1 standards working group, which aims at defining a framework for the Tactile Internet. Among others, the key principles envision to (*i*) develop a generic Tactile Internet reference architecture, (*ii*) support local area as well as wide area connectivity through wireless (e.g., cellular, WiFi) or hybrid wireless/wired networking, and (*iii*) leverage computing resources from cloud variants at the edge of the network. The IEEE P1918.1 standards working group was approved by the IEEE Standards Association in March 2016. The group defines the Tactile Internet as follows: "*A network, or a network of networks, for remotely accessing, perceiving, manipulating or controlling real and virtual objects or processes in perceived real-time.* Some of the key use cases considered in IEEE P1918.1 include teleoperation, haptic communications, immersive augmented/virtual reality (AR/VR), and automotive control. Such applications may require the processing of large amounts of computation-intensive, delay-sensitive tasks. Mobile devices, however, are subject to limited hardware resources (e.g., battery life, CPU, and storage) and therefore may not be able to satisfy the stringent latency requirements of complex tasks.

To fill the gap between the increasing demands of computation-intensive, delay-sensitive tasks driven by emerging Tactile Internet applications and the availability of limited resources on smart mobile devices, mobile cloud computing (MCC) has emerged to reduce the computational burden of mobile devices and broaden their capabilities by extending the concept of cloud computing to the mobile environment by means of full and/or partial computation offloading. The MCC paradigm enables mobile devices to use infrastructures, platforms, and software packages offered by cloud providers at affordable costs to save battery power and accelerate task execution. We note, however, that the applicability of MCC to delay-sensitive tasks raises several technical challenges due to additional communication overhead and poor reliability that remote computation offloading may introduce. To cope with these limitations, mobile edge computing has recently emerged to provide cloud computing capabilities at the edge of access networks, leveraging the physical proximity of edge servers and mobile users to achieve reduced communication latency and increased reliability, e.g., Chen et al. (2016). As stated by Taleb et al. (2017), the European Telecommunications Standards Institute (ETSI) has recently dropped the word "mobile" and introduced the term multi-access edge computing (MEC) in order to broaden its applicability to heterogeneous networks, including WiFi and fixed access technologies (e.g., fiber).

Although a conventional (remote) cloud can provide high storage and computational resources, its applicability to immersive applications is often limited, which is due to large incurred latency, as task inputs have to travel all the way through the backhaul to reach the processing units. On the other hand, MEC may offer a reduced communication induced latency due to its proximity to end users, but it may suffer from an increased processing latency due to limited available computational resources. Therefore, MEC and remote cloud can be complementary to each other, creating a hierarchical computing paradigm to help end users experience an ultra low response time. In addition to the discussion above, we note that an important aspect of the 5G vision is decentralization. While 2G-3G-4G cellular networks were built under the design premise of having complete control at the infrastructure side, 5G systems may drop this design assumption and evolve the cell-centric architecture into a more device-centric one. Coexistence of MEC and remote cloud, along with on-device processing, gives rise to the so-called *hierarchical cooperative computing* (HCC), where the proximity of the MEC serves on one hand and strong computational capabilities of the remote cloud on the other hand may be leveraged to augment the limited on-device processing capabilities of end devices to give way to a flexible computing paradigm, which is able to satisfy different quality-of-experience (QoE) requirements of offloaded tasks generated by different types of emerging applications.

It is evident that future 5G mobile networks will lead to an increasing integration of cellular and WiFi technologies and standards, giving rise to so-called heterogenous networks (HetNets), which mandates the need for addressing the backhaul bottleneck challenge. Recently, Beyranvand et al. (2017) have explored the performance gains obtained from unifying coverage-centric 4G LTE-Advanced (LTE-A) HetNets and capacity-centric fiber-wireless (FiWi) access networks based on data-centric Ethernet technologies with resulting fiber backhaul sharing and WiFi offloading capabilities towards realizing future 5G networks. By means of probabilistic analysis and verifying simulations based on recent and comprehensive smartphone traces, Beyranvand et al. (2017) showed that an average end-to-end latency of <10 ms can be achieved for a wide range of traffic loads and that mobile users can be provided with highly fault-tolerant FiWi connectivity for reliable low-latency fiber backhaul sharing and WiFi offloading. Note, however, that Beyranvand et al. (2017) considered only data offloading without any computation offloading via MEC. Furthermore, Rimal et al. (2016) and Rimal et al. (2017) have investigated the feasibility of implementing conventional cloud and MEC in FiWi access networks, where the main objective was

to design a unified resource management scheme to integrate offloading activities with the underlying FiWi operations. While much of the effort in these papers has been devoted to the management of networking resources, cooperation between mobile devices, MEC servers, the remote cloud and the problem of offloading decision making have not been investigated.

In this chapter, we examine the performance gains obtained by the decentralization of computation resources using our proposed hierarchical cooperative computation offloading in MEC enabled FiWi enhanced HetNets, which relies not only on the computational capabilities of edge/cloud servers but also on the limited local computing resources at the device side. More specifically, we aim to design a two-tier MEC enabled FiWi enhanced HetNet architecture, where the mobile devices as well as the edge servers cooperatively offload their computation tasks towards achieving a reduced average response time. In our design approach, we take into account the limitations stemming from both communications and computation via accurate modeling of the fronthaul/backhaul as well as edge/cloud servers, while paying particular attention to the offloading decision making between mobile users and edge servers as well as edge servers and the remote cloud.

The remainder of the chapter is structured as follows. In Section II, we revisit FiWi access networks in the context of conventional clouds and emerging cloudlets, thereby highlighting the limitations of centralized C-RAN in light of future 5G networks moving toward decentralization based on cloudlets and MEC. In Section III we present our proposed hierarchical cooperative computing scheme for FiWi enhanced HetNets, which leverages on a two-level non-local computing hierarchy as well as local computing to obtain a reduced response time in a cooperative manner. In Section VI, we present our analytical framework for estimating the energy-delay performance of our proposed cooperative task offloading scheme. We present the numerical results in Section V. Finally, Section VI draws conclusions.

MEC ENABLED FIWI ACCESS NETWORKS

Although a few FiWi architectural studies exist on the integration of passive optical network (PON) with LTE or WiMAX wireless front-end networks, the vast majority of studies such as Aurzada et al. (2014) have considered FiWi access networks consisting of a conventional IEEE 802.3ah Ethernet PON (EPON) fiber backhaul and an IEEE 802.11b/g/n/s wireless local area network (WLAN) mesh front-end, which may be further upgraded by leveraging

NG-PONs, notably 10+ Gb/s TDM/WDM PONs, and Gigabit-class IEEE 802.11ac very high throughput (VHT) WLAN technologies. Most FiWi access architectures thus rely on low-cost data-centric optical fiber Ethernet (i.e., EPON) and wireless Ethernet (i.e., WLAN) technologies, which provide a number of important benefits, as elaborated in the following. First, economic considerations are expected to play an even more critical role in 5G networks compared to previous generations, due to an unprecedented increase of the number of mobile devices. Such economic considerations, along with the fact that today's service providers have to cope with an unprecedented growth of mobile data traffic worldwide, have spurred a great deal of interest toward complementing 4G LTE-A HetNets with already widely deployed WiFi access points. This represents a key aspect of the strategy of today's operators to offload mobile data traffic from their cellular networks, a technique also known as *WiFi offloading*. Clearly, FiWi access networks with a WLAN based front-end represent a promising approach to realize WiFi offloading in a cost-efficient manner.

We note that, unlike LTE, WLANs use a *distributed* medium access control (MAC) protocol for arbitrating access to the wireless medium among stations. Specifically, the so-called distributed coordination function (DCF) typically deployed in WLANs may suffer from a seriously deteriorated throughput performance due to the propagation delay of the fiber backhaul. These limitations of WLAN based FiWi access networks can be avoided by controlling access to the optical fiber and wireless media separately from each other, giving rise to so-called radio-and-fiber (R&F) networks. R\&F networks use in general two different MAC protocols, with protocol translation taking place at their interface. As a consequence, wireless MAC frames do not have to travel along the backhaul fiber to be processed at any central control station, but simply traverse their associated access point and remain in the WLAN. Access control is done locally inside the WLAN in a fully decentralized fashion. Note that in doing so, WLAN based FiWi access networks of extended coverage can be built without imposing stringent limits on the size of the fiber backhaul. Recall that this holds only for distributed MAC protocols such as DCF, but not for MAC protocols that deploy centralized polling and scheduling such as EPON and LTE. Thus, in a typical R&F based FiWi access network consisting of a cascaded EPON backhaul and WLAN front-end for WiFi offloading, the end-to-end coordination of both fiber and wireless network resources may be done by a co-dynamic bandwidth allocation (co-DBA) algorithm that uses the centralized IEEE 802.3ah multipoint control protocol (MPCP) for EPON and the decentralized DCF for WiFi, with MAC

protocol translation taking place at the optical-wireless interface. Note that the decentralized nature of WLAN's access protocol DCF is instrumental in realizing one of the key attributes of future 5G networks, decentralization.

Maier and Rimal (2015) studied FiWi access networks in the context of both conventional clouds and emerging cloudlets, paying particular attention to the difference of R&F and traditional radio-over-fiber (RoF) networks. RoF networks have been studied for decades and were also used in China Mobile's C-RAN, which relies on a centralized cloud infrastructure and moves baseband units (BBUs) away from remote radio heads (RRHs), rendering the latter ones intentionally as simple as possible without any processing and storage capabilities. In contrast, beside MAC protocol translation, the distributed processing and storage capabilities inherently built into R&F networks may be exploited for a number of additional tasks. Therefore, Maier and Rimal (2015) argued that R&F based FiWi access networks may become the solution of choice in light of the aforementioned trends of future 5G mobile networks toward decentralization based on cloudlets and MEC. Note however that Rimal et al. (2017), Rimal et al. (2017), and Rimal (2018) have argued that R&F and RoF technologies may be also used jointly together in FiWi access networks for providing multi-tier cloud computing services.

Maier et al. (2018) have put forward the idea that the Tactile Internet may be the harbinger of human augmentation and human-machine symbiosis envisioned by contemporary and early-day Internet pioneers. More specifically, they explored the idea of treating the human as a "member" of a team of intelligent machines rather than keep viewing him as a conventional "user." In addition, they elaborated on the role of artificial intelligence (AI) enhanced agents in supporting humans in their task coordination between humans and machines. Toward achieving advanced human-machine coordination, we developed a distributed allocation algorithm of computational and physical tasks for fluidly orchestrating human-agent-robot teamwork (HART) coactivities, e.g., the shared use of user- and/or network-owned robots. In their design approach, all HART members established through communication a collective self-awareness with the objective of minimizing the task completion time.

Tan et al. (2017) proposed a scalable online algorithm for task scheduling in an edge-cloud system, which was verified by simulations using real-world traces from Google. Tong et al. presented a hierarchical MEC-based architecture with a focus on the workload placement problem. Chen et al. (2017) presented an optimization framework for solving the problem of joint offloading decision and allocation of computation and communication resources with the aim

of minimizing a weighted sum of the costs of energy, cost of computation, and the delay for all users. More recently, Xiao and Krunz (2018) studied the computation offloading problem for cooperative fog computing networks and investigated the fundamental tradeoff between QoE of mobile users and power efficiency of fog nodes. Guo et al. (2018) presented a collaborative computation offloading scheme for MEC over FiWi networks. All mentioned papers, however, mainly focused on the management of computing resources without further investigating the impact of the capacity-limited backhaul.

While computation offloading for mobile computing systems has been around for almost a decade, the edge/fog computing paradigm has emerged only recently. Sun et al. (2017) proposed a novel cloudlet cellular network architecture to enable mobile users to offload their computation workload to nearby cloudlets and then designed a latency-aware workload offloading strategy to allocate the offloaded workloads to suitable cloudlets. Fan et al. (2018) extended the research done by Sun et al. (2017) by incorporating a two-tier hierarchical architecture for cloudlets. Liu et al. (2018) formulated a multiobjective optimization problem for fog computing systems with the joint objective of minimizing energy consumption, execution delay, and payment cost by finding the optimal offloading probability and transmit power of mobile devices. Note, however, that in the research done by Liu et al. (2018), the cooperation between edge servers and remote cloud is limited to the case when the edge servers are overloaded with the offloaded tasks from mobile devices, thus not fully reaping the benefits of the two-tier hierarchical edge computing architecture. Rodriguez et al. (2017) aimed to minimize the response time in a scenario with two MEC servers by focusing on both computation and communication latencies through virtual machine migration and transmission power control, respectively. Rodriguez et al. (2018) extended the research of Rodriguez et al. (2017) to further reduce the average response time of users by using a particle swarm optimization approach to balance the workload between MEC servers. Note that these studies considered only the cellular access mode without any computation offloading through WiFi. Muoz et al. (2015) jointly optimized the transmit power, precoder, and computation load distribution for femto-cloud computing systems, where the cloud server is formed by a set of femto access points. Guo et al. (2016) were one of the first to address the joint computation offloading and resource scheduling problem with task dependencies for mobile cloud computing.

Note that the placement of MEC servers on a FiWi based networking architecture may have a significant impact on the resultant user experience. Thus, the problem of MEC server placement represents one of the important design issues from a network planning viewpoint. Toward this end, Wong et al. (2017), Mondal et al. (2017), Mondal et al. (2018), and Mondal et al. (2018) have argued that proactive placement stands as a promising approach, where the network planner builds a model for placing MEC servers after analyzing the traffic and mobility history of mobile users. In this context, Xu et al. (2016) explored the exact solution of the ILP formulation of the capacitated cloudlet placement problem. Due to poor scalability of the optimal approach to the developed ILP, Xu et al. (2016) proposed an efficient solution to obtain satisfactory results in terms of reduced complexity. Jia et al. (2017) elaborated on the shortcomings of the heaviest access point-first placement method and proposed the so-called density-based clustering placement heuristic, which was shown to achieve near optimal results.

HIERARCHICAL COOPERATIVE COMPUTING

As discussed in Section I, one of the key attributes of future 5G networks is decentralization from both communications and computation viewpoints. While much attention has been devoted to designing distributed wireless access mechanisms (e.g., WLAN), decentralization of computational resources has not been explored in great depth. Contributing to this effort, we elaborate on our proposed decentralized hierarchical cooperative computing scheme for FiWi enhanced HetNets, where the entire set of available computational resources, including the remote cloud, MEC serves, and end devices' local CPUs are leveraged to allow mobile users to experience a reduced response time as well as decreased energy consumption.

Figure 1 depicts the generic architecture of the considered FiWi enhanced LTE-A HetNets. The fiber backhaul consists of a time or wavelength division multiplexing (TDM/WDM) IEEE 802.3ah/av 1/10 Gbps Ethernet PON (EPON) with a typical fiber range of 20 km between the central optical line terminal (OLT) and remote optical network units (ONUs). The EPON may comprise multiple stages, each separated by a wavelength broadcasting splitter/combiner or a wavelength multiplexer/demultiplexer. There are three different subsets

Figure 1. Generic MEC-enabled FiWi enhanced LTE-A HetNets architecture

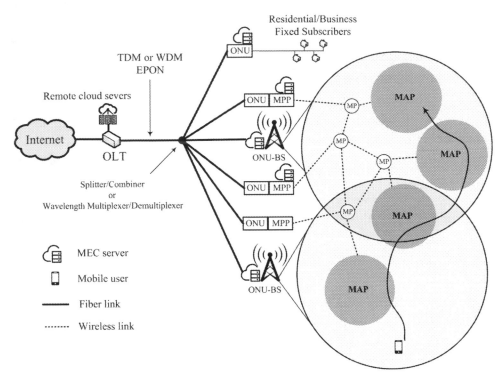

of ONUs. An ONU may either serve fixed (wired) subscribers. Alternatively, it may connect to a cellular network base station (BS) or an IEEE 802.11n/ac/s WLAN mesh portal point (MPP), giving rise to a collocated ONU-BS or ONU-MPP, respectively. Depending on her trajectory, a mobile user (MU) may communicate through the cellular network and/or WLAN mesh front-end, which consists of ONU-MPPs, intermediate mesh points (MPs), and mesh access points (MAPs).

We equip selected ONU-BSs/MPPs with MEC servers (or simply called *edge servers[1]* hereafter) collocated at the optical-wireless interface. MUs may offload fully or portion of their incoming computational tasks to nearby edge servers. In addition to edge servers, the OLT is equipped with cloud computing facilities, which consist of multiple servers dedicated to processing mobile tasks. Each MU uses a task scheduler that decides whether to offload a task to an edge server or execute it locally in its local CPU. We model the

task scheduler in each MU by a queuing system, as illustrated in Figure 2. We assume that in each mobile device there are two servers, namely, the CPU and the wireless interface (i.e., WiFi or LTE-A). The former server is used to model the local task execution at the MU's CPU, whereas the latter is responsible for offloading tasks to an edge server in proximity. We assume that tasks arrive at MU_i's scheduler at rate λ_{MU_i}.

The task scheduler at MU_i makes its decision based on the value of the so-called *offloading probability, β_i,* which is defined as the probability that an incoming task is offloaded to the edge server. Tasks generated by MU i are characterized by B_i^l and D_i^l, which denote the average size of computation input data (e.g., program codes and input parameters) and average number of CPU cycles required, respectively. Computation tasks are assumed to be atomic and thus cannot be divided into sub-tasks. We also assume that each edge server is equipped with a task scheduler, which decides whether to execute an incoming task or further offload it to the remote cloud. Similarly to MUs, a task arriving at edge server j is further offloaded to the remote cloud with probability α_j or executed locally with probability $(1 - \alpha_j)$.

Figure 2. Schematic diagram of the proposed hierarchical cooperative computing scheme, leveraging local-, edge-, and remote cloud-computing. Task scheduler and queueing system of MU i includes two disjoint queues served by local CPU and WiFi/ LTE-A wireless interface. Likewise, the queueing system of ONU j comprises two disjoint queues served by MEC server j and optical interface to offload the tasks to the remote cloud in the upstream direction of the backhaul EPON.

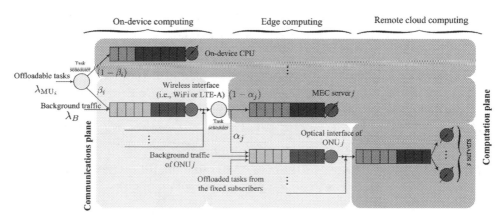

ENERGY-LATENCY ANALYSIS

In this section, we analyze the performance of our proposed cooperative MEC enabled FiWi enhanced LTE-A HetNets in terms of average response time and energy consumption for task offloading coexistent with conventional H2H traffic.

Assumptions

In the analysis, we make the following assumptions.

- We assume a Poisson task arrival model and an exponentially distributed number of required CPU cycles for task execution. Further, tasks are assumed to be computationally intensive, mutually independent, and can be executed either locally or remotely on an edge server or the remote cloud via computation offloading. According to Xiao and Krunz (2018) and Sun et al. (2017), each edge server has a limited computational capability and can serve a single task at a time. Besides, the remote cloud comprises a limited number of high-performance computing servers, each of which can serve a single task at a time.
- Similar to Chen et al. (2016), Guo et al. (2018), Liu et al. (2018), and Guo et al. (2016), we neglect the time overhead for sending the computation result back to the mobile users due to the fact that for many applications (e.g., face/object recognition) the size of the computation result is generally smaller than that of the computation input data.
- Each MU is directly associated with an ONU-AP or a cellular BS via a wireless single hop, whereby ONU-MPPs serve as ONU-APs. The WiFi connection and interconnection times of MUs are assumed to fit a truncated Pareto distribution, as validated by Beyranvand et al. (2017) via recent smartphone traces. The probability P_{temp}^{MU} that an MU is temporarily connected to an ONU-AP is estimated as $\bar{T}_{on} / \left(\bar{T}_{on} + \bar{T}_{off} \right)$, whereby $\bar{T}_{on}$ and $\bar{T}_{off}$ denote the average WiFi connection and interconnection time, respectively. In this chapter, we assume that $\bar{T}_{on}$ =28.1 minute and $\bar{T}_{off}$ =10.3 minute, which are consistent with the measurements of PhoneLab traces (see Beyranvand et al. (2017) for further details).

- In addition to the conventional MUs that generate Poisson H2H traffic at rate λ_B, background traffic coming from ONUs with attached fixed (wired) subscribers is set to $\alpha_{PON} \lambda_B$, where $\alpha_{PON} > 1$ is a traffic scaling factor for fixed subscribers that are directly connected to the backhaul EPON.

Average Response Time

In the proposed HCC scheme, both computation and communication induced latencies may contribute to the resultant response time experienced by MUs. Note that under the proposed HCC scheme, MUs can be either fully decentralized, partially decentralized, or fully centralized. While fully decentralized MUs rely on their local computing capabilities without offloading any task to the edge or remote cloud, fully centralized MUs rely only on the computing capabilities of the edge/remote cloud by offloading all the incoming tasks. In contrast, partially decentralized MUs rely on both local and non-local computing capabilities in a cooperative manner, as elaborated in Section III.

First, we estimate the latencies due to computation for both local and nonlocal computing. For a given MU_i, who is involved in task offloading, assuming i.i.d exponentially distributed task interarrival times and given the offloading probability β_i, the tasks arriving at the CPU queue for local computing follow a Poisson process with rate $(1 - \beta_i) \cdot \lambda_{MU_i}$, whereas the offloaded tasks arriving at the wireless interface queue follow a Poisson process with rate $\beta_i \cdot \lambda_{MU_i}$. This is because thinning a Poisson process with a fixed probability results in another Poisson process. Let D_i^l be the average number of required CPU cycles to execute a task arriving at MU i. The average local task execution time τ_i^l at MU i is given by

$$\tau_i^l = \frac{D_i^l}{f_i}, \tag{1}$$

where f_i is the clock frequency (in CPU cycles per second) of MU i. Assuming that the number of required CPU cycles per task follows an exponential distribution, we can model the local CPU server of MU i as an M/M/1 queue with mean arrival rate $(1 - \beta_i) \lambda_{MU_i}$ and mean task execution time τ_i^l. The

average delay Δ_{MU_i} of local task execution (which includes both queueing and service times) at MU i's CPU is then given by

$$\Delta_{\mathrm{MU}_i} = \frac{1}{\mu_i^l - \left(1 - \beta_i\right)\lambda_{\mathrm{MU}_i}}, \tag{2}$$

where μ_i^l, which is equal to $1/\tau_i^l$, is the rate at which the executed tasks depart from MU i' CPU.

Let R_j denote the set of MUs that are served by edge server j. Further, let $\lambda_{o,j}^e$ be the mean arrival rate and $D_{o,j}^e$ denote the required number of CPU cycles of offloaded tasks from the fixed (wired) subscribers, if any, which may be directly connected to edge server j. Given the offloading probabilities β_i, $\forall \mathrm{MU}_i \in R_j$, the mean arrival rate λ_{MEC_j} at the task scheduler of edge server j is computed as follows:

$$\lambda_{\mathrm{MEC}_j} = \lambda_{0,j}^e + \sum_{\mathrm{MU}_i \in R_j} \beta_i \lambda_{\mathrm{MU}_i}, \tag{3}$$

Let τ_j^e denote the average task execution time at edge server j. For estimating τ_j^e, we compute the average number $D_{o,j}^e$ of CPU cycles required to execute a task at edge sever j as follows:

$$\bar{D}_j^e = \frac{\lambda_{0,j}^e D_{0,j}^e + \sum_{\mathrm{MU}_i \in R_j} \beta_i \lambda_{\mathrm{MU}_i} D_i^l}{\lambda_{0,j}^e + \sum_{\mathrm{MU}_i \in R_j} \beta_i \lambda_{\mathrm{MU}_i}}, \tag{4}$$

which is then used to calculate τ_j^e, which is given by

$$\tau_j^e = \frac{\bar{D}_j^e}{f_j^e}, \tag{5}$$

where f_j^e is the computational capability (in CPU cycles per second) of edge server j. Modeling edge server j as an M/M/1 queue with mean arrival rate $(1 - \alpha_j) \lambda_{\text{MEC}_j}$ and mean service time τ_j^e, the average delay Δ_{MEC_j} of task execution at edge server j is calculated as follows:

$$\Delta_{\text{MEC}_j} = \frac{1}{\mu_j^e - \left(1 - \alpha_j\right) \lambda_{\text{MEC}_j}}, \tag{6}$$

whereby $\mu_j^e = 1 / \tau_j^e$. Substituting Equation (3) in Equation (6) provides the following expression:

$$\Delta_{\text{MEC}_j} = \frac{1}{\mu_j^e - \left(1 - \alpha_j\right)\left(\lambda_{0,j}^e + \displaystyle\sum_{\text{MU}_i \in R_j} \beta_i \lambda_{\text{MU}_i}\right)}, \tag{7}$$

which is valid only if

$$\mu_j^e - \left(1 - \alpha_j\right)\left(\lambda_{0,j}^e + \sum_{\text{MU}_i \in R_j} \beta_i \lambda_{\text{MU}_i}\right) < 1.$$

Next, we proceed to estimate the task execution delay at the remote cloud. Let R denote the set of edge servers that are connected to the remote cloud. The mean arrival rate λ_c at the remote cloud is obtained as follows:

$$\lambda_c = \lambda_{BKGD}^{cloud} + \sum_{\text{MEC}_j \in R} \alpha_j \lambda_{\text{MEC}_j}, \tag{8}$$

Let λ_{BKGD}^{cloud} and D_0^c denote the arrival rate and number of CPU cycles required to execute the background tasks at the remote cloud, respectively. Moreover, let τ_c denote the average task execution time at the remote cloud. In order to estimate τ_c, we first calculate the average number $\bar{D}_c$ of CPU cycles required to execute a task at the remote cloud, which is given by

$$\bar{D}_c = \frac{\lambda_0^c D_0^c + \sum_{\text{MEC}_j \in R} \alpha_j \lambda_{\text{MEC}_j} \bar{D}_j^e}{\lambda_{BKGD}^{cloud} + \sum_{\text{MEC}_j \in R} \alpha_j \lambda_{\text{MEC}_j}}, \tag{9}$$

which is then used to estimate τ_c as follows:

$$\tau_c = \frac{\bar{D}_c}{f^c}, \tag{10}$$

where f^c is the computational capability of each of the s homogeneous servers deployed at the remote cloud. We can thus model the remote cloud as an M/M/s queue with mean arrival rate λ_c (given by Equation (8)) and mean service time τ_c (given by Equation (10)). The average delay Δ_c experienced by an arbitrary task in the remote cloud is then estimated by the well-known

Erlang-C formula:

$$\Delta_c = \frac{c(s,a).\tau_c}{s-a} + \tau_c, \tag{11}$$

where a is equal to $\lambda_c.\tau_c$ and $C(s,a)$ is given by:

$$C(s,a) = \frac{\dfrac{a^s.s}{s!(s-a)}}{\displaystyle\sum_{k=1}^{s-1} \dfrac{a^k}{k!} + \dfrac{a^s.s}{s!(s-a)}}, \tag{12}$$

Next, we turn our attention to calculating the communication induced latency in our cooperative task offloading scheme. Recall from above that the offloaded tasks arrive at the wireless interface of MU i with rate $\beta_i . \lambda_{\text{MU}_i}$. With L_m denoting the maximum payload size of a single packet, the number of packets per task is equal to $\left\lceil \dfrac{B_i^l}{L_m} \right\rceil$. We can then estimate the rate Γ_{MU_i} at which packets arrive at the wireless interface of MU i as follows:

$$\Gamma_{\mathrm{MU}_i} = \lambda_B + \left\lceil \frac{B_i^l}{L_m} \right\rceil \cdot \beta_i \cdot \lambda_{\mathrm{MU}_i}, \tag{13}$$

where λ_B denotes the background H2H traffic (see also Figure 2).

In the following, we calculate the average packet delay Θ_i^{WiFi} in the uplink for MU i, who is associated with an ONU-AP through WiFi. Similar to Aurzada et al. (2014), for a given set of network model parameters, we can estimate Θ_i^{WiFi} as

$$\Theta_i^{\mathrm{WiFi}} = \frac{1}{\dfrac{1}{\Delta_i} - \Gamma_{\mathrm{MU}_i}}, \tag{14}$$

where Δ_i denotes the average channel access delay and Γ_{MU_i} is given by Equation (13). Note that

Equation (14) accounts for both queueing and channel access delay. We also note that the average access delay Δ_i consists of time delays due to carrier sensing, exponential back-offs, collided and erroneous (if any) attempts, successful transmission, and acknowledgement. To compute the average channel access delay, we define a two-dimensional Markov process $(s(t), b(t))$ under unsaturated conditions and estimate the average service time Δ_i in a WLAN using the IEEE 802.11 distributed coordination function (DCF) for access control, whereby $b(t)$ and $s(t)$ denote the random back-off counter and size of the contention window at time t, respectively. Due to given space constraints, we don't provide further details, but for completeness briefly note that Δ_i is obtained as follows:

$$\Delta_i = \sum_{k=0}^{\infty} p_{e,i}^k \left(1 - p_{e,i}\right) \left[\sum_{j=0}^{\infty} p_{c,i}^j \left(1 - p_{c,i}\right) \right.$$
$$\left. \left(\left(\sum_{b=0}^{k+j} \frac{2^{\min(b,m)} W_0 - 1}{2} E_s \right) + j T_{c,i} + k T_{e,i} + T_{s,i} \right) \right], \tag{15}$$

where $p_{e,i}$ is the probability of an erroneous transmission, $p_{c,i}$ is the probability of a collision, W_0 is the initial contention window size, E_s is the expected time-

slot duration, and $T_{c,i}$, $T_{e,i}$, and $T_{s,i}$ denote the average duration of a collided, erroneous, successful transmission of MU i, respectively.

Next, we assume a 4G LTE-A cellular network and estimate its uplink delay. Let p_i^{tx} denote the transmission power of MU i. We use the Shannon-Hartley Theorem to estimate the uplink data rate r_i^{LTE} of MU i transmitting to BS k via 4G LTE-A cellular network as follows:

$$r_i^{\text{LTE}} = \omega \log_2 \left(1 + \frac{p_i^{tx} G_{i,k}}{\overline{\omega}_0^2 + \sum_{j \neq i} p_j^{tx} G_{j,k}} \right), \tag{16}$$

where ω and $\overline{\omega}_0^2$ are the channel bandwidth and background noise power, respectively; $G_{i,k}$ denotes the channel gain between MU i and BS k. Similar to Beyranvand et al. (2017), the uplink delay of LTE-A users can be estimated by

$$\Theta_i^{\text{LTE}} = \frac{\rho_{BS}^u}{2 r_i^{\text{LTE}} \left(1 - \rho_{BS}^u \right)} \left(\frac{\varsigma_L^2}{\overline{L}} + \overline{L} \right) + \frac{\overline{L}}{r_i^{\text{LTE}}} + D_{RA}^{up} + D_{setup} + \tau_{BS}, \tag{17}$$

where D_{RA}^{up} is the initial random access delay, D_{setup} denotes the connection setup delay after passing the random access process successfully, ρ_{BS}^{up} denotes the uplink traffic intensity, τ_{BS} is the propagation delay in the cellular network, and $\overline{L}$ and ς_L^2 denote the mean and variance of the packet length, respectively.

Considering the user mobility model in the assumptions above, MU i is either connected to an ONU-AP through WiFi with probability P_{temp}^{MU} or an ONU-BS through cellular network with probability $\left(1 - P_{temp}^{\text{MU}} \right)$. The average task transmission delay Θ_i^{UL} in the uplink is then computed as follows:

$$\Theta_i^{\text{UL}} = \left(P_{temp}^{\text{MU}} . \Theta_i^{\text{WiFi}} + \left(1 - P_{temp}^{\text{MU}} \right) . \Theta_i^{\text{LTE}} \right) . \left\lceil \frac{B_i^l}{L_m} \right\rceil. \tag{18}$$

Next, we present the delay analysis of backhaul EPON. Let D_{PON}^u denote the average packet delay in the backhaul EPON in the upstream direction.

The average task transmission delay Θ^{PON} in the backhaul is then equal to $D_{\mathrm{PON}}^{u} \cdot \left\lceil \dfrac{B_i^l}{L_m} \right\rceil$, where D_{PON}^{u} is given by Aurzada et al. (2014):

$$D_{\mathrm{PON}}^{u} = \Phi\left(\rho^{u}, \bar{L}, \varsigma_L^2, c_{PON}\right) + \frac{\bar{L}}{c_{PON}} + 2\tau_{PON}\frac{2-\rho^{u}}{1-\rho^{u}} - B^{u}, \tag{19}$$

whereby ρ^{u} is the upstream traffic intensity, τ_{PON} is the propagation delay between ONUs and OLT, c_{PON} is the EPON data rate, $\Phi(.)$ denotes the well-known Pollaczek-Khintchine formula, and B^{u} is obtained as

$$\Phi\left(\frac{1}{\Lambda c_{PON}}\sum_{i=1}^{O}\sum_{q=1}^{O}\Gamma_{iq}^{PON}, \bar{L}, \varsigma_L^2, c_{PON}\right),$$

where O is the number of ONUs and Γ_{iq}^{PON} is the traffic coming from ONU_i to ONU_j, and Λ denotes the number of wavelengths in the WDM PON.

After calculating the computation and communication delay components, we proceed to compute the total average response time Ψ_i of MU i as follows:

$$\Psi_i = \left(1-\beta_i\right).\Delta_{\mathrm{MU}_i} + \beta_i.\left(\Theta_i^{\mathrm{UL}} + \left(1-\alpha_j\right)\Delta_{\mathrm{MEC}_j} + \alpha_j\left(\Theta^{\mathrm{PON}} + \Delta_c\right)\right), \tag{20}$$

where the terms denoted by Δ and Θ represent the latency components of computation and communication, respectively. Note that the communication-induced latency terms Θ_i^{UL} and Θ_i^{PON} depend on the offloading probabilities β_i and α_i, respectively. More specifically, if MUs decide to offload a large portion of their incoming tasks to the edge servers, the average task transmission delay in the uplink as well as the waiting times in the edge server may increase significantly. On the other hand, if the edge servers also decide to further offload a large portion of their tasks arriving from MUs and fixed subscribers to the remote cloud, the backhaul upstream delay as well as waiting delay at the cloud servers may increase as a result. Therefore, in order for the MUs to benefit from the powerful computational capabilities of the edge/remote servers and experience a low response time, it is important for both device and edge-server schedulers to optimally adjust their offloading probabilities.

Average Energy Consumption

Similar to Xiao and Krunz (2018), we model the power consumption of MU i's CPU as κf_i^3, where κ is the effective switched capacitance related to the chip architecture, as argued by Wang et al. (2016). The energy consumption per CPU cycle is thus equal to κf_i^3, as f_i represents the number of CPU cycles per second. The average energy consumption E_i^l for local execution of a task at MU i is then given by

$$E_i^l = \kappa . f_i^3 . D_i^l, \tag{21}$$

Recall from above that an incoming task at MU i is either executed locally with probability $(1 - \beta_i)$ or it is offloaded for nonlocal execution with probability β_i. Let E_i^o denote the average energy consumption of MU i to offload an incoming task, which is calculated as follows:

$$E_i^o = \left(k_1^{tx} + k_2^{tx} . p_i^{tx} \right) . \Theta_i^{\mathrm{UL}}, \tag{22}$$

where k_1^{tx} represents the static power consumption for having the radio frequency (RF) transmission circuitries switched on and k_1^{tx} measures the linear increase of the transmitter power consumption with radiated power p_i^{tx}. The average energy consumption E_i (for either executing a task locally or transmitting its input data to an edge server) of MU i is then estimated as

$$E_i = (1 - \beta_i) . E_i^l + \beta_i E_i^o. \tag{23}$$

By substituting Eqs. (21) and (22) into Equation (23), we have

$$E_i = (1 - \beta_i) . \left(\kappa . f_i^3 . D_i^l \right) + \beta_i \left(k_1^{tx} + k_2^{tx} . p_i^{tx} \right) . \Theta_i^{\mathrm{UL}}. \tag{24}$$

RESULTS

The following numerical results were obtained by using the LTE-A and FiWi network and traffic parameter settings listed in Table 1, which are consistent with those in the researches of Beyranvand et al. (2017), Aurzada et al. (2014), Muoz et al. (2015), Guo et al. (2016), and Wang et al. (2016). In our considered scenario, 50 MUs are scattered randomly within the range of 50 m from each ONU-BS. Besides, we consider four MUs within the coverage area of each ONU-AP. In the cellular access mode, we set the channel gain to $G_{i,k} = d_{i,k}^{-\zeta}$

Table 1. MEC-enabled FiWi enhanced HetNet Parameters and Default Values

Parameter	Value	Parameter	Value
Traffic Model Parameters			
L_m	1500 Bytes	λ_B	30 packets/s
α_{PON}	100	$\overline{L}, \varsigma_L^2$	1500 Bytes, 0
Backhaul EPON			
l_{PON}	100 km	c_{PON}	10 Gbps
N_{ONU}	12	Λ	1
WiFi Parameters			
DIFS	34 μsec	SIFS	16 μsec
PHY Header	20 μsec	W_0, H	16 slots, 6
ϵ	9 μsec	RTS	20 Bytes
CTS	14 bytes	ACK	14 Bytes
r in WMN	300 Mbps	ONU-AP radius	15 m
LTE-A Parameters			
p^{tx}	100 mW	ω	5 Mhz
$\overline{\omega}_0^2$	-100 dBm	k_1^{tx}	0.4 W
k_2^{tx}	18	ONU-BS radius	50 m
p^{rx}	200 mW		
Task and Edge/Cloud Server Parameters			
λ_{MU}	25 tasks/min	f_i	185 MHz
λ_0^e	12 tasks/min	f_j^e	1.44 GHz
λ_{BKGD}^{cloud}	480 tasks/min	s	6
f^c	1.44 GHz	B^l	66 KB
D^l, D_0^e, D_0^c	400 Mcycles	κ	10^{-26}

between MU i and BS k, where $d_{i,k}$ is the distance between MU i and BS k, and $\zeta = 4$ is the path loss factor. Further, we set $\beta_i = \beta \left(\forall i = 1, 2, ... \right)$ and $\alpha_j = \alpha \left(\forall j = 1, 2, ... \right)$. We consider N_{edge}=4 MEC servers, each associated with 8 end-users, whereof $1 \leq N_{PD} \leq 8$ partially decentralized end-users can flexibly control the amount of offloaded tasks by varying their computation offloading probability. The remaining 8-N_{PD} are fully centralized end-users that rely on edge computing only (i.e., their computation offloading probability equals 1).

For completeness, we first illustrate the average response time of fully decentralized MUs, who use only their local CPUs for computation, as well as the fully centralized ones, who rely on either edge- or cloud-only computing. The average response time vs. task arrival rate is depicted in Figure 3, which is helpful to compare the delay performance of local-, edge-, and cloud-computing without any hierarchical cooperation. We observe that

Figure 3. Performance comparison of local vs. non-local computing in terms of average response time for different values of background task arrival rate λ_{BKGD}^{cloud} (in tasks per second) to remote cloud

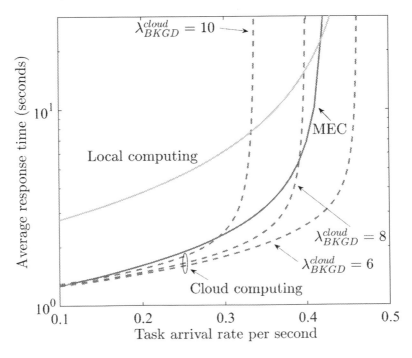

cloud computing, among others, is a promising solution toward achieving the smallest average response time if the background task arrival rate to the cloud doesn't exceed 6. Otherwise, depending on the rate which tasks arrive at MUs, we observe that either local-, edge-, or cloud-computing can yield the smallest average response time. Our major takeaway from Figure 3 is that although cloud- or edge-computing often results in a reduced response time, MUs may be able to experience a small response time even if they rely on their local CPUs, especially when the edge and/or cloud servers are over-utilized.

Next, we consider the cooperation between device and edge servers, which is characterized by the offloading probability β of N_{PD} partially decentralized MUs. Figures 4(a) and (b) illustrate the average response time and energy consumption vs. offloading probability β of partially decentralized MUs, respectively. We observe from Figure 4(a) that the average response time is a strictly convex function of offloading probability β, having a global optimum for a given N_{PD}. For instance, for N_{PD}=8, the MUs, on average, can experience a response time of 2.4 s when the partially distributed MUs set their offloading probability to β^*=0.65, which represents a significant reduction of 89.6% compared with 23.5 s for the case where β is set to 0, i.e., local computing. Also, note that β^* increases as the number N_{PD} of

Figure 4. Device-edge cooperative offloading: (a) average response time of MUs vs. offloading probability β for different number of partially distributed MUs, $N_{PD}=[1,2,3,4,8]$; (b) energy consumption vs. offloading probability β (λ_{MU} =25 tasks per minute and $\alpha=0$).

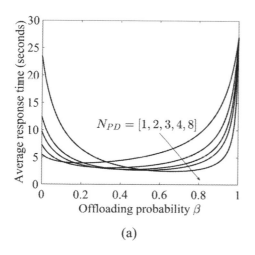

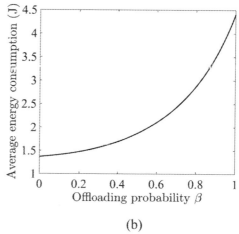

(a)   (b)

partially decentralized MUs increases. This happens in light of the fact that increasing N_{PD} leaves fewer fully centralized MUs that offload their entire incoming tasks, thus alleviating the burden on edge servers. This, in turn, allows other MUs to benefit from the computational resources of the edge servers by optimally adjusting their offloading probabilities, resulting in a reduced response time. More interestingly, Figures 4(a) and (b) characterize the energy-delay trade-off in our proposed device-edge cooperative computing scheme. More specifically, given an energy budget, Figure 4(b) determines the feasible set for β, which, together with Figure 4(a), can be used to find β^* that minimizes the average response time.

Finally, we consider the cooperation between device, edge, and cloud and investigate the average response time and energy consumption vs. α for different number N_{PD} of partially decentralized MUs in Figures 5(a) and (b), respectively. Note that for a given α and N_{PD}, each point shown on the curves in Figures 5(a)-(b) is obtained by setting the offloading probability to $\beta=\beta^*$ for a given network configuration and traffic scenario. First, we observe that the cooperation between device, edge, and cloud yields even better results in terms of average response time compared with the device-edge cooperation (see Figs 4(a) and 5(a)). Second, we observe from Figures 5(a)-(b) that increasing the number of partially decentralized MUs reduces

Figure 5. Device-edge-cloud cooperative computing: (a) average response time of MUs vs. offloading probability α for different number of partially distributed MUs, $N_{PD}=[1,4,8]$; (b) energy consumption vs. offloading probability α ($N_{edge}=4$ fixed and $\beta=\beta^*$).

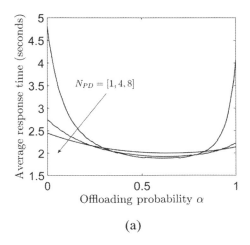

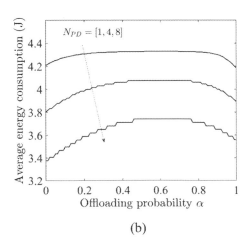

(a)

(b)

the average response time as well as energy consumption. More interestingly, our findings demonstrate that decentralization of computation decreases the sensitivity of the average response time to the fluctuations of the offloading probability α. More specifically, when all MUs are partially decentralized, i.e., $N_{PD}=8$, a slight deviation from the optimal setting of α doesn't have a significant detrimental impact on the average response time, provided that the MUs locally set their offloading probabilities β to the optimal value β^*.

CONCLUSION

This chapter studied the hierarchical cooperative computation offloading in MEC enabled FiWi enhanced HetNets from both network architecture and offlading mechanism design perspectives. We revisited FiWi access networks in the context of conventional clouds and emerging cloudlets, thereby highlighting the limitations of centralized C-RAN in light of future 5G networks moving toward decentralization based on cloudlets and MEC. Importantly, we elaborated on which implications wireless access via WiFi has for the design of decentralized co-DBA algorithms in support of future 5G low-latency applications. After compiling and classifying the research work conducted for the MEC in the context of the Tactile Internet, we presented our simple but efficient offloading strategy that leverages trilateral cooperation among device, edge server, and remote cloud. We developed an analytical framework to estimate the average response time and energy consumption of mobile users in a FiWi based MEC enabled network infrastructure. Our results demonstrate that the proposed hierarchical cooperative computing scheme outperforms edge- or cloud-only solutions.

REFERENCES

Aijaz, A., Dohler, M., Aghvami, A. H., Friderikos, V., & Frodigh, M. (2017). Realizing the Tactile Internet: Haptic communications over next generation 5G cellular networks. *IEEE Wireless Communications, 24*(2), 82–89. doi:10.1109/MWC.2016.1500157RP

Andrews, J. G. (2013). Seven ways that HetNets are a cellular paradigm shift. *IEEE Communications Magazine, 51*(3), 136–144. doi:10.1109/MCOM.2013.6476878

Andrews, J. G., Buzzi, S., Choi, W., Hanly, S. V., Lozano, A., Soong, A. C., & Zhang, J. C. (2014). What will 5G be? *IEEE Journal on Selected Areas in Communications*, *32*(6), 1065–1082. doi:10.1109/JSAC.2014.2328098

Aurzada, F., Lévesque, M., Maier, M., & Reisslein, M. (2014). FiWi access networks based on next-generation PON and gigabit-class WLAN technologies: A capacity and delay analysis. *IEEE/ACM Transactions on Networking*, *22*(4), 1176–1189. doi:10.1109/TNET.2013.2270360

Beyranvand, H., Lévesque, M., Maier, M., Salehi, J. A., Verikoukis, C., & Tipper, D. (2017). Toward 5G: FiWi enhanced LTE-A HetNets with reliable low-latency fiber backhaul sharing and WiFi offloading. *IEEE/ACM Transactions on Networking*, *25*(2), 690–707. doi:10.1109/TNET.2016.2599780

Chen, M. H., Liang, B., & Dong, M. (2017, May). Joint offloading and resource allocation for computation and communication in mobile cloud with computing access point. In *INFOCOM 2017-IEEE Conference on Computer Communications, IEEE* (pp. 1-9). IEEE. doi:10.1109/INFOCOM.2016.7524340

Chen, X., Jiao, L., Li, W., & Fu, X. (2016). Efficient multi-user computation offloading for mobile-edge cloud computing. *IEEE/ACM Transactions on Networking*, *24*(5), 2795–2808. doi:10.1109/TNET.2015.2487344

Fan, Q., & Ansari, N. (2018). Workload allocation in hierarchical cloudlet networks. *IEEE Communications Letters*, *22*(4), 820–823. doi:10.1109/LCOMM.2018.2801866

Fettweis, G. P. (2014). The Tactile Internet: Applications and Challenges. *IEEE Vehicular Technology Magazine*, *9*(1), 64–70. doi:10.1109/MVT.2013.2295069

Guo, H., & Liu, J. (2018). Collaborative computation offloading for multi-access edge computing over fiber-wireless networks. *IEEE Transactions on Vehicular Technology, 67*(5).

Guo, S., Xiao, B., Yang, Y., & Yang, Y. (2016, April). Energy-efficient dynamic offloading and resource scheduling in mobile cloud computing. In *INFOCOM 2016-The 35th Annual IEEE International Conference on Computer Communications, IEEE* (pp. 1-9). IEEE. 10.1109/INFOCOM.2016.7524497

Jia, M., Cao, J., & Liang, W. (2017). Optimal cloudlet placement and user to cloudlet allocation in wireless metropolitan area networks. *IEEE Transactions on Cloud Computing*, *5*(4), 725–737. doi:10.1109/TCC.2015.2449834

Liu, L., Chang, Z., Guo, X., Mao, S., & Ristaniemi, T. (2018). Multiobjective optimization for computation offloading in fog computing. *IEEE Internet of Things Journal*, *5*(1), 283–294. doi:10.1109/JIOT.2017.2780236

Maier, M., Chowdhury, M., Rimal, B. P., & Van, D. P. (2016). The Tactile Internet: Vision, recent progress, and open challenges. *IEEE Communications Magazine*, *54*(5), 138–145. doi:10.1109/MCOM.2016.7470948

Maier, M., Ebrahimzadeh, A., & Chowdhury, M. (2018). The Tactile Internet: Automation or Augmentation of the Human? *IEEE Access: Practical Innovations, Open Solutions*, *6*, 41607–41618. doi:10.1109/ACCESS.2018.2861768

Maier, M., & Rimal, B. P. (2015). The audacity of fiber-wireless (FiWi) networks: Revisited for clouds and cloudlets. *China Communications*, *12*(8), 33–45. doi:10.1109/CC.2015.7224704

Miettinen, A. P., & Nurminen, J. K. (2010). Energy Efficiency of Mobile Clients in Cloud Computing. *HotCloud*, *10*, 1–7.

Mondal, S., Das, G., & Wong, E. (2017, December). A Novel Cost Optimization Framework for Multi-Cloudlet Environment over Optical Access Networks. In *GLOBECOM 2017-2017 IEEE Global Communications Conference* (pp. 1-7). IEEE. 10.1109/GLOCOM.2017.8254251

Mondal, S., Das, G., & Wong, E. (2018, April). CCOMPASSION: A hybrid cloudlet placement framework over passive optical access networks. In *IEEE INFOCOM 2018-IEEE Conference on Computer Communications* (pp. 216-224). IEEE. 10.1109/INFOCOM.2018.8485846

Mondal, S., Das, G., & Wong, E. (2018, July). Supporting Low-Latency Applications through Hybrid Cost-Optimised Cloudlet Placement. In *2018 20th International Conference on Transparent Optical Networks (ICTON)* (pp. 1-4). IEEE. 10.1109/ICTON.2018.8473911

Munoz, O., Pascual-Iserte, A., & Vidal, J. (2015). Optimization of radio and computational resources for energy efficiency in latency-constrained application offloading. *IEEE Transactions on Vehicular Technology*, *64*(10), 4738–4755. doi:10.1109/TVT.2014.2372852

Rimal, B. P., Maier, M., & Satyanarayanan, M. (2018). Experimental Testbed for Edge Computing in Fiber-Wireless Broadband Access Networks. *IEEE Communications Magazine, 56*(8), 160–167. doi:10.1109/MCOM.2018.1700793

Rimal, B. P., Van, D. P., & Maier, M. (2016, April). Mobile-edge computing vs. centralized cloud computing in fiber-wireless access networks. In *Computer Communications Workshops (INFOCOM WKSHPS), 2016 IEEE Conference on* (pp. 991-996). IEEE. 10.1109/INFCOMW.2016.7562226

Rimal, B. P., Van, D. P., & Maier, M. (2017). Mobile edge computing empowered fiber-wireless access networks in the 5G era. *IEEE Communications Magazine, 55*(2), 192–200. doi:10.1109/MCOM.2017.1600156CM

Rimal, B. P., Van, D. P., & Maier, M. (2017). Cloudlet enhanced fiber-wireless access networks for mobile-edge computing. *IEEE Transactions on Wireless Communications, 16*(6), 3601–3618. doi:10.1109/TWC.2017.2685578

Rimal, B. P., Van, D. P., & Maier, M. (2017). Mobile-edge computing versus centralized cloud computing over a converged FiWi access network. *IEEE eTransactions on Network and Service Management, 14*(3), 498–513. doi:10.1109/TNSM.2017.2706085

Rodrigues, T. G., Suto, K., Nishiyama, H., & Kato, N. (2017). Hybrid method for minimizing service delay in edge cloud computing through VM migration and transmission power control. *IEEE Transactions on Computers, 66*(5), 810–819. doi:10.1109/TC.2016.2620469

Rodrigues, T. G., Suto, K., Nishiyama, H., Kato, N., & Temma, K. (2018). Cloudlets Activation Scheme for Scalable Mobile Edge Computing with Transmission Power Control and Virtual Machine Migration. *IEEE Transactions on Computers, 67*(9), 1287–1300. doi:10.1109/TC.2018.2818144

Simsek, M., Aijaz, A., Dohler, M., Sachs, J., & Fettweis, G. (2016). 5G-enabled Tactile Internet. *IEEE Journal on Selected Areas in Communications, 34*(3), 460–473. doi:10.1109/JSAC.2016.2525398

Sun, X., & Ansari, N. (2017). Latency aware workload offloading in the cloudlet network. *IEEE Communications Letters, 21*(7), 1481–1484. doi:10.1109/LCOMM.2017.2690678

Taleb, T., Samdanis, K., Mada, B., Flinck, H., Dutta, S., & Sabella, D. (2017). On multi-access edge computing: A survey of the emerging 5G network edge cloud architecture and orchestration. *IEEE Communications Surveys and Tutorials, 19*(3), 1657–1681. doi:10.1109/COMST.2017.2705720

Tan, H., Han, Z., Li, X. Y., & Lau, F. C. (2017, May). Online job dispatching and scheduling in edge-clouds. In *INFOCOM 2017-IEEE Conference on Computer Communications, IEEE* (pp. 1-9). IEEE. 10.1109/INFOCOM.2017.8057116

ITU-T Technology Watch Report. (2014). *The Tactile Internet*. ITU-T.

Tong, L., Li, Y., & Gao, W. (2016, April). A hierarchical edge cloud architecture for mobile computing. In *INFOCOM 2016-The 35th Annual IEEE International Conference on Computer Communications, IEEE* (pp. 1-9). IEEE.

Wang, Y., Sheng, M., Wang, X., Wang, L., & Li, J. (2016). Mobile-edge computing: Partial computation offloading using dynamic voltage scaling. *IEEE Transactions on Communications, 64*(10), 4268–4282.

Wong, E., Mondal, S., & Das, G. (2017, July). Latency-aware optimisation framework for cloudlet placement. In *Transparent Optical Networks (ICTON), 2017 19th International Conference on* (pp. 1-2). IEEE. 10.1109/ICTON.2017.8024881

Xiao, Y., & Krunz, M. (2018). Distributed Optimization for Energy-efficient Fog Computing in the Tactile Internet. *IEEE Journal on Selected Areas in Communications*.

Xu, Z., Liang, W., Xu, W., Jia, M., & Guo, S. (2016). Efficient algorithms for capacitated cloudlet placements. *IEEE Transactions on Parallel and Distributed Systems, 27*(10), 2866–2880. doi:10.1109/TPDS.2015.2510638

ENDNOTE

[1]   A cloudlet or edge server is defined as a trusted cluster of computers that comprise resources available to use for nearby mobile devices. A cloudlet can be treated as data center in a box, running a virtual machine capable of provisioning resources to end devices in real time.

Chapter 3
An Introduction to LiFi and Review of Prototypes Designed on FPGA and Other Hardware

Faisal Khan Khaskheli
Dawood University of Engineering and Technology, Pakistan

Fahim Aziz Umrani
Mehran University of Engineering and Technology, Pakistan

Attiya Baqai
Mehran University of Engineering and Technology, Pakistan

ABSTRACT

The current wireless networks are highly deficient when it comes to catering to the needs of the modern world with applications such as IoT and online interactive gaming. LiFi (visible light communication) has attracted interest as a solution to this problem due to its high data rate, wider spectrum, low power consumption, higher security, lower cost, and immunity to EMI. The idea behind LiFi is to use LED lights already available for space lighting for the purpose of transmitting. The chapter begins with a brief introduction to LiFI and then takes the reader through the history and market status of the technology all the way through to popular modulation techniques and finally ends with summarizing the transceiver prototypes designed previously with special emphasis on FPGA-based prototypes. The chapter provides a starting point for young budding researchers interested in LiFi and its implementation.

DOI: 10.4018/978-1-5225-9767-4.ch003

INTRODUCTION

It has been three decades since the wireless mobile communication systems became commercially available and the technology has already become an essential part of our everyday life, becoming a fundamental commodity. The past two decades have seen an exponential increase in mobile data traffic and have gone through a massive deployment of wireless communication systems. Technology advancements such as Internet of Things and Virtual reality have put huge pressure on currently available Radio frequency spectrum and the limited availability of RF spectrum is pointing towards a looming 'RF spectrum crisis' (Ofcom, 2013 ; Tsonev, Videv & Haas, 2013). This has prompted researchers to look to move towards higher frequencies and smaller cell sizes, exploring the millimeter wave part of the spectrum. While a smaller cell size is not a problem as far as system performance is concerned as it significantly improves performance. It does create other problems. Providing infrastructure to each cell and increased power consumptions are major issues in such networks. One of the possible solutions suggested to these problems is Visible Light Communication (VLC). It is just the next logical step in the move towards higher frequencies and takes one into the Nanometer range. VLC has attracted particular interest because lighting has virtually become a basic commodity for every home and place of work. Especially since LED has become a common device for illumination, it has made the dream of combining communication and illumination a reality. The existing infrastructure means the VLC Access points area readily available and existing technologies like Power Line Communication (PLC) and Power over Ethernet (PoE) mean the technology required for backhaul connectivity is also ready at hand. Also because light is on most of the times in indoor environment, the technology is power efficient since data is piggy backing illumination in most cases. Other benefits of VLC in addition to these include inherent security and immunity to Electromagnetic Interference (EMI).

Li-Fi is a relatively new subclass under the larger umbrella of VLC. Most of the research available is simulation based. However, some prototypes have been developed on various platforms that shall be discussed later in this chapter. Designers have implemented prototype Li-Fi/VLC transceivers on microcontrollers, FPGAs, Raspberry Pi and Arduino using a range of physical layer devices from expensive LED packages including drive circuits to cheap off the shelf devices. Data rates of around 1 Gbps and 3.4 Gbps have been reported using phosphorous coated white LED (Khalid, Cossu, Corsini,

Choudhury & Ciaramella, 2012) and off the shelf RGB LED (Cossu, Khalid, Choudhury, Corsini & Ciaramella, 2012). The technology allegedly has the potential to hit 10 Gbps mark.

VLC mostly deals with the physical implementation of Optical Wireless Communications. However, for a VLC system capable of complimenting the existing RF wireless networks and providing significant spectrum relief, a full network solution is required. This is what we call Li Fi. The term was first used by Harald Haas, a German physicist working at the University of Edinburgh. The Idea is to use the existing LED lights available for Illumination, for the purpose of data transfer. If the LED is modulated at a very high speed and it switches on and off quicker than the human eye can detect the same LED can be used for Illumination as well as data transfer without any considerable compromises.

History

Humans have been using light for communication in some form or the other for thousands of years. All the way from primitive smoke signals and beacon fires to Semaphore. (Huurdeman A.A., 2003) It was ancient Greeks and Romans who first used sunlight for long distance communication by polishing their shields and using them as reflectors during battles. (Holzmann G. J. & Pehrson B., 1994) Gauss invented his heliograph in 1810 to transmitted a beam of sunlight through mirrors, to a distant station However, in more recent history the idea of using light to transmit something as complex as voice for example, has also been around for over a century. It was 1880 when Graham Bell first proposed his design of a photophone but it never caught on. The technology available at the time made this nothing more than a dream. The dream, however did not die with Graham Bell. The first practical use of Free Space Optical Communication was seen in 1904 when the German military used heliograph transmitter technology which was later followed by US, British and French troops deploying similar technology in field. The German army also used to deploy an optical Morse code based communication during world war I when conventional communication lines were cut. It was also the German Military that developed a photophone in 1935 using tungsten filament lamp. (Mike, 1987) In 1962 MIT Lincoln Labs reported transmission of TV signals over a 30 Km Distance with an experimental OWC system.(Khan, L. U., 2017). However the development was slow and ultimately faded away due to the arrival of low loss optical fibers in 1970s.

Goodwin, F. E. (1970) provides a review of Optical Wireless Communication (OWC) research throughout the 60's decade. In the past two decades OWC communication has really taken off.

The more recent research in Visible Light Communication began in 2003 when in Kieo university data was transmitted using LEDs, through Visible Light.(LEE C.G., 2011) By 2010 a data rate of 500 Mbps had been reported over a short distance.

It was professor Harald Haas who first used the term Li-Fi for a short range indoor optical network using VLC. (pureVLC, 2013) Professor Haas is Co-founder of pure Li-Fi and is also the chair professor of Wireless Communication at Edinburgh University.

Li-Fi Consortium was formed in 2011 by industry groups, to promote high-speed optical wireless systems and to overcome the limited amount of radio-based wireless spectrum available by exploiting a completely different part of the electromagnetic spectrum.(Abdulhafid, Nizar, Simon & Sameeh, 2015) Single color LEDs were shown to produce data rates of 1.6 Gbps in 2013. (pureVLC, 2013) A Mexican company, Sisoft reported data rates of 10 Gbps in 2014. Li-Fi is standardized by IEEE under IEEE 802.15.7r1.

Abdulhafid et al, (2015) ; & FN Division, TEC (2015) mention some of the projects already underway and present a view of the future of Li-Fi based on the author's understanding. The history and future vision for Li-Fi is also discussed by Benlachtar et al, (2009). Prof. Haas also started the D light project in which the aim is to provide data rates of over 10 Mbps through Li-Fi using OFDM as the modulation technique, which is much speedier than the average broadband connection. Li-Fi has become a keen business interest for companies around the world. Listed below are some of the use cases.

1. A UK based Company, Pure Li-Fi claims to be one of the market leader in Li-Fi Technology. Their products include:

    ◦   Li-Flame Ceiling Unit which connects to an LED light
    ◦   Li-Flame Desktop Unit which uses USB to connect to a device.

A next generation system to Li-Flame called Li-Fi-X offers a complete networked solution, supporting roaming, multiple access and mobility. It provides a user experience that is far superior to existing wireless technologies.

Li-Fi-X claims to deliver full duplex communication with downlink and Uplink speeds of 40Mbps with full mobility.

Li-Fi-X Access Point (AP)

- Support for Power over Ethernet (PoE) or Power Line Communications (PLC).
- Connect to a wide range of LED light fixture to form an atto-cell.
- Handover control enables seamless switching between Aps.

Li-Fi-X Station (STA)

- Powered by USB 2.0.
- Supports handover.

2. A French company OLEDCOMM designs Li-Fi routers for LED based lighting systems. The products and services offered by OLEDCOMM are:

   ○ *GEOLi-Fi- Indoor Location Based Services:* It is a high efficiency dimmable LED driver connected with an Indoor Positioning System (IPS) and works as a Li-Fi broadcast system. It can convert the LED lights in a building into an IPS to locate people and Objects and create location based services such as mobile marketing. A consumer inside a shopping mall could be guided to his/her desired object based on the indoor map of the mall. It can also allow physical tracking of the customer and help deal with problems like shop lifting.

   ○ *Li-FiNET - Unlimited bandwidth for connecting people and IoT:* It combines a high efficiency dimmable LED driver with a bidirectional Li-Fi communication for people and IoT. It enables secure communication for IoT. This system aims to solve some of the major problems which hinder unleashing of the potential of the Internet of Things such as high power consumption and signal leakage. OLEDCOMM also claimed to have developed the first Li-Fi enabled car in 2007 using Li-Fi for car to car communication.

Future Vision

If the technology continues to develop at this pace very soon every LED would be connected to a Li-Fi network providing a cleaner, greener high-speed data connection.

SYSTEM ARCHITECTURE

IEEE 802.15.7 specifies VLC consisting of 3 types of communication. Mobile to Mobile, Fixed to Mobile, and Infrastructure to Mobile. The VLC mainly focuses on medium range communication at low speeds and short range at high speeds for Fixed to Mobile and Mobile to Mobile Communications. (FN Division, TEC, 2015).

Khan, (2017); Ramadhani & Mahardika, (2018) categorize Li-Fi based on a layered architecture shown in figure 1.

In this architecture Li-Fi consists of 3 layers; physical layer, MAC layer and application layer. The IEEE 802.15.7 only defines two layers for Li FI i.e. physical layer and MAC layer.

PHY Layer

The PHY layer is responsible for detection of the state of communication channel (idle or busy), activation and deactivation of optical transceiver and the actual transmission and reception. It has three modes of operation PHY I, PHY II and PHY III as specified in table 1. The modulation schemes that are

Figure 1. Layered network architecture of Li-Fi system according to IEEE 802.15.7 standard

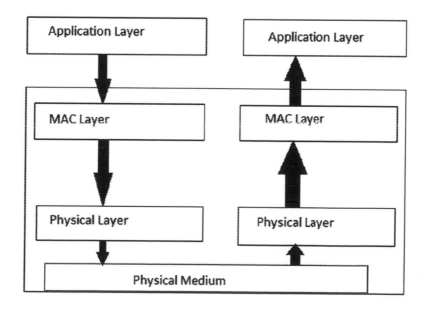

Table 1. Three modes of operation of Li-Fi physical layer (Carlos, Itziar, David, Carlos, 2016)

Operation mode	Usage	Category	Rates
PHY I	Outdoor	Low	11.6 Kbps-266.6 Kbps
PHY II	Indoor	Moderate	1.25 Mbps-96 Mbps
PHY III	Multiple transceiver	CSK Modulation	12 Mbps-96Mbps

recognized for PHY I and PHY II are Variable Pulse Position Modulation and On Off Keying. There is a DC component included to avoid light extinction in case of a long run of 0's since the system also has to ensure an uninterrupted illumination.

There are also two Japanese standards for VLC networking (JEITA CP-1221 and CP-1222). (FN Division, TEC, 2015)

MAC Layer

Three network topologies are described here, peer-to-peer, star and broadcast. (Khan, 2017)

1. **Peer to Peer**: Two devices communicating with each other.
2. **Star**: Communication between several devices.
3. **Broadcast**: A single devices sends data to multiple devices. Communication is one way.

A Li-Fi communication system could be deployed in any of the above configurations. Figure 2 gives one such deployment.

Propagation Channel

The Li-Fi propagation channel can be characterized as being Line Of Sight and Non Line Of Sight. LOS is a condition where a clear, unobstructed path is available between the transmitter and the receiver, and a NLOS is the situation where no such path exists. In NLOS channel, light is spread via reflections from walls and ceiling. Table 2 summarizes the characteristics of each criterion:

Figure 2. Li-Fi network (Satyanarayana, Mathew & Sathyashree, 2016)

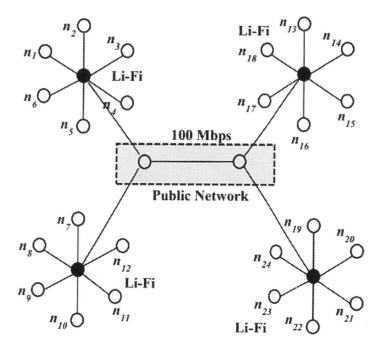

Table 2. Li-Fi channel characterization (Ramadhani & Mahardika,2018)

	Directed	Hybrid	Non Directed
Line of Sight	• Maximize power efficiency • Minimize path loss	• Combining Transmitter and Receivers with different degrees of directionality.	• Wide angles Transmitters and receivers. • Convenient to use for mobile terminals.
Non Line of Sight	• Rely upon reflections from ceilings or walls etc. • Increased link robustness and ease of use. • Allow operation even in the presence of obstacles.		

Hardware

Since a large number of optical front end devices are required to deploy a Li-Fi system that can provide complete coverage the only suitable candidate is LEDs. Cheap off the shelf devices are also good enough for this purpose as they are inexpensive and have a wide enough beam width they can be used in large enough numbers and can be expected provide the desired amount of coverage.

Both phosphorous coated white LEDs and off the Shelf RGB LEDs have been used in downlink for early Li-Fi systems producing good data rates and error performance.

The uplink of a Li-Fi system could be a wireless broadband link making it a Li-Fi/Wi-Fi hybrid system or it could also be an infrared link. Both seem quite promising since the bandwidth requirement for uplink is not expected to be anywhere near as large as it is for the downlink.

LI-FI VS. WI-FI

The true merits of any new technology can only be clearly observable when compared with already existing competing technologies and for Li-Fi the biggest competitor is Wi-Fi. Therefore, a lot of published material is available, comparing Li-Fi with Wi-Fi. Verma et al (2015) ; Hadi, (2016) compare these two technologies and highlight the various shortcomings of Wi-Fi and how Li-Fi overcomes those short comings. Wi Fi has been the technology of choice for providing user end connectivity for over a decade now but the advent of 5 G and technologies such as VR and IoT has severely exposed its limitations.

It is therefore, necessary to compare the two technologies here. Listed below are some of the major flaws of Wi-Fi and how Li-Fi maybe able to overcome them.

1. *Capacity:* Wi-Fi is looking increasingly deficient in providing the sufficient bandwidth. Li-Fi on the other hand offers thousands of times wider bandwidth as it operates in the visible part of the EM spectrum. (George W, 2012)
2. *Power Efficiency:* In Li-Fi, most of the times data is piggy backing illumination and the power consumed is almost zero since the light is on for the purpose of illumination anyway. It consumes very little power compared with Wi-Fi.
3. *Availability:* It is not advisable to use Wi-Fi in certain places such as aero planes, petrochemical plants and hospitals, due to Chances of interference with critical equipment and risk of accidents. Light sources are available virtually everywhere and since Li-Fi operates in the optical part of the EM spectrum, there is no chance of any interference with other equipment and it can be safely used inside hospitals and nuclear power plants etc.

4. *Security:* Due to the ability of radio waves to penetrate walls, security is a major concern for Wi-Fi. Light does not penetrate walls and it is inherently more secure than Wi-Fi.

Table 3 and Table 4 show comparison between Li-Fi and Wi-Fi.

A hybrid network, combining both Wi-Fi and Li-Fi may be a good option as it would combine the best of both technologies. Since Li-Fi is sensitive to ambient light, it is predominantly an indoor technology. Wi-Fi can help extend the network to outdoor environment. It could also be considered an option to provide uplink connectivity in a Li-Fi system.

Table 3. Comparing Li-Fi to Wi-Fi (Sharma et al, 2014)

Technology	Physical layer	Security	Bandwidth	Cost
Wi-Fi	Electromagnetic waves (2.5-5 Ghz)	Good	Limited	Moderate
Li-Fi	Light	Excellent	Exceptional	Low

Table 4. Li-Fi vs Wi-Fi (Akshika & Arvind, 2016 ; Prateek, Aditya &Prashant 2016)

	Li-Fi	Wi-Fi
Mode of Operation	Data transmitted using light through LEDs.	Data Transmitted using radio waves through a Wi-Fi router
Interference	No interference issues	Interferes with other nearby access points
Technology	Present IrDA compliant devices	802.11 a/b/g/n/ac/ad standard compliant devices
Merits	Less interference, high bandwidth	Immune to ambient light can work well outdoors
Applications	Inside aircrafts, hospitals, nuclear reactors and other places where EMI is an issue	Used for accessing the internet in public places such as bus stops etc
Privacy	Cannot pass through walls	Can pass through walls
Speed	About 1 Gbps	About 150 Mbps to 250 Mbps
Ecological Impact	Low	High
Network Topology	Point-to-point	Point-to-multipoint

MODULATION

When discussing performance improvement of any communication system the first thing that comes to mind is a change in the modulation technique. It is pivotal when it comes to increasing the amount of data that can be transferred or improving the error performance of a communication system. An all optical network that can provide seamless coverage would require a large number of front end optical devices. For such devices the most suited candidates are solid state LEDs. The problem with such devices is that information can only be coded in the intensity, and the amplitude and phase may not be changed. VLC can only be deployed as an IM/DD system and the signal has to be both unipolar as well as real valued. This greatly limits the available modulation techniques for Li-Fi. Several modulation techniques have been suggested by researchers, both in their original form as well as with some variations. In addition to this some novel techniques have also been explored that better suit the specific needs of an indoor visible light communication system. In this regard Haas, Yin, Wang, & Chen, (2016) Have done one of the most comprehensive works in which the authors discuss the most commonly used modulation techniques for Li-Fi. Sufyan & Haas, (2016) discuss several single carrier (OOK,PPM,PAM) and multicarrier (OFDM and its variants) modulation techniques separately and compare the advantages and limitations of each, very briefly. Li-Fi specific modulation techniques such as Color Shift Keying and Color Intensity Modulation are also touched upon. It also touches upon multiple accessing and suggests a Li-Fi-Wi-Fi hybrid system. Tsonev, Videv & Haas, (2013) also discuss multiple access and modulation and then briefly discuss Li-Fi atto-cell.

Monteiro & Hranilovic, (2014) set their aim, as mentioned by the authors to reduce cost through selection of appropriate modulation, coding and filtering. The objective was to achieve a desirable Bit Error Rate (BER) with a low cost system. The authors managed to analyze the BER performance and its dependence on distance and angles of incidence and irradiance for various modulation techniques.

Single Carrier Modulation Techniques

As discussed previously, several single carrier techniques have been explored successfully for use in a Li-Fi communication system. Some of them are discussed in this section.

On-Off Keying

On-Off Keying is the simplest form of Amplitude Shift Keying (ASK) and is probably one of the most commonly used techniques for optical communication systems. In its simplest form two distinct voltage levels are defined a low (0) and a high (1). An LED is modulated to transition between these voltages. The advantages are low complexity and cost. Where as the drawbacks include low power efficiency and susceptibility to noise.

Pulse Width Modulation

PWM works by modulating the width of pulses in accordance with the amplitude of the information signal. The idea is for the signal to have a constant frequency but a variable duty cycle, according to the message signal. It offers moderate complexity and is more robust against noise. On the flip side, since it requires devices with high switching speed, the components are expensive. PWM also suffers from high switching losses at high frequencies.

Pulse Amplitude Modulation

PAM works by varying the amplitude of a series of pulses according to the value of an analog signal. It is used very commonly in VLC systems due to very good bandwidth efficiency however it comes with its own problems. For example the difference between the highest and lowest amplitude pulse may be very large and the brightness of the LED may vary greatly.

Pulse Position Modulation

PPM is a modulation technique in which M bits are transmitted by encoding them in a pulse transmitted during one of the 2^M available time slots. It is used very commonly in optical communication systems. This technique is sensitive to synchronization errors and multipath interference effects. Since the position of the pulse in time is what contains the data, loss of synchronization or presence of multiple time delayed reflected version of the same signal can make it almost impossible to correctly decode data. PPM consumes much less power than OOK due to a very narrow pulse transmitted but consumes a lot more bandwidth.

Digital Pulse Interval Modulation

DPIM is a modulation technique which is seen as an alternative to the more established, OOK and PPM.(Ghassemlooy, Aldibbiat & Hayes, 2007) In this technique a block of M bits is encoded on one of the 2^M DPIM symbols. (Ghassemlooy, Aldibbiat & Hayes, 2007) Each symbol starts with a short pulse that is then followed by a number of empty slots representing the decimal value of the information block of M bits. It has a distinct advantage over PPM as the symbol length is variable rather than fixed. This results in greater throughput. To counter the effects of multipath reflections a guard band may be inserted after the pulse.

Multi-Carrier Modulation Techniques

The single carrier modulation schemes are fairly simple to implement and less costly for a low to moderate data rate application. However, as the data rates increase the non flat frequency response of the optical channel comes into play and they suffer severely from Inter Symbol Interference. A more resilient modulation scheme is required for such cases. OFDM and its several variants seem to be the most suitable candidates for such a situation.

Optical OFDM

Over the last few years we have seen a dramatically increased interest in OFDM for optical communication. OOFDM uses the same principle of dividing a communication channel into several smaller overlapping subcarriers which do not interfere due to the fact that they are orthogonal to each other.

Optical OFDM provides the same benefits as its electrical counterpart. The most significant of these being immunity to ISI and frequency selective behavior of the optical channel. This feature is going to come in very handy as in the indoor environment multiple reflections off walls and ceiling are very much a given.

SIM-OFDM

Subcarrier index modulation is a technique that attempts to make use of an additional dimension of the OFDM frame. In conventional OFDM different frequency carriers are modulated using a signal following a scheme such as

QAM. SIM OFDM encodes another OOK modulated data stream in the index of the subcarrier that is active. Each subcarrier thus receives the energy of the QAM as well as the OOK bit rendering the technique more power efficient.

DCO-OFDM

Since it is a feature of optical devices that they are inherently unipolar, OFDM which is a bipolar technique is not directly suited to optical communication. Techniques need to be explored, to convert bipolar OFDM signal to a unipolar one. DCO-OFDM is one such technique. The idea is to provide the OFDM signal with a strong enough DC bias to shift the entire signal up and remove the negative peaks. The technique is fairly simple but is inefficient in terms of power consumed.

ACO-OFDM

ACO-OFDM reduces the power requirement of an Optical OFDM system since no power is wasted in DC biasing in order to convert bipolar OFDM into unipolar for use in an optical communication system. The negative values on ACO-OFDM are simply set to zero. This offers a much greater electrical SNR for a given optical power than DCO-OFDM. Several variants of ACO-OFDM can also be used including a DCO-OFDM, ACO-OFDM hybrid often called ADO-OFDM.

In literature, comparisons have been performed between Asymmetrically Clipped Optical OFDM and DC- Biased Optical OFDM. As the modulation order increases DCO-OFDM suffers from distortion, whereas this effect is much less significant in ACO OFDM.

Modulation Techniques Specific to LI FI

Color Shift Keying (CSK)

This is a modulation technique defined in section 8.2 of IEEE 802.15.7 standard and is designed to be used with RGB LEDs. The symbols are selected such that the instantaneous chromaticity varies while the average luminosity remains constant and the information is coded in the instantaneous

color of the transmitter light. CSK has two major advantages over intensity modulation. firstly, there is no flicker and it guarantees a constant luminosity. Secondly, there is an almost constant drive current which means there is no sudden inrush of high current when data is being sent. This reduces chances of inductance and isolates the communication signal from the power line. (Monteiro & Hranilovic, 2014)

ADVANTAGES AND CHALLENGES FOR LI-FI

Advantages

Li-Fi has huge benefits to power efficiency, capacity and security. It is the ideal option for high density wireless coverage in closed indoor environments since it has no radio interference issues. Let us now examine each one of these advantages individually. (Prerna, Ritika & Rani 2012 ; Parmar, Khushbu & Jay, 2014)

Efficiency

Most of the energy in a radio station is used for cooling purpose and the actual efficiency is around 5%. LEDs consume very little energy making Li-Fi a far more efficient system. Some of the efficiency related benefits are listed below:

Low Cost

Li-Fi system could be established using cheap off the shelf LEDs and the over all cost of the system is much lower than that of a comparable radio system. The supporting components are also much cheaper than those for microwave.

Energy

LEDs require very little energy anyway, when compared with other lighting sources and data does not require much additional energy since the LED is already on for Illumination.

Environment

Li-Fi works in environment such as underwater communication where RF transmission is very difficult.

Capacity

Any source of light can be used as a hotspot to carry data in a Li-Fi system such as car headlights, street lights etc. this makes Li-Fi cheaper and easy to deploy. (Parmar, Khushbu & Jay, 2014)

The most important Factors when discussing capacity of a Li-Fi system are Bandwidth, Data density and speed.

Bandwidth

Since Li-Fi operates in the visible part of the spectrum there is an abundance of bandwidth available, more than 10,000 times larger than there is for RF systems.

Data Density

The Data density achievable for Li-Fi systems is many times greater than that for Wi-Fi systems since the light is contained within a small area, whereas RF tends to spread out and cause interference.

High Speed

Large bandwidth, low interference and a high data density naturally make very large data rates of around 500 Mbps a possibility.

Safety

Light does not carry the health concerns typically associated with microwave and radio communication. Due to the fact that it does not interfere with other electronic circuits, it can safely be used inside hospitals and aero planes etc.

Security

Li-Fi systems are inherently more secure since the transmission is confined in a tight space and the signal is unable to penetrate walls. The Li-Fi signal is very difficult to eavesdrop on. It can be clearly seen where the data is going.

Limitations

Hadi, (2016) ; Aftab, (2016) mention some applications of Li-Fi and discuss some of its limitations. Chauhan & Kulai, (2015) present obstruction as a major source of errors and suggests a feedback system to detect this obstruction and a pause in both transmission and reception until the obstruction clears. The pioneer in Li-Fi technology is Prof. Harald Haas, who was the first to coin the term Li-Fi. Khandal, & Jain, (2014) give a brief review of his work before going into details of possible applications and limitations of Li-Fi

Some of the major limitations of Li-Fi are:

- Network can only be accessed where an LED light source is available which restricts the environments and situation where Li-Fi can be used.
- Requires a clear line of sight to transmit.
- Opaque obstacles on pathways can affect data transmission.
- Ambient light like sunlight and light from other artificial sources can cause interference.

Implementation Issue in High Speed Li-Fi Systems

Most of the research until now has been focused on providing high data rates using Li-Fi, however a couple of major concerns for such system is lighting quality and power consumption. The lighting specification for indoor units is generally application specific. Conference rooms and restaurants can require light levels as low as 1 percent of maximum illumination for aesthetic and comfort purposes. An illuminance level of 300 lux (lumen per square meter) is suggested for reading and writing tasks, whereas 30 lux is sufficient for computer task. (Gancarz Elgala & Little, 2013 ; Zafar, Karunatilaka & Parthiban, 2015) The average optical power may change during communication producing a flicker. Which is periodic or nonperiodic

output power (brightness) fluctuation that the eyes can perceive. Although very little work has been done on this, some methods have been suggested to overcome this flicker and dimming problem.

- **Idle Pattern and Compensation Time Dimming:** The IEEE 802.15.7 standard allows an idle pattern to be inserted between the data frames for light dimming. It can be in band or out of band. An in-band pattern does not require any clock changes and the receiver can see it. An out-of-band pattern is sent at a lower optical clock and is not detected by the receiver.
- **Visibility Pattern Dimming:** These are in-band patterns that are used in the payload of a CVD (color visibility dimming) frame. The CVD frame is a frame used for color, visibility and dimming support. It provides information such as channel quality to the user. The CVD frame may also be sent during idle mode for continuous visibility and dimming support.
- **VPPM Dimming:** VPPM offers protection from intra-frame flicker. Since the pulse amplitude is always constant in VPPM, it does not give rise to the color-shift in the light source that can arise from amplitude dimming and the dimming control is not performed by amplitude but rather by pulse width. Bits "1" and "0" in VPPM are distinguished by the pulse position within a unit period and have the same pulse width within their respective unit periods. Dimming and full brightness in VPPM is achieved by controlling the "on" time pulse width.
- **Pulse Dual Slope Modulation:** The binary input bit "0" stream changes only the slope of the rising edge of the pulse In PSDM, keeping the slope of the falling edge fixed and vice versa for a bit "1". During the idle period, the slope of the both rising and falling edges changes by the equal amount.

In FEC codes the probability of 1's and 0's is not guaranteed to be equal which may give rise to need for dimming control. Also FEC codes cannot avoid continuous runs of 1's and 0's which may cause fluctuations in the short run causing noticeable flicker. In (Fang et al, 2017) a capacity-achieving and flicker-free FEC coding scheme using polar codes is proposed for dimmable VLC. the proposed method can achieve both, a high coding efficiency as well as a simplicity of design.

REVIEW OF LI-FI PROTOTYPE SYSTEMS

Mathematics and simulations are one thing but ultimately Li-Fi is a communication system designed for practical use. The next logical step is of simulation results as well as to come up with an optimal hardware platform for developing a Li-Fi communication system. This section reviews a few such prototypes. The focus here shall be FPGA based prototypes, however other platforms shall also be touched upon briefly.

Microcontrollers

Nikashep & Sowmya, (2016) aimed to analyze the performance of a Li-Fi system established using Atmel AT89 microcontroller which is less powerful than the AT90 Microcontroller based on Intel 8051 core. Industry Standard instruction set allows the reuse of legacy code. The applicability of the system was demonstrated and guidelines for future systems were also suggested. Shah, Purohit, Samant & Karani, (2015) also managed to transit images using a system based on the same controller.

Kolhe & Mandavgane, (2007) ; Lakshmisudha, D. Nair, A. Nair & Garg, *(2016)*both use Atmega 16 Microcontroller for encoding and decoding purpose.Lakshmisudha et al, (2016) design a system that can transmit text, video and audio at 115200 baud rate. The system can also be connected with sensors like a thermostat and MQ6 for detecting flammable gases and used for industrial safety system.

Kala, & Sathishkumar, (2017); Siva, Raju, Mohana, & Sai, (2017); Doori, et al (2017); Suraj, Sagar & Pankaj (2016); Mrs. Singh & Prof. (Dr) Singh (2014); Rashmi, Rajalaxmi & Mr.Balaji (2015) & Kumawat, & Verma, (2017). all use PIC 16F877 A micro controller for the purpose of encoding data. Kala, & Sathishkumar, (2017), Mrs. Singh & Prof. (Dr) Singh (2014) & Rashmi, Rajalaxmi & Mr.Balaji (2015) All demonstrate the workability of the transceiver using the PIC controller. In Suraj, Sagar & Pankaj (2016) report having transmitted both stored data from memory and real time input from a keyboard with speed up to 1Kbps. In Doori, et al (2017) the transmission of data and audio is demonstrated using PCM and MP3 streaming using VLC. Siva, Raju, Mohana, & Sai, (2017) transmitted Encrypted text and images successfully up to a distance of 4 meters. Kumawat, & Verma, (2017) report a transmission distance for audio ranging up to 20 meters.

A prototype that transmits Image files is designed and tested by Bharadwaj, (2017) using the PIC 18F46K22 Microcontroller.

Krishnan (2017) has designed and implemented a prototype for vehicle-2-vehicle communication using the Atmega 328 P controller, with the aim to provide an open source system for vehicles regardless of their manufacturers. The system is aimed to exchange information like vehicle speeds and when the brakes are applied etc.

The limited processing power, smaller memory and complexity of programming are some of the issues that were obvious in the above designs. The issues were caused by the limitations of the microcontrollers. These limitations restrict one from testing the true potential of a high speed communication system such as Li-Fi.

Raspberry Pi

Mangesh ct al (2016) ; Dayalakshmi & Ivareddy, (2016) ; Kodama, & Haruyama, (2017) ; Fergusson, (2016) all use raspberry pi as the platform to develop a Li-Fi prototype. Fergusson, (2016) aims to show a proof of concept, and the designer was able to develop a prototype transceiver using Raspberry Pi 2B. It was also found that the use of addressable LEDs was only feasible in heavily constrained environments.

The aim of the authors in Kodama, & Haruyama, (2017)was to develop a fine grain positioning system over Raspberry Pi 3 using a Digital Micrometer Device Projector. The prototype system was deployed in a cloth shop and was shown to work within an accuracy of a few millimeters.

Mangesh et al (2016) aimed to develop a Li-Fi system for Hospitals and other constrained environments using Raspberry Pi 3. Two transceiver modules were tested. A unidirectional data rate of 100 Mbps was reported on LAN using *Research Design Lab Module*. Whereas the module by the vendor Firefly was able to produce speeds of 350-400 Mbps and up to 500 Mbps over short range.

Dayalakshmi & Ivareddy, (2016). discusses the development of a Li-Fi system using Raspberry Pi Model B for the transmitter and a PIC microcontroller for the receiver part. A baud rate of 38400 was reported and the system was reported to work over a range of 3 meters.

Other Processing Devices

Goswami, & Shukla (2017) use the Audrino UNO R3 to develop a prototype transceiver that can transmit Text, Audio and video. The modulation technique used by the designers was OOK. The system was a unidirectional one and therefore suited for broadcasting. A speed of 115,200 bps was achieved. The authors suggest use of Higher end devices to improve the speed of the system.

A bidirectional communication system is designed in Kamsula, (2015) using the USRP. The designers of the prototype reported maximum data rates of 12.5 Mbps, which were limited only by the sample rate of USRP. Transmission was successfully received up to a range of 7 meters. The authors also established an internet connection using Powel Line Communication (PLC). The modulation technique of choice was GMSK. However initial testing for future work was also done on GFSK, QPSK, 8-PSK, 16-QAM and OFDM.

DSP Development Board

Professor Harald Haas and his fellow authors in Elgala, Mesleh,& Haas, (2009). present a hardware prototype based on DSP development board. The prototype uses OFDM as the modulation technique of choice to investigate the effects of SNR, channel coding and Constellation order on the BER performance. After detailing the system model the authors present their results in terms of relative position of transmitter and receiver. BER performance for different modulation schemes were investigated.

FPGA

Mohie et al (2016) used the Spartan-6 Xilinx XC 6SLX4ST device providing large speed internet access using more than one serial communication protocol that will be used to cover a medium sized room . It was found that UART has limited data rates and SPI was not supported by the FPGA device and in the end they settled for GB Ethernet.

The designers Guo et al (2017) propose a fundamental design and implementation of data communication of VLC on the MAC layer based on FPGA. The authors demonstrated the working of a UWB MAC Controller for VLC using a Cyclone II 2C20 device.

Xilinx Spartan 6 Valent FX Mark-1 Board was the platform of choice for Videv, S., & Haas, H. (2014). The aim of this paper is to show practical implementation of Spatial Shift Keying (SSK) for VLC. The paper reports a BER of less than 2×10^{-3} which allows for error free communication if FEC is used. Maintaining sufficient symbol separation was identified as the main problem with using SSK and suggested solution such as using polarization filters at both transmitter and receiver, using spatial geometrical positioning of LEDs and PDs to ensure minimum overlap or introducing a power imbalance at the transmitter to better distinguish different symbols.

Ghassemlooy, Aldibbiat &Hayes (2007) attempt to design a diffuse optical link using Digital Pulse Interval Modulation (DPIM). The model used for this purpose was Xilinx XC4005B. Slot Error Rate (SER) and Packet Error Rate (PER) are used as performance indicators. . Performance shown to improve slightly with optical filter, for daylight. For low frequency electronic ballast performance was improved with use of optical filter whereas for a bulb it remained unchanged. A data rate of 2.5 Mbps was reported.

Baeza, Sánchez-Fernández, Armada, & Royo, (2015) designed a testbed for VLC downlink where the transmitter is mounted on street lights. The FPGA model used for this purpose was Spartan 3E-Xc3s500E. Different combinations of modulation techniques and line codes were tested and the results were reported.

In Anguita, Brizzolara, & Parodi, (2010) two different models of FPGA, having different clock speeds were used namely, Spartan 3 and Actel IGLOO AGLN250 for an underwater VLC system. Several modulation techniques such as OOK, 4-PPM and 8-PPM were tested. After considering constraints like speed, power consumption and design complexity, 8-PPM was seen as the most efficient technique out of those tested. Apart from this the performance of different colored LEDs was tested and it was seen that at different distances the performance of each LED in the RGB configuration varied.

The main goal of Kumar & Nirubama, (2012) was to implement an adaptive PPM technique for OWC using Altera Cyclone III EP3 C16F484 FPGA. The designers used fuzzy logic to implement the system that could switch between PPM,DPPM and MPPM. The switched would be performed based on whether, bandwidth efficiency, data rates or power was the concern.

Hagem (2016) tested 4-PPM and 16-PPM for optical underwater communication and concluded that PPM is highly suited for the purpose.

Aly et al (2015) reports data rates of up to 24 Mbps using OOK modulation. The authors also suggest PPM, PWM and PAM as other possible modulation techniques to be explored.

Table 5. Summary of Hardware implementations of VLC prototypes

Platform	Year	Data rates	Modulation	Range
FPGA	2016	2.3Gbps (BER x^{-10})	-	Average room size
	2017	-	-	-
	2014	1 Mbps for testing(BER < 2×10^{-3})	SSK (as IM/DD)	Up to 35 cm
	2007	2.5 Mbps	DPIM	-
	2015	Up to 266 Kbps	OOK, VPPM	Up to 50 cm
	2010	1-2 Mbps	4-PPM, 8-PPM, 16-PPM	4-5 m
	2016	-	4-PPM and 16-PPM	-
	2012	-	PPM, DPPM, MPPM	-
	2015	Up to 24Mbps	OOK	1-2 meters
	2017	-	PPM	25 m
	2011	-	4-QAM	20 cm
Raspberry Pi				
	2017	Up to 500 Mbps	OOK	
	2016	38400 (baud rate)	-	3 m
	2016	1 Mbps	OOK (Manchester & Differential Manchester)	
	2017		2PPM	2.5 m
Arduino	2017	115Kbps	OOK	
USRP	2015	12.5 Mbps	GMSK	7 m
Micro Controller	2016		DTMF	
	2017			
	2017	9600 Kbps	OOK	4 m
	2017		OOK	Several meters
	2017			
	2016	1Kbps	OOK	
	2016	115200 (baud rate)	-	-
	2015	-	OOK	-
	2017	-	Intensity Modulation	-
	2014	-	PPM,FSK	-
	2015	-	-	-
	2017	-	OOK	20 m
	2017	-	OOK	-
DSP board	2009	-	OFDM	1 m

A system using pulse position modulation and Reed-Solomon codec was designed using FPGA board in Chen, Guo, Xu, & Liang, (2017). A video was transmitted and viewed at the receiver in real time at a distance of 5 m. it was observed that communication is possible over much longer distances with very little BER. The maximum distance was reported to be 25 meters with a BER of 6.30 x 10^{-6}.

Non-linearity effects of LEDs are tested by Stefan, Elgala, Mesleh, O'Brien, & Haas(2011) for OFDM based VLC system. The purpose of the research is to identify the optimum value for Biasing point and OFDM signal amplitude. the DSP Development Kit, Stratix II Edition is the platform of choice.

REFERENCES

Abdulhafid, E., Nizar, Z., Simon, T., & Sameeh, D. (2015). *Overview Li-Fi Technology.* . doi:10.13140/RG.2.1.1440.0080

Aftab, F. (2016). Potentials and Challenges of Light Fidelity Based Indoor Communication System. *International Journal of New Computer Architectures and Their Applications*, 6(3), 91–102. doi:10.17781/P002152

Akshika, A., & Arvind, S. (2016). Light fidelity (Li-Fi): Future of Wireless Technology. *International Journal of Computer Science Trends and Technology*, 4(2).

Aly, M. A., El-Desouky, M. I., Roushdy, M., Hamdy, A., & Mahmoud, M. (2015). *Visible Light Communication Systems over FPGA*. Retrieved from https://www.wpi.edu/Pubs/E-project/Available/E-project-032814-001416/unrestricted/MQP_Report_Final_Draft_3_27_14.pdf

Anguita, D., Brizzolara, D., & Parodi, G. (2010). VHDL Modules and Circuits for Underwater Optical Wireless Communication Systems The State of the Art of Underwater Optical Communication. *Wseas Transactions On Communications*, 9(9), 1–26.

Baeza, V. M., Sánchez-Fernández, M., Armada, A. G., & Royo, A. (2015). Testbed for a Li-Fi system integrated in streetlights. *2015 European Conference on Networks and Communications, EuCNC 2015*, 517–521. 10.1109/EuCNC.2015.7194129

Benlachtar, Y., Watts, P. M., Bouzian, R., Milder, P., Koutsoyannis, R., Hoe, J. C., & Killey, R. I. (2009). 21.4 GS/s real-time DSP-based optical OFDM signal generation and transmission over 1600 km of uncompensated fibre. *2009 35th European Conference on Optical Communication,* (3), 5–6.

Bharadwaj, A. (2017). High Speed Data Transmission of Images over Visible Light Spectrum using PIC Microcontroller. *International Journal of Advance Research in Computer Science and Management Studies*, 5(10), 43–49.

Carlos, L., Itziar, A., David, S., & Carlos, R. (2016). Evaluation of the Effects of Hidden Node Problems in IEEE 802.15.7 Uplink Performance. *Sensors (Basel)*, 16(2), 216. doi:10.339016020216 PMID:26861352

Chauhan, M., & Kulai, A. (2015). Li-Fi – Let There Be Light. *International Journal of Engineering Trends and Technology*, 28(4), 163–165. doi:10.14445/22315381/IJETT-V28P231

Chen, M., Guo, J., Xu, X., & Liang, M. (2017). Real-Time Video Transmission of Visible Light Communication Based on LED. *International Journal of Communications, Network and System Sciences*, 10(8), 58–68. doi:10.4236/ijcns.2017.108B007

Cossu, G., Khalid, A., Choudhury, P., Corsini, R., & Ciaramella, E. (2012). 3.4 Gbit/s visible optical wireless transmission based on RGB LED. *Optics Express*, 20(26), B501–B506. doi:10.1364/OE.20.00B501 PMID:23262894

Dayalakshmi & Ivareddy. (2016). Design and Implementation of Smart Illumination CUM Communication to Power Lines via Li-Fi using Raspberry Pi. *International Journal of Advanced Technology and Innovative Research,* 8(20), 3911–3913.

Doori, V. D., Dhibakar, C., Nandhakumar, S., Prabhakaran, V., & Sivakrubakaran, S. (2017). Li-Fi (light fidelity) based smart communication system. *International Journal of Latest Engineering Research and Applications,* 43–48.

Elgala, H., Mesleh, R., & Haas, H. (2009). Indoor broadcasting via white LEDs and OFDM. *IEEE Transactions on Consumer Electronics*, 55(3), 1127–1134. doi:10.1109/TCE.2009.5277966

Fang, J., Che, Z., Jiang, Z. L., Yu, X., Yiu-Ming, S., Ren, K., & Chen, Z. (2017). An efficient flicker-Free FEC coding scheme for dimmable visible light communication based on polar codes. *IEEE Photonics Journal, 9*(3), 1–8. doi:10.1109/JPHOT.2017.2689744

Fergusson, P. (2016, October). Light Fidelity (Li-Fi) Prototype with Raspberry Pi, University of Southern Queensland Faculty of Health. *Engineering and Science*, 116.

FN Division, TEC. (2015). *Li-Fi (Light Fidelity) & its Applications FN*. Author.

Gancarz, J., Elgala, H., & Little, T. (2013). Impact of Lighting Requirements on VLC Systems. *IEEE Communications Magazine, 51*(12), 34–41. doi:10.1109/MCOM.2013.6685755

George, W. (2012). *'Li-Fi' provides a light bulb moment for wireless web.* Academic Press.

Ghassemlooy, Z., Aldibbiat, N. M., & Hayes, A. R. (2007). An experimental diffuse optical wireless link employing DPIM. *International Journal of Electronics, 94*(10), 961–971. doi:10.1080/00207210701685683

Goodwin, F. E. (1970). A Review of Operational Laser Communication Systems. *Proceedings of the IEEE, 58*(10), 1746–1752. doi:10.1109/PROC.1970.7998

Goswami, P., & Shukla, M. K. (2017). Design of a Li-Fi Transceiver. *Wireless Engineering and Technology, 08*(04), 71–86. doi:10.4236/wet.2017.84006

Guo, H., Man, K. L., Ren, Q., Huang, Q., Hahanov, V., Litvinova, E., & Chumachenko, S. (2017). FPGA implementation of VLC communication technology. *Proceedings - 31st IEEE International Conference on Advanced Information Networking and Applications Workshops,* 586–590. 10.1109/WAINA.2017.54

Haas, H., Yin, L., Wang, Y., & Chen, C. (2016). What is Li-Fi? *Journal of Lightwave Technology, 34*(6), 1533–1544. doi:10.1109/JLT.2015.2510021

Hadi, M. A. (2016). Wireless Communication tends to Smart Technology Li-Fi and its comparison with Wi-Fi. *American Journal of Engineering Research, 5*(5), 40–47.

Hagem, R. M. (2016). FPGA Based Implementation of Pulse Position Modulation for Underwater Optical Wireless Communication. *International Journal of Engineering and Innovative Technology*, 6(5), 47–50.

Holzmann, G. J., & Pehrson, B. (1994). *The Early History of Data Networks*. Wiley-IEEE Computer Society Press.

Huurdeman, A. A. (2003). *The Worldwide History of Telecommunications*. Wiley Interscience. doi:10.1002/0471722243

Kala, V., & Sathishkumar, D. (2017). *Wireless Communication Using Li-Fi Technology in Transmission of Audio Signal*. Academic Press.

Kamsula, P. (2015). *Design and Implementation of a Bi - Directional Visible Light Communication Testbed*. University of Oulu.

Khalid, A. M., Cossu, G., Corsini, R., Choudhury, P., & Ciaramella, E. (2012, October). 1-Gb/s Transmission Over a Phosphorescent White LED by Using Rate-Adaptive Discrete Multitone Modulation. *IEEE Photonics Journal*, 4(5), 1465–1473. doi:10.1109/JPHOT.2012.2210397

Khan, L. U. (2017). Visible light communication: Applications, architecture, standardization and research challenges. *Digital Communications and Networks*, 3(2), 78–88. doi:10.1016/j.dcan.2016.07.004

Khan, L. U. (2017). Visible light communication: Applications, architecture, standardization and research challenges. *Digital Communications and Networks*, 3(2), 78–88. doi:10.1016/j.dcan.2016.07.004

Khandal, D., & Jain, S. (2014). *Li-Fi (Light Fidelity): The Future Technology in Wireless*. Academic Press.

Kodama, M., & Haruyama, S. (2017). A Fine-Grained Visible Light Communication Position Detection System Embedded in One-Colored Light Using DMD Projector. *Mobile Information Systems*, 2017, 1–10. doi:10.1155/2017/9708154

Kolhe, A. B., & Mandavgane, R. N. (2007). Data Transmission Using Li-Fi System. *International Journal of Innovative Research in Science, Engineering and Technology, 3297*(11), 53–60. Retrieved from www.ijirset.com

Krishnan, G. V., Nagarajan, R., Durka, T., Kalaiselvi, M., Pushpa, M., & Priya, S. S. (2017). *Vehicle Communication System Using Li-Fi Technology. International Journal of Engineering and Computer Science*. doi:10.18535/ijecs/v6i3.47

Kumar, V., & Nirubama. (2012). A FPGA Implementation of Adaptive PPM Modulation Schemes for Wireless Optical Communication. *International Journal of Scientific and Engineering Research, 3*(4), 1–5.

Kumawat, H., & Verma, S. (2017). Audio Transmission Through Visible Light Communication. *International Journal of Science Engineering and Technology Research, 6*(5), 798–801.

Lakshmisudha K., Nair D., Nair A., & Garg P. (*2016)*: Li-Fi (Light Fidelity). *International Journal of Computer Applications, 146*(15).

Lee, C. G. (2011). Visible Light Communication. Advanced Trends In Wireless Communication, 327-338. doi:10.5772/16034

Mangesh, H., Nathalal, P., Paras, B., Parth, V., Parekh, M., Prerna, G., & Kerawalla, A.K.M. (2016). Li-Fi – A revolution in the field of wireless-communication. *International Journal of Advanced Research in Engineering and Applied Sciences*.

Mike, G. (1987). Photophones Revisited: A review of amateur optical communications. *Amateur Radio*, 12 – 17.

Mohie, G., Elhafez, E. A., Mohamed, R. A., Mohamed, R. N., Attia, S. M., & Mohamed, S. H. (2016). *Internet Access Over Visible Light (Grad Project Report)*. Cairo University.

Monteiro, E., & Hranilovic, S. (2014). Design and Implementation of Color-Shift Keying for Visible Light Communications. *Journal of Lightwave Technology, 32*(10), 2053–2060. doi:10.1109/JLT.2014.2314358

Nikshep, K. N., & Sowmya, G. (2016). Voice and data communication using Li-Fi. *International Journal of Advanced Computational Engineering and Networking, 4*(10).

Ofcom. (2013). Study on the future UK spectrum demand for terrestrial mobile broadband applications. *Realwireless*.

Parmar, D. N., Khushbu, M., & Jay, B. H. (2014). *LI-FI Technology – A Visible Light Communication. International Journal of Engineering Development and Research.*

Prateek, G., Aditya, S., & Prashant, K. (2016, November). Various Modulation Techniques for Li-Fi. *International Journal of Advanced Research in Computer and Communication Engineering, 5*(SI), 3.

Prerna, C., Ritika, T., & Rani, J. (2012). Li-Fi (Light Fidelity)-The future technology In Wireless communication. *International Journal of Applied Engineering Research.*

PureVLC. (2013). *pureVLC Demonstrates Li-Fi Streaming along with Research Supporting World's Fastest Li-Fi Speeds up to 6 Gbit/s.* Press release. Author.

Ramadhani, E., & Mahardika, P. (2018). The Technology of Li-Fi: A Brief Introduction. *IOP Conference Series. Materials Science and Engineering, 325,* 012013. doi:10.1088/1757-899X/325/1/012013

Rashmi, T., Rajalaxmi, R., & Balaji, V.R. (2015). Prototype Model of Li-Fi Technology using Visible Light Communication. *International Journal of Electrical, Computing Engineering and Communication, 1*(4). Retrieved from http://iisrt.com/wp-content/uploads/2015/09/1-IISRT_Rashmi.pdf

Satyanarayana, D., Mathew, A. R., & Sathyashree, S. (2016). An Architecture for Wireless Communication Systems using Li-Fi technology. *8th International Conference on Latest Trends in Engineering and Technology (ICLTET'2016),* 37–41. 10.15242/IIE.E0516026

Shah, V., Purohit, D., Samant, P., & Karani, R. (2015). *2D Image Transmission using Light Fidelity Technology.* Academic Press.

Sharma, R. R., Sanganal, A., & ... (2014). Li-Fi Technology: Transmission of data through light. *International Journal of Computer Technology and Applications, 5*(1), 150–154.

Shetty, A. (2016). A Comparative Study and Analysis on Li-Fi and Wi-Fi. *International Journal of Computers and Applications, 150*(6), 975–8887.

Singh, S., & Singh, Y. P. (2014). An Innovative and energy efficient Designing of communication System Based on Light Fidelity (LI-FI). *International Journal of Scientific Research Engineering & Technology,* 30–31.

Siva, K., Raju, S., Mohana, V., & Sai, V. (2017). PC to PC Transfer of Text, Images Using Visible Light Communication (VLC). *International Journal of Advanced Engineering Management Science*, (5), 446–449.

Stefan, I., Elgala, H., Mesleh, R., O'Brien, D., & Haas, H. (2011): Optical Wireless OFDM System on FPGA: Study of LED Nonlinearity Effects. *Vehicular Technology Conference (VTC Spring)*. 10.1109/VETECS.2011.5956691

Sufyan, I. M., & Haas, H. (2016). *Modulation Techniques for Li-Fi*. Retrieved from http://www.cnki.net/kcms/detail/34.1294.TN.20160413.1658.002.html

Suraj, V. S., Sagar, D., & Pankaj, S.L. (2016). Li-Fi: Data Transmission through Light. *International Journal of Innovative Research in Computer and Communication Engineering, 4*(3).

Tsonev, D., Videv, S., & Haas, H. (2013). Light fidelity (Li-Fi): Towards all-optical networking. *Proceedings of SPIE - The International Society for Optical Engineering*. 10.1117/12.2044649

Verma, P. (2015). *Light-Fidelity (Li-Fi): Transmission of Data through Light of Future Technology*. Academic Press.

Videv, S., & Haas, H. (2014). Practical space shift keying VLC system. *IEEE Wireless Communications and Networking Conference, WCNC*, 405–409. 10.1109/WCNC.2014.6952042

Zafar, F., Karunatilaka, D., & Parthiban, R. (2015). Dimming schemes for visible light communication: The state of research. *IEEE Wireless Communications, 22*(2), 29–35. doi:10.1109/MWC.2015.7096282

KEY TERMS AND DEFINITIONS

BER: Bit error ratio is the number of bits in error divided by the total received bits (probability of error) while Bit Error Rate is the number of bits in error per unit time.

Downlink: It is the connection from the base station to the mobile device.

Electromagnetic Interference: It is the interference created by external sources affecting a circuit or device through electromagnetic induction.

IM/DD: It is the technique where the intensity of light is modulated and the demodulation is done through direct detection of optical signal through a photodetector.

OFDM: It is a digital modulation technique in which a single data stream is split into multiple parallel streams and transmitted over narrow overlapping subcarriers.

Power Line Communication (PLC): It is the communication technology that uses available power lines to transmit data. The cables that power up a device can also carry data and no extra cabling is required.

Power Over Ethernet: It is the technology that transmits power as well as data over the twisted pair cables allowing a single cable to provide data as well as power to devices such as wireless access points.

QAM: A modulation technique where two signals are modulated using amplitude shift keying and then transmitted over same frequency with a 90-degree phase.

Uplink: It is the connection from the mobile device to the base station.

Chapter 4
Performance Analysis of FSO Links in Turbulent Atmosphere

Banibrata Bag
Haldia Institute of Technology, India

Akinchan Das
Haldia Institute of Technology, India

Aniruddha Chandra
National Institute of Technology Durgapur, India

Rastislav Róka
iD https://orcid.org/0000-0001-9767-9547
Slovak University of Technology in Bratislava, Slovakia

ABSTRACT

The free-space optical communications technology is emerging as an attractive substitute to RF communications. It can satisfy the current demands for higher bandwidth to the customer. Atmospheric turbulence is a major obstacle in wireless optical communication systems. To fully utilize the terabit capacity of FSO system, it has to overcome various challenges offered by the heterogeneous nature of the atmospheric channel. Currently, FSO communication through atmospheric turbulence under adverse weather conditions is an active research topic. A lot of studies and experiments have been carried out on the effect of attenuation due to atmospheric turbulence; but still, much more research is necessary for fulfilling the current demands and commercial needs for implementing this technology successfully. This chapter discussed the various limitations of FSO system which are faced during data transmission through the atmospheric channel and various ways to improve the performance regarding BER, outage probability, and channel capacity.

DOI: 10.4018/978-1-5225-9767-4.ch004

INTRODUCTION

Free Space Optical communication (FSOC) or optical wireless communication (OWC) is an emerging technology that transmits data wirelessly under free space using the laser beam in Line Of Sight (LOS) connectivity. In recent years, free space optical (FSO) communication has gained notable interest over the other wireless RF technologies due to its unique features like significantly increased data rates, large bandwidth, license-free operation, easy and quick deployability, less power requirement, low maintenance cost, low mass requirement and improved security. The FSO technology is ideal and very much useful where the physical connections are impractical due to high cost or other considerations including temporary and rapid installation requirement for disaster recovery. Free-space optical links serve as a promising alternative to the conventional fiber optic cables used for backhaul links. Recent developments of optical technology have advanced FSO to make it an alternative to RF wireless communication.

Theoretically, FSO communication is the same as fiber optic transmission as both use the laser beam as the carrier. The only difference is the medium, where FSO technology sends the signal through the unguided medium (air or free space) rather than guided fiber optic cables. To provide a full-duplex transmission system using FSO technology it requires two systems, each consists of a low-power laser transmitter to transmit signal and a telescope used to receive the signal at the receiver. From the source terminal, the optically modulated signal is transmitted via laser beam and at the receiving point (consist of a high-sensitivity receiver telescope) a photo detector intercepts the beam, and the data is extracted by demodulation process.

Deployment of DWDM-based optical metropolitan area networks (MANs) is not sufficient to attain the high bandwidth demand. Therefore the wireless operators and service providers are forced to look for alternative way rather than RF spectrum to connect cells that may provide the high bandwidth demand. In this scenario, the free-space optical transmission is an excellent alternative to conventional communication technology. The FSO technology has proven itself a great success for LAN/ campus connectivity within short distance like a link between a newsroom and a broadcasting station, or a dedicated link between two high-traffic nodes in a large building complex.

Figure 1a shows the block diagram of a typical FSO communication system, where at the source terminal, the information source is optically

Figure 1. The block diagram of a) an optical communication system b) passive optical network.

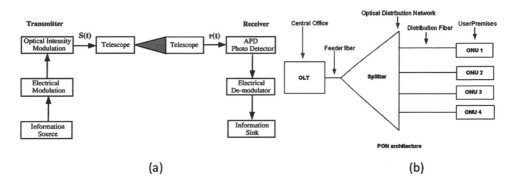

(a)   (b)

modulated followed by electrically modulation and then transmitted via a telescope through the free space or air in a LOS manner towards the destination telescope. In the destination there exist a receiver telescope interconnected with a photo detector that intercepts the laser beam and after demodulation original information is extracted.

A typical passive optical network (PON) shown in Figure 1b generally works with the principal of CWDM (coarse/ coarse wavelength division multiplexing) technique through a single optical fibre. In this network, the information is sent from source to user premises without any active opto-electronic components. Today, worldwide billions of people are using a different standard of the passive optical network to send the information at a high data transmission rate. Nowadays network providers regularly use different PON standard like BPON (Broadband PON), EPON (Ethernet Passive Optical Network), GPON (Gigabit PON), WDM PON (Wavelength Division Multiplexing-Passive Optical Network) etc., to send the information to user point with high data rate up to 10 Gbps. FSO communication system is the other platform of future 5G cellular communication which also offer a massive amount of bandwidth and fantastic data rate. To provide a better quality of service to the user for video transmission, video calling, group conferencing, the system must have the capacity to offer a gigantic bandwidth and data transmission rate. In (Chen, 2018) (Ali Shahpari, 2014) the authors proposed and demonstrated a FSO communication system with 10 Gbits/s using on-off keying traffic, integrating with a PON for broadcasting wireless data. The International Telecommunication Union (ITU-T) Focus Group on

Network 2030 forecasts that the convergence of terrestrial and space networks is essential for the future generation communication system to achieve the goal of providing communication service for everyone everywhere at any time (Li, 2018).

CURRENT STATUS

In 1960 with the discovery of first working laser at Hughes Research Laboratories, Malibu, California (Hecht, 2005), a lot of advancement is noted in FSO technology (Khalighi, 2014) and commercially available FSO equipment. In recent days with the advancement of FSO technology, it becomes one of the promising solutions for addressing the large bandwidth requirements and the 'last mile bottleneck' problem. FSO link has been demonstrated in the laboratory to provide 80 Gbps data rate with an average BER of 10^{-6}. Optical wireless communications are already commercially available which can provide high-speed data transmission (100 Mbps - 10 Gbps) without forward error correction (FEC) coding.

In general, for high-speed broadband data communications using FSO technology, one needs to increase the transmission power for optical signals. The development of high powered laser technology enhances the possibility to cope up with the degrading effects caused by scattering and fading in atmospheric turbulence. However, from a practical viewpoint, the speed of conventional FSO system with multiple of 10 Gbps transmission bandwidth cannot be achieved by only increasing the optical power, due to safety standards meant for protecting human eyes. Even relatively small amounts of laser light can lead to permanent eye injuries. Moderate and high-power lasers are potentially hazardous because they can burn the retina of the eye or even the skin. Therefore the government imposes regulations on sale and usage of lasers to ensure the safe design, use and implementation of lasers to minimize the risk of laser accidents. The standard FSO link setups cannot easily upgrade their speed due to such administrative and technical problems. To enhance the data transmission speed over a diffraction limited FSO channel, narrow laser beam is being used to minimize the beam divergence in some recent FSO communication systems. Due to uses of narrow laser beam, data can be transmitted over several kilometers with low output power and at a reasonable data rate. The data speed is near about same as that offered by the optical fiber communication system for a 100m link ($\sim$ 1.8 Tbps) (Arimoto, 2010).

ADVANTAGES OF FSO COMMUNICATION

FSO communication system offers several advantages over the traditional radio frequency communication technology or optical fiber transmission.

Low Cost

Unlike the high-cost optical fiber cables or highly expensive RF spectrum, the FSO communication technology uses economic unguided channel free-space. During network installations using optical fiber cables, trenching streets or digging ground is mandatory which incurs huge amount of extra cost. Again there is a high chance of damaging the expensive optical fiber cable during installations process.

License-Free Operation

Unlike RF communication for long-range operation, FSO communication is free from any licensing issues.

High Speed

FSO links offer much better data rates than RF links with lower latency. The latest development of this technology enables data (voice and video) transmission up to 2.5 Gbps through the air at distances up to 4 km, without the botheration of expensive deployment of fiber-optic cable or scarcity of the spectrum licenses. In modern systems, FSO can achieve a data rate of 1.28 Tbps using WDM transmission with 32 signals, each having a capacity of 40 Gbps (Ciaramella, 2009).

High Throughput

FSO links are capable of satisfying the most demanding throughput requirements of today's several bandwidth-hungry applications and mobile applications like voice and video calling, video chat, mobile TV, high definition television (HDTV) etc.

Last-Mile Access

In busy metro cities or the mountainous regions, it is hardly possible to lay out the optical fiber cable by simply laying the optical fiber cable or by digging/trenching the roads. In this scenario, the high-speed FSO links can be used to solve this "last mile" problem by bridging the gap between the end user and the existing fiber optic infrastructure.

High Security

Compared to RF or other wireless transmission technologies, free space optics is more secure and favored over conventional wireless technology. In FSO communication normally laser beam is used which is highly directional with very narrow beam divergence that becomes undetected by any of the existing spectrum analyzers, therefore any kind of interception is pretty challenging. Moreover unlike the RF signal, in FSO signal eavesdropping is also not possible due to its impossibility to penetrate walls [3]. Therefore in FSO communication, with an added degree of security, data can be transmitted over an encrypted connection.

DISADVANTAGES OF FSO COMMUNICATION

However, despite many attractive features, there is one big challenge for optical wireless communication, and that is the atmospheric turbulence of the communicating medium which causes signal fading. Other disadvantages of FSO communication are:

Attenuation of Optical Signals

The FSO transmission attenuates by atmospheric attenuation at a changeable rate which is weather-dependent and commonly caused by fog, clouds, dust, sandstorms, smoke, haze and rain etc. The measurement of atmospheric attenuation loss may be varied from 0.2 dB/km to 350 dB/km in sunny weather conditions with long-range visibility and relatively low attenuation to a very dense mist or fog, heavy cloudy weather condition with very low-range visibility and high attenuation.

The fog is another deterioration factor in atmospheric attenuation. During dense fog conditions at visibility less than 50 m, attenuation can be more than 350 dB/km (Nadeem E. L. F, 2010) that restrain the availability of FSO communication link. During the transmission of the optical source from the transmitting end through the atmospheric channel, the attenuation faced usually follows the negative exponential Beer's-Lambert law with the mathematical definition like the following:

$$h_l(z) = \exp(-\sigma z) \tag{1}$$

where $h_l(z)$ indicate that the loss due to attenuation in the propagation path with length z, σ is represented the attenuation constant. Typically, $h_l(z)$ is considered the constant parameter for long haul communication with the absence of randomness behavior in the channel for a long period. The numerical value must be dependent on the size and distribution of the scattering particles. This particular attenuation of the optical signal due to fog and haze at a distance R, can be determined by the Beer-Lambert law.

$$A_{fog} = e^{-a_{fog}(R)} \tag{2}$$

where R is the distance of the optical beam and a_{fog} is the attenuation coefficient in (km^{-1}), which is given by (Nadeem, Kvicera, Leitgeb, Muhammad, & Kandus, 2009)

$$a_{fog} = \frac{3.912}{V} \left(\frac{\lambda}{\lambda_0}\right)^q \tag{3}$$

where V is the visibility distance (in km) in open eye, λ and λ_0 are the wavelengths of the transmitted signal and the visibility reference, and q is the distribution coefficient of scattering according to Kruse's model (McQuistan, 1962).

The impact of rain in FSO communication is not much effective as the size of rain droplets are quite larger (100 to 10000 μm) than the wavelength used in FSO communication (850 nm and 1500 nm). The attenuation loss ranges from 1 dB/km to 10 dB/km for rainfall (2.5 mm/hr) and heavy rainfall

(25 mm/hr) respectively. For an FSO link the attenuation due to rain, α_{rain} is given by (Ghasemi, 2012)

$$\alpha_{rain} = k_1 \left(R\right)^{k_2} \tag{4}$$

where R is the rainfall rate per hour and $k1$, and $k2$ are the parameters depends on the size of the droplet and rain temperature.

Physical Obstructions

As FSO works in line of sight (LOS) of transmission, it may be blocked temporarily by flying objects, birds or by trees and tall buildings. Anything crossing he beam may affect the transmission.

Scintillation

FSO link is very much sensitive to atmospheric conditions. By the heat rising from the earth and by the different heating ducts creates temperature variations among different air pockets which causes fluctuations in signal amplitude leads to "image dancing" at the FSO receiver. It is the most challenging part of the FSO system to resolve the fluctuation problems and hitting the laser beam precisely at the centre point of the receiver telescope.

Geometric Losses

For FSO line of sight (LOS) communication laser beam should be narrow enough. During transmission from transmitted end to receiver end, due to the spreading of the laser beam, the power level of signal reduced and optical beam attenuated. This phenomenon is known as a geometric loss. This loss is proportional to the link length at a fixed receiver aperture.

Absorption

In the atmospheric channel absorption mainly caused by the water molecules, carbon dioxide and ozone that absorb the photons power would lead to a decrease in the power density of the optical beam and affect the FSO transmission system. This atmospheric loss can be quantified in terms of

Figure 2. a) A typical beam divergence of conventional FSO system. b) Classification of FSO Communication.

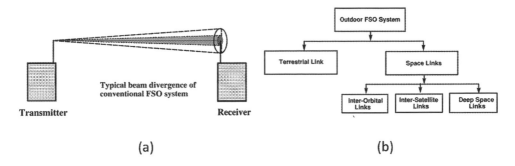

(a)　　　　　　　　　　　　　　　(b)

optical depth τ which correlates with power at the receiver P_R and the transmitted power P_T as

$$P_R = \left(P_T \right) e^{-\tau} \tag{5}$$

The atmospheric transmittance (*Ta*) is the ratio of power received to the power transmitted in the optical link.

$$T_a = \frac{P_R}{P_T} \tag{6}$$

Moreover, this absorption phenomenon depends on the wavelength of the laser beam. Therefore for FSO communication system the range of wavelength (known as transmission windows) must be chosen to have minimal absorption where the attenuation due to the absorption must be less than 0.2 dB/km. Out of several existing transmission windows within the range of 700-1600 nm, the majority of FSO systems are designed at 780-850 nm or 1520-1600 nm. It has been noticed that the BER concerning operating wavelength of 1550 nm is much lesser than that of 780 nm and 850 nm. Moreover in this 1550 nm wavelength the optical beam less affected by scattering and atmospheric attenuation. Therefore this operating wavelength is the most suitable and adequate for FSO links in all weather conditions. Most of the commercially available FSO systems operate at these two windows to use the corresponding available off-the-shelf components.

Scattering

Scattering happens when the optical beam collides with the various scattering particles present in the atmosphere results only in the directional redistribution of the optical energy which leads to the reduction in the intensity of laser beam for longer distance. Therefore, it plays an influential role in the attenuation of an optical signal and FSO communication system as well. In FSO communication, the scattering phenomenon mainly happens due to mist and fog when the size of particles that collided with the light beam is of the same order of magnitude as the wavelength of the transmitted wave. Therefore, this is one of the most significant barrier factors to long distance FSO system deployment. If the radius of the particles is r and the wavelength of the beam is λ then, for $r < \lambda$ the scattering process is known as Rayleigh scattering, for $r \approx \lambda$ the scattering process is known as Mie scattering and when $r > \lambda$ the scattering process can be explained using diffraction theory.

Types of FSO Communication

The FSO communication is one of the broad categories of "Wireless optical communication" (WOC) that is mainly outdoor type and uses an optical carrier to transfer information from one point to point LOS communication link through free space an unguided medium. The FSO communication systems are further classified into terrestrial and space optical links that include building-to-building, ground-to-satellite, satellite-to-ground, satellite-to-satellite, satellite-to-airborne platforms (unmanned aerial vehicles (UAVs) or balloons), (Popoola, 2010) etc. Figure 2(b). illustrates the classification of WOC system.

ATMOSPHERIC TURBULENCE INDUCED FSO CHANNEL AND CHALLENGES

Channel Characterization

Atmospheric Turbulence is the main obstacle to the communicating medium between the transmitter and the receiver of the FSO communication system. Both the intensity and the phase of the received light signal fluctuates randomly due to the effect of turbulence, and therefore the performance

of the system rigorously affected (Kahn J. M, 2003; Amon, 2004). Hence to combat with the atmospheric turbulence which is random, for a reliable FSO communication, it is very much essential to have a detail understanding about the different factors that are the major cause of power loss during the laser beam propagation through the turbulent environment. Some of the relevant parameters or terms to describe the channel when the optical beam is propagating through the atmosphere are:

Link Margin

Undoubtedly in FSO communication during data transmission, the power used at transmitter gradually reduce along the channel due to the different attenuation effects presents within the turbulent channel. In quantifying the performance an FSO link, the link margin is one of the most vital parameters which is essentially the amount of light over and above which is required at the destination to keep the link active. The link margin must be positive and should be maximized for reliable connections. The link margin is commonly scaled in dB (decibels). The link margin determines the system's ability to deliver sufficient optical power in the worst atmospheric conditions by considering the other channel characteristics of the FSO link. At a very adverse atmospheric condition, link margin is usually low ($\approx$30 dB). This can be determined by the three factors, (i) transmit power, (ii) transmitting antenna gain, and (iii) receiving antenna gain.

Refractive Index and Scintillation

Scintillation is the temporal and spatial fluctuations of the laser beam due to thermal turbulence of the transmission medium. The thermal characteristic of the atmosphere at building's roof level and near the ground surface changes along the path of the optical link causes the non-homogeneities of the refractive index results scintillation and beam wandering. The scintillation index is one of the essential measures of turbulence severity. The value of which (near the ground) is higher for strong turbulence ($1 \times 10^{-13} \text{m}^{-2/3}$) and smaller for weak turbulence ($1 \times 10^{-17} \text{ m}^{-2/3}$) whereas typical average value is ($1 \times 10^{-15} \text{ m}^{-2/3}$), and remain constant for a particular type of turbulence (Kahn & Zhu, 2003). It increases as the refractive-index structure parameter (C_n^2) increases. The fluctuation of refractive index is high at minimum temperatures and low at maximum temperatures.

The scintillation is described by the Rytov variance (σ_x^2) for a plane wave can be expressed as

$$\sigma_x^2 = 1.23 C_n^2 \left(\frac{2\pi}{\lambda}\right)^{\frac{7}{6}} L^{11/6} \tag{7}$$

where λ represents the wavelength (in nm) of the source, L is the length of the FSO link and C_n^2 is an altitude-dependent index of the refractive structure parameter. In FSO system a narrow beam the small diverging beam is appropriate, and thus plane wave expression is more appropriate than the spherical beam expression which is somewhat different. Figure 3 represent the standard deviation (σ_x^2) of Log-amplitude fluctuation to propagation distance (L) for a plane wave and spherical wave respectively.

Pointing Error

Another major cause of sharp deterioration of the channel performance in an FSO system is the misalignment between the transmitter and the receiver telescope known as pointing error, the main reason behind it is the thermal expansion, wind loads, and weak earthquakes (Arnon, 2003; Sandalidis, Tsiftsis, & Uysal, 2008). Therefore proper investigation on the impact of pointing error (jitter) in the performance of an FSO link is an essential issue for designing and deployment of a reliable and available FSO communication

Figure 3. Standard deviation of Log-amplitude fluctuation with respect to propagation distance for a a) Plane waves b) spherical waves

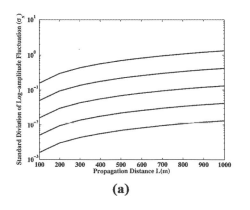

(a)

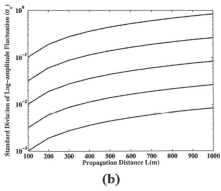

(b)

system. A small change in pointing error can cause high power losses. Considering a circular detection aperture of radius a and a Gaussian beam profile at the receiver I_{beam}, the attenuation due to geometric spread with pointing error r is expressed as

$$h_p(r,z) = \int I_{beam}(\rho - r; z) d\rho \tag{8}$$

where $h_p(\cdot)$ represents the fraction of the power collected by the detector of radius a, the beam shape and the detector area are symmetrical; therefore $h_p(r,z)$ depends only on the radial distance $r = \|r\|$ can be expressed approximately as (Farid & Hranilovic, 2007)

$$h_p(r,z) \approx A_0 \exp\left(-\frac{2r^2}{W_{z_{eq}}^2}\right) \tag{9}$$

where $A_0 = \left[\text{erf}(v)\right]^2$ is the fraction of the collected power at $r = 0$ denoting $erf(\cdot)$ as the error function, W_{zeq} is the equivalent beam width with $W_{z_{eq}}^2 = \dfrac{W_z^2 \sqrt{\pi}}{2v\exp(-v^2)} erf(v)$, W_z is the beam waist calculated at distance z, and $v = \dfrac{r\sqrt{\pi}}{W_z\sqrt{2}}$. Considering the elevation and the horizontal displacement are subject to independent and identical Gaussian distributions (Arnon, 2003), the radial displacement r at receiver, modelled by a Rayleigh distribution can be expressed as

$$f_r(r) = \frac{r}{\sigma_s^2} \exp\left(\frac{r^2}{2\sigma_s^2}\right) \tag{10}$$

where σ_s^2 is the jitter variance at the receiver.

Now combining (9) and (10), the authors in (Farid & Hranilovic, 2007) have derived the probability distribution (PDF) of attenuation due to pointing errors hp for a Gaussian beam and a circular detection aperture of radius r as

$$f_{h_p}\left(h_p\right) = \frac{\gamma^2}{A_0^{\gamma^2}}\left(h_p\right)^{\gamma^2-1} \tag{11}$$

where $\gamma = W_{z_{eq}}/2\sigma_s$ represents the ratio of the equivalent beam radius at the receiver to the pointing error displacement.

Aperture Averaging

In FSO Communication due to atmospheric turbulence at the receiver telescope, the intensity of the laser beam fluctuates over the point receiver that leads to significant signal fades. It is possible to reduce the received power variance by increasing the receiver aperture size. The technique to mitigate the effect of atmospheric turbulence by increasing the size of the receiver aperture is known as "aperture averaging". When the receiver aperture diameter (D) is considered as point receiver, i.e., $D \ll \sqrt{\lambda L}$, where L is the propagation length, the aperture averaging factor A can be defined as (Davis, 2005),

$$A = \frac{\sigma_1^2\left(D\right)}{\sigma_1^2\left(0\right)} \tag{12}$$

where $\sigma_1^2\left(D\right)$ and $\sigma_1^2\left(0\right)$ are the normalized intensity variance of the signal at receiver with diameter D and at a point receiver with an infinite small aperture ($D \approx 0$).

The aperture averaging technique reduces the BER performance of the system with multiple orders. According to the result of experiment conducted by NASA on aperture averaging using operating wavelength of $\lambda = 1550$ nm, the transmit aperture 2.5 cm and propagation path $L=1$ km using Gaussian beam with varying receiver aperture it shows that for small aperture diameter 2 inches BER was around 10-3 and increasing it to 8 inches, BER performance reached up to 10^{-12}. It has been observed that the amount of background noise collected by the receiver also increase with the increase of receiver aperture diameter leads to a reduction of the SNR. Therefore aperture averaging or optimum aperture diameter is the only practical way to get better performance in the FSO system.

Statistical Models for Turbulence Induced Fading Channel

The main challenge faced by the FSO technology is atmospheric turbulence since it uses the laser through the air as its medium of communication. As FSO works in free space LOS link, it is weather dependent and affected by the atmospheric turbulence in adverse weather condition. To get a reliable FSO communication, designing an accurate probabilistic model for the turbulence induced fading channel is very much essential. As it is hardly possible to guess correctly about the turbulence distribution, adopting the statistical moments of the turbulence is the best possible way to determine and make use of it. In recent technical report, authors adopt different statistical models to corresponding to different severity of atmospheric turbulence. The Log-normal distribution is suitable to model weak turbulent conditions whereas gamma-gamma and negative exponential distributions are widely accepted to model strong turbulence induced fading channel. Nowadays the new direction of the research in this area is to use a generalized distribution so that it can be used to model all other well-known distribution for modeling the ever-changing atmospheric turbulence condition appropriately. Therefore, rather than adopting the different distributions for different turbulent environment, many authors are interested in designing a statistical model with a generalized distribution like I-K distribution, double GG distribution, η - μ distribution, Malaga distribution etc.

Log-Normal Distribution

The common statistical models that are used to characterize the weak turbulence channels is the Log-normal and is suitable for characterizing FSO communications in clear sky links over several hundred meters (Kahn & Zhu, 2003; Lee & Chan, 2004). The probability density function (PDF) of the Log-normal distribution can be expressed as

$$f\left(x\right) = \frac{1}{x\sigma\sqrt{2\pi}} \exp\left[\frac{-\left(\ln\left(x\right)-\mu\right)^{2}}{2\sigma^{2}}\right]; x > 0. \tag{13}$$

where μ and σ are the mean and standard deviation of the logarithm.

The mean is

$$E(X) = \exp(\mu + 1/2\sigma^2),$$

and the variance

$$Var(x) = \exp(2\mu + \sigma^2)(\exp(\sigma^2) - 1),$$

and hence the coefficient of variation is $\sqrt{\exp(\sigma^2) - 1}$, which is approximately σ when that is small (e.g., $\sigma < 1=2$).

The intensity of light is related to log-amplitude, X by

$$I = I_0 \exp(2X - 2X) \tag{14}$$

Figure 4. PDF of Log-normal distribution at different parameter values

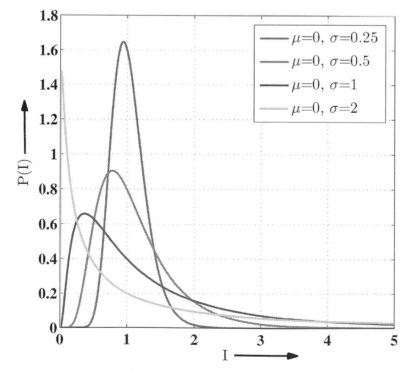

For a more accurate representation see the electronic version.

where $\langle X \rangle$ is the ensemble average. To estimate the fading occur at any single point in space and at a single point of time, we need to find the marginal distribution of light intensity caused by turbulence Log-normally distributes as (Kahn & Zhu, 2003)

$$f_I\left(I\right) = \frac{1}{2I\sqrt{2\pi\sigma^2}} \exp\left[\frac{-\left\{\ln\left(I\right) - \ln\left(I_0\right)\right\}^2}{8\sigma^2}\right] \tag{15}$$

Gamma-Gamma Distribution

The Gamma-Gamma distribution is a generalized model that can be applied to a wide range of turbulence (both weak, moderate and strong) conditions (Al-Habash, Andrews, & Phillips, 2001). The irradiance of the optical beam can be defined as the product of two random phenomena, i.e., $I = I_x I_y$, where I_x and I_y are responsible for bigger and smaller eddies presents in the turbulent medium. Specifically, G-G distribution is used to model both small-scale fluctuation and large-scale fluctuation. The statistical PDF of which is expressed regarding irradiance (I) as

$$f_I\left(I\right) = \frac{2\left(\alpha_t\beta_t\right)^{\frac{\left(\alpha_t+\beta_t\right)}{2}}}{\Gamma\left(\alpha_t\right)\Gamma\left(\beta_t\right)}\left(I\right)^{\frac{\left(\alpha_t+\beta_t\right)}{2}} K_{\alpha_t-\beta_t}\left(2\sqrt{\alpha_t\beta_t I}\right) \tag{16}$$

where $\Gamma(\cdot)$ is the gamma function, and $K_v(\cdot)$ is the modified Bessel function of the second kind of order v. The turbulence parameters, α_t and β_t, represent the number of large-scale and small-scale eddies in the turbulent environment. These two parameters together define the scintillation index (SI) as,

$$SI = \frac{1}{\alpha_t} + \frac{1}{\beta_t} + \frac{1}{\alpha_t\beta_t} \tag{17}$$

which are used for measuring the optical intensity variation by atmospheric turbulence, and can be associated with other physical quantities in the following manner [17]:

$$\alpha_t = \left[\exp\left\{ \frac{0.49\chi^2}{\left(1 + 0.65d^2 + 1.1\chi^{12/5}\right)^{7/6}} \right\} - 1 \right]^{-1} \tag{18}$$

$$\beta_t = \left[\exp\left\{ \frac{0.51\chi^2 \left(1 + 0.69\chi^{12/5}\right)^{-5/6}}{\left(1 + 0.9d^2 + 6.2d^2\chi^{12/5}\right)^{7/6}} \right\} - 1 \right]^{-1} \tag{19}$$

where, $\chi^2 = 1.23C_n^2 k^{7/6} L^{11/6}$ is the Rytov variance, C_n^2 is an altitude-dependent index of the refractive structure parameter, and $d = \left(kD^2 / 4L\right)^{1/2}$, where D is the diameter of the receiver collecting lens aperture, L is the propagation distance, $k = 2\pi / \lambda$, representing optical wave number, where λ is the wavelength (in nm) of the source.

The instantaneous electrical SNR can be defined as $\gamma = \frac{\left(\eta I\right)^2}{N_0}$. The average

electrical SNR is defined as, $\bar{\gamma} = \frac{\left(\eta E[I]\right)^2}{N_0}$. (Kahn X. Z., Free-space optical

communication through atmospheric turbulence channels, 2002). After a simple power transformation of the random variable (rv) I, the PDF in terms of average and instantaneous SNR can be written as (Uysal & T.Li, 2004; Datsikas, Peppas, Sagias, & .Tombras, 2010; Bag, Das, & Chandra, 2014) modelled by gamma-gamma distribution (without taking into account the pointing error effect for any FSO link),

$$f_\gamma(\gamma) = \frac{2\left(\alpha_t\beta_t\right)^{\frac{(\alpha_t+\beta_t)}{2}}}{\Gamma(\alpha_t)\Gamma(\beta_t)\sqrt{\gamma\bar{\gamma}}} \left(\sqrt{\frac{\gamma}{\bar{\gamma}}}\right)^{\frac{(\alpha_t+\beta_t)}{2}-1} K_{\alpha_t-\beta_t}\left(2\sqrt{\alpha_t\beta_t\sqrt{\frac{\gamma}{\bar{\gamma}}}}\right) \tag{20}$$

where $\Gamma(.)$ and $K_v(.)$ represents the same as in Equation(14).

For any FSO channel considering both the turbulence-induced scintillation modelled by gamma-gamma distribution and misalignment-induced fading (i.e., pointing error effect), the corresponding unconditional PDF can be obtained by calculating the mixture of the two distributions as follows

$$f_{h}\left(h\right) = \int f_{h|h_{a}}\left(h \mid h_{a}\right) f_{h_{a}}\left(h_{a}\right) dh_{a} \tag{21}$$

where $f_{h|h_{a}}\left(h \mid h_{a}\right)$ is the conditional probability given a turbulence state ha. Finally, after some mathematical manipulation, the corresponding PDF can be expressed as (Zedini, Soury, & Alouini, On the performance analysis of dual-hop mixed FSO/RF systems, 2016)

$$f_{\gamma fso} = \frac{\xi^2}{2\Gamma\left(\alpha_t\right)\Gamma\left(\beta_t\right)\gamma} G_{13}^{30}\left[\alpha_t\beta_t k\sqrt{\frac{\gamma}{\overline{\gamma}_{fso}}} \middle| \begin{matrix} \xi^2+1 \\ \xi^2, \alpha_t, \beta_t \end{matrix}\right] \tag{22}$$

where, $G_{pq}^{mn}\left[z \middle| \begin{matrix} \left(a_p\right) \\ \left(b_q\right) \end{matrix}\right]$ is the Meijer's G-function (Prudnikov, Brychkov, & Marichev, 1990 equation 8.2.1), $k = \dfrac{\xi^2+1}{\xi^2}$ and ξ^2 is related to the effect of pointing error as $\xi^2 = \dfrac{W_{z_{eq}}}{2\sigma_s}$ is the ratio between equivalent beam diameter and pointing error displacement standard deviation (jitter) at the receiver. The cumulative distribution function (CDF) of gamma-gamma distribution with pointing error effect is as follows (Zedini, Soury, & Alouini, On the performance analysis of dual-hop mixed FSO/RF systems, 2016)

$$F_{\gamma fso} = \frac{\xi^2}{\Gamma\left(\alpha_t\right)\Gamma\left(\beta_t\right)\gamma} G_{24}^{31}\left[\alpha_t\beta_t k\sqrt{\frac{\gamma}{\overline{\gamma}_{fso}}} \middle| \begin{matrix} 1, \xi^2+1 \\ \xi^2, \alpha_t, \beta_t, 0 \end{matrix}\right] \tag{23}$$

Malaga Distribution

Recently, another new generalized statistical distribution called M-distribution or Malaga distribution has been proposed to characterize the irradiance fluctuations of an optical beam propagating through a turbulent medium under all turbulence conditions. Different distribution model like Rice-Nakagami, gamma-gamma, shadowed-Rician, K-distribution, homodyned-K, exponential or Gamma-Rician etc., can be constructed from M-distribution (Jurado-Navas

Figure 5. a) PDF of Gamma-Gamma distribution b) PDF of Malaga distribution.

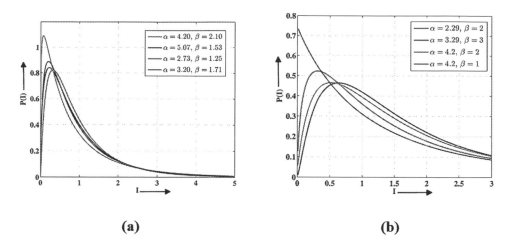

(a)   **(b)**

For a more accurate representation see the electronic version.

A., Garrido-Balsells, Paris, azquez, & Puerta-Notario, 2012) encompassing all the channel conditions. The Malaga distribution has been proposed in (Jurado-Navas A., Garrido-Balsells, Paris, & Puerta-Notario, 2011) by Navas at. all. They introduced this unified distribution technique and also find the relation between other distribution techniques with Malaga. Trigui et all in (Trigui, Cherif, & Affes, 2017) have shown for the first time that Malaga distribution can be applied suitably in FSO system for commensurate with the atmospheric effects like fading and turbulence.

The PDF for the FSO channel with M statistical turbulence with irradiance I is given by the standard mathematical equation as (Ansari I. S., 2016):

$$f_I\left(I\right) = \wedge \sum_{k_t}^{\beta_t} a_k \left(I\right)^{\frac{\left(\alpha_t + k_t\right)}{2} - 1} K_{\alpha_t - k_t}\left(2\sqrt{\frac{\alpha_t k_t I}{g_t \beta_t + \overline{\Omega}_t}}\right) \tag{24}$$

where

$$\wedge \triangleq \frac{2\left(\alpha_t\right)^{\frac{\alpha_t}{2}}}{\left(g_t\right)^{1+\frac{\alpha_t}{2}} \Gamma\left(\alpha_t\right)}\left(\frac{g_t \beta_t}{g_t \beta_t + \overline{\Omega}_t}\right)^{\beta_t + \frac{\alpha_t}{2}},$$

$$a_k \triangleq \left(\begin{array}{c} \beta_t - 1 \\ k_t - 1 \end{array} \right) \frac{\left(g_t \beta_t + \overline{\Omega}_t \right)^{1-\frac{k_t}{2}}}{\left(k_t - 1 \right)!} \left(\frac{\overline{\Omega}_t}{g_t} \right)^{k_t - 1} \left(\frac{\alpha_t}{\beta_t} \right)^{\frac{k_t}{2}},$$

and

$$\overline{\Omega}_t = \Omega_t + 2b_0 \rho_t + 2\sqrt{2b_0 \rho_t \Omega_t} \cos\left(\phi_A - \phi_B \right).$$

where $\alpha t, \beta t, g t$ and t are the fading parameters associated with the atmospheric turbulence conditions (Ansari I. S., 2016). α_t is a positive parameter related to the effective number of the large-scale scattering process. β_t is the amount of fading parameter and is a natural number. g_t denotes the average power of the scattering component received by off-axis eddies which are associated with both average powers of the total scatter components ($2b_0$) and the amount of scattering (ρ_t). The value of the amount of scattering typically lies between zero and one. Ω_t represents the amount of average power of the line of sight (LOS) components between channels. $K_{\alpha_t - k_t} (\cdot)$ is the modified Bessel function of the second kind of order ($\alpha_t - k_t$). The outage probability, average BER and the average capacity with considering pointing error effect are depicted in Figure 6(a) - Figure 6(c), considering $\xi = 0.5422, 0.6890,$ and $0.9129,$ with turbulence parameters $\alpha = 2.296, \beta = 2.0.$

Figure 6. a) Outage Probability at $\xi_{th} = 2dB$ with considering pointing error in Malaga distribution. b) BER with considering pointing error in Malaga distribution. c) Capacity with considering pointing error in Malaga distribution.

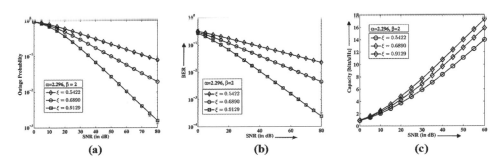

Modulation Techniques for Optical Wireless

A laser beam is only a fixed light beam bearing no information. Modulation is the process through which light characteristics vary, and this variation carries the information. Therefore modulation is an essential part to transmit message signal for long-haul communication for every communication system. With the knowledge of modulation to send the information from source to destination using FSO communication system, message signal superimposed with the carrier components (like LASER source or LED source). Several types of electronic modulation scheme have been used in this communication purpose like On-Off-Keying (OOK), Pulse Position Modulation (PPM), Differential Pulse Position Modulation (DPPM), Subcarrier Intensity Modulation, Trellis Coded PPM (TC-PPM), M-QAM etc. The data transmission in FSO communication typically used is intensity modulation and direct detection (IM/DD) technique. Here in this chapter, the authors discuss some of the above techniques briefly with their corresponding resultant bit-error rate.

Figure 7 shows a simple block diagram to transmit the message signal to the user end with the FSO communication system. In this figure, any types of electronic modulation (those are previously discussed) may be employed before transmitting the message signal to the destination end. Now the modulated waveform mixing with the high-frequency optical signal by MZM (Mach-Zehnder modulator-Optical Modulator). The high-frequency optical signal generated by an optical source like LASER or LED. Here the researchers have to use IM/DD technique to transmit and receive the modulated optical signal at transmitting and receiving end respectively. At the user end, the researchers have to use electronic demodulation scheme to find the original information. To get the pure result receiver end sometime used different types of receiver diversity techniques.

Figure 7. Typical block diagram of Optical Modulation process.

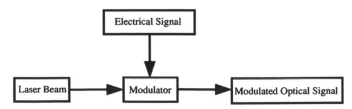

On-Off-Keying (OOK)

At first, the authors would like to discuss the more useful modulation technique called On-Off-Keying (OOK). In this technique, one bit is solely represented by an optical pulse that occupies the entire or part of the bit duration while the absence of an optical pulse represents a bit zero. Due to the effect of additive white Gaussian noise (AWGN) in the communication channel, the optimum receiver for an OOK waveform is the matched filter followed by a threshold detector between the zero bit and one-bit energies level. In diffuse optical links, multipath induced dispersion limits the achievable data rate. The maximum likelihood sequence detector should be adapted to perform optimally in the multipath channel for OOK. The implementation of which is not practical because of its complexity and the preventing processing time. A sub-optimal but practical approach would be to use an equalizer The BER for this technique in AWGN channel is $Q\left(\sqrt{\gamma}\right)$ where γ is the average SNR between transmitter and receiver and $Q(\cdot)$ is called the Gaussian Q-function.

M-PPM: The block diagram model for transmitting the data using pulse modulation is shown in Figure 7. For M-PPM $\log_2(M)$ number information bit has been transmitted through the channel. Typically it's a train of M chips with chip one has been set by the current level of $\sqrt{MPs}$ and other rest chips are fixed to zero where P_s indicate the average electrical power of M-PPM symbol. So the average electrical power of each bit can be defined in terms of P_s is $E_b = \dfrac{MP_s}{\log_2\left(M\right)}$. To evaluate the BER of the system using any types of modulation techniques the researchers have to find the average electrical SNR for each bit. The average electrical SNR must be a function of electrical power of each bit of the M-PPM scheme, and it's also related with power spectral density of the AWGN channel. After some mathematical manipulation, the researchers may derive the average electrical SNR for M-PPM by $\gamma_b = \dfrac{E_b}{N_0}$ where $N0$ is the Gaussian noise present in the channel. However, the analytical BER (P_e) performance of this decoder can be obtained regarding SER (Symbol Error Rate) like following

$$P_e = \frac{M \log_2\left(M\right)}{2\left(M - 1\right)} SER \qquad (25)$$

where SER can be written with its mathematical derivation for equally probable $(s_i \, ; \, i=1;2;:::M)$ of each M number of chips of M-PPM scheme is $SER \leq (M - 1)P(s_2|s_1)$.

M-PAM

Another modulation technique called M-PAM is discussed here with the help of the same block diagram in Figure 7. Now, like the M-PPM, $\log_2(M)$ is the number of equiprobable bits transmitted through the channel where the symbols are carried with the current levels and The energy of each bit for PAM defined by and the average SNR for each bit is same as M-PPM scheme. The probability of error can be defined as

$$P_e = \frac{2(M-1)}{M \log_2 M} Q\left(\sqrt{\frac{6\gamma \log_2 (M)}{(M+1)(M-1)}}\right) \tag{26}$$

Performance Metrics

Outage Probability

The outage probability (OP) is the probability of end-to-end SNR that falls below under a specific threshold value (that specify a minimum SNR value, above which it satisfies the quality of service (QoS), expressed mathematically as

$$P_{out}\left(\gamma_{th}\right) = Pr\left(\gamma \leq \gamma_{th}\right) = \int_0^{\gamma_{th}} f_\gamma\left(\gamma\right) d\gamma \tag{27}$$

where, $f_\gamma(\gamma)$ is indicating the PDF of the different statistical model for different turbulent induced FSO communication system or any types of wireless communication system like gamma-gamma, negative exponential, Malaga etc.

The outage probability for single FSO link under Gamma-Gamma turbulence induced fading channel considering pointing error is shown in Figure 8.

Figure 8. BER for single FSO link under Gamma-Gamma turbulence induced fading channel considering pointing error

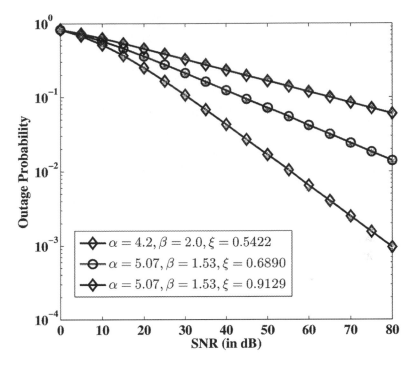

Bit-Error Rate

The probability of error or the bit-error rate (BER) is one of the main relevant performances metric under consideration to design a communication system. BER is the number of errors that occur during a time interval relative to the total number of transferred bits. In a noisy channel, the BER is often expressed as a function of the normalized carrier-to-noise ratio denoted by $E_b = N_0$ where E_b and N_0 signify the energy per bit and the noise power spectral density respectively. The researchers can derive the analytical calculation for this metric by a couple of ways, one is by PDF based approach, and another is MGF based approach.

PDF Based Approach

The researchers assume that the probability of error through the AWGN channel is $P_e(\gamma)$ where γ indicate that electrical SNR of the system for per

bits in the message signal. The values of $P_e(\gamma)$ is typically depend upon the modulation techniques. For example, if the system used ASK modulation technique then $P_e(\gamma) = Q(\sqrt{\gamma})$ and for BPSK modulation scheme this would be $\sqrt{Q(2\gamma)}$, and so on, where Q(·) is called the Gaussian Q function. So the BER of the overall system with system's PDF can be expressed mathematically as

$$P_e = \int_0^{\infty} P_e(\gamma) f_\gamma(\gamma) d\gamma \tag{28}$$

where $f_\gamma(\gamma)$ is the PDF of any of the various statistical model mostly used for FSO communication system, like gamma-gamma, negative Exponential, Malaga etc. In our previous section, the authors have already discussed elaborately on the statistical distribution of different types with its corresponding mathematical expression for PDF or CDF.

MGF Based Approach

The standard equation for deriving the BER is as follows

$$P_e = \int_0^{\infty} P_e(x) f_x(X) dx \tag{29}$$

where $f_x(X)$ is the PDF of the statistical channel, and the error probability for the AWGN channel can be expressed in terms of Gaussian Q function as its standard integral form as (Bayaki, Schobe, & Mallik, 2009)

$$P_e(x) = Q(x) = \frac{1}{\pi} \int_0^{\frac{\pi}{2}} \exp\left(-\frac{gx}{2(\sin\theta)^2}\right) d\theta \tag{30}$$

where g is the positive numerical value depends upon the modulation technique.

Therefore using (29) and (30) it becomes

$$P_e = \int\limits_0^\infty \left[\frac{1}{\pi} \int\limits_0^{\frac{\pi}{2}} \exp\left(-\frac{gx}{2(\sin\theta)^2} \right) d\theta \right] f_x(X)\, dx \tag{31}$$

Now changing the integral position of the above equation, it may be rewritten as

$$P_e = \frac{1}{\pi} \int\limits_0^{\frac{\pi}{2}} \left[\int\limits_0^\infty \exp\left(-\frac{gx}{2(\sin\theta)^2} \right) f_x(X)\, dx \right] d\theta \tag{32}$$

On the other hand, from the mathematical definition of MGF it may be written as

$$\mathcal{M}_x(s) \int\limits_0^\infty \exp(-xs) f_x(X)\, dx \tag{33}$$

Therefore, rewriting the equation using MGF-based approach (33) as

$$P_e = \frac{1}{\pi} \int\limits_0^{\frac{\pi}{2}} \mathcal{M}_x\left(-\frac{g}{2(\sin\theta)^2} \right) d\theta \tag{34}$$

A single FSO link under weak turbulent channel modelled by Log-normal statistical distribution, the average BER is shown in Figure 9(a). The BER for single FSO link under Gamma-Gamma turbulence induced fading channel considering pointing error is shown in Figure 9(b).

Channel Capacity

The channel capacity is another important parameter in any communication system and indeed in FSO link to determine the maximum data rates achievable

Figure 9. a) BER for single FSO link under Log-normal (weak) turbulence induced fading channel b) BER for single FSO link under Gamma-Gamma turbulence induced fading channel considering pointing error.

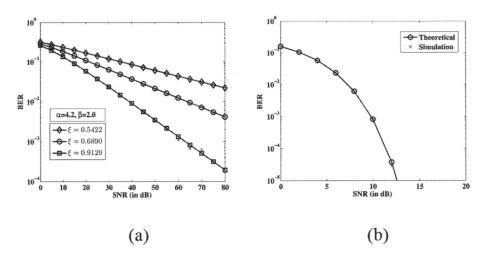

(a)   (b)

during transmission under turbulence induced fading. The average capacity for single FSO link under Gamma-Gamma turbulence induced fading channel considering pointing error is shown in Figure 10(a). Different adaptation policies can be adopted subject to the availability of channel state information (CSI) at transmitter and receiver and the average transmitting power that can be classified by (i) Optimal Rate Adaption (ORA) with constant transmit power (ii) simultaneous Optimal Power and Rate Adaptation (OPRA) (iii) Channel Inversion with Fixed Rate (CIFR) and (iv) Truncated Channel Inversion with Fixed Rate (TCIFR).

A fully adaptive transmission policy results in optimum capacity by exploiting the full CSI but requires a feedback path from destination to source, complex hardware architectures, and advanced decoding techniques. Suboptimal adaptive transmission policies significantly reduce the complexity through implementing channel inversion techniques.

Optimal Rate Adaptation (ORA)

Under constant transmits power and optimal rate adaptation, when CSI is available only at the receiver side, the policy is known as the Optimal Rate Adaption (ORA) policy (Yilmaz, Kucur, & Alouini, 2010). The channel

Figure 10. a) Capacity for single FSO link under Gamma-Gamma turbulence induced fading channel considering pointing error b) Normalized average capacity as a function of average SNR for different adaptation policies at $\alpha_t = 5.07$ and $\beta_t = 1.53$.

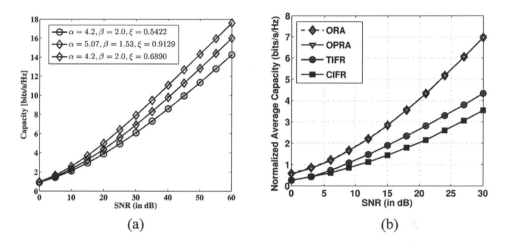

(a)   (b)

capacity (in bits/s/Hz), C_{ora}, can be obtained by averaging the instantaneous capacity over the fading SNR PDF, can be written as follows:

$$C_{ora} = \int_0^\infty \log_2\left(1 + \Omega\right) f_\gamma\left(\Omega\right) d\Omega \tag{35}$$

Optimal Power and Rate Adaptation (OPRA)

When the CSI is available both at receiver and transmitter (i.e., there exist a feedback path from the receiver to transmitter end), it is possible to adjust both the transmit power and rate with the channel variations. The optimal power and rate adaptation (OPRA) policy is implemented with a constraint on average transmitting power (Goldsmith & Alouini, 1999). Also, there exists a minimum cut-off SNR, γ_0, below which further data transmission is prevented. The channel capacity, C_{opra}, in this case, can be expressed as

$$C_{opra} = \int_{\gamma_0}^\infty \log_2\left(\Omega \Big/ \gamma_0\right) f_\gamma\left(\Omega\right) d\Omega \tag{36}$$

where the optimal cut-off SNR must qualify the condition,

$$\int_{\gamma_0}^{\infty} \left(1/\gamma_0 - 1/\Omega\right) f_{\gamma}\left(\Omega\right) d\Omega = 1$$

(Alouni & Simon, 2005). Usually, γ_0 increases as Ω increases and γ_0 always lie in between zero and one since no data are sent when $\Omega < \gamma_0$, the optimum policy suffers a probability of outage P_{out}, equal to the probability of no transmission.

Channel Inversion With Fixed Rate (CIFR)

In this case, the source adapts its power to sustain a fixed transmission rate for all channel conditions by inverting the channel fading effects. The channel capacity for CIFR policy can be expressed as

$$C_{cifr} = \log_2\left(1 + \frac{1}{R_{cifr}}\right) \tag{37}$$

where, $R_{cifr} = \varepsilon\left\{\frac{1}{\Omega}\right\} = \int_0^{\infty} \left(\frac{1}{\Omega}\right) f_{\gamma}\left(\Omega\right) d\Omega$ with $\varepsilon(\cdot)$ denoting the expectation operator (Varaiya, 1997).

Truncated Channel Inversion With Fixed Rate (TCIFR)

To overcome the shortcomings in the CIFR policy, truncated channel inversion with fixed rate (TCIFR) policy is preferred where the transmitter attempts to invert the channel fading only above a fixed cutoff SNR, γ_0 (Varaiya, 1997). If the received SNR (Ω) falls below the specified cutoff SNR (γ_0), data transmission is terminated. The channel capacity with TCIFR strategy is expressed analytically as (Varaiya, 1997),

$$C_{tcifr} = \log_2\left(1 + \frac{1}{R_{tifr}}\right) \times \left[1 - P_{out}\left(\gamma_0\right)\right] \tag{38}$$

where $R_{tifr} \triangleq \int\limits_{\gamma_0}^{\infty} (1/\Omega) f_{\gamma}(\Omega) d\Omega$ and $P_{out}(\cdot)$ is the outage probability. The average capacity of the FSO link (in bits/sec/Hz) is given as

$$C_{avg} = \int\limits_{0}^{\infty} \log_2 (1+\Omega) f_{\gamma}(\Omega) d\Omega \qquad (39)$$

DIVERSITY AND CODING: MITIGATING THE TURBULENCE EFFECTS

Spatial Diversity in Fading Channels

The overall performance of any communication systems mostly depends upon its received signal at the receiver side of the system. As the authors have discussed earlier, the received signal power may be affected by multi-path fading and atmospheric turbulence, presence in the communicating medium of the FSO system. The received signal power may be empowered at the receiver end of the system by using different types of transmitting and receiving diversity techniques at the transmitter and receiver end of the communication system. It can be developed using any types of spatial diversity techniques like Multi-Input Multi-Output (MIMO), Multi-Input Single-Output (MISO) or Single-Input Multi-Output (SIMO) antenna diversity techniques.

The overall signal-to-noise ratio (SNR) weakens due to the effect of multipath fading on the received signal at the receiver end, and the researchers have to utilize some types of spatial diversity techniques at the transmitter and receiver terminal of the communication system to lessen the effect of multipath fading. To implements, the diversity techniques, either multiple numbers of transmitting antennas or receiving antennas are used where sub channels carry the duplicate version of the same transmitted signal; technically diversity techniques are called transmitter diversity and receiver diversity respectively. Some time both diversity techniques are implemented concurrently to get a better impact. It's verified that the diversity technique enhances the overall gain of the base-band signal at the receiver. This gain depends on the initial SNR and the numbers of transmitting and receiving antennas of the system. The diversity combining technique is combining the

replicas of same transmitting data at receiver side using multiple receiving antennas. Thus the overall SNR becomes upgraded. Hence the performance of the system regarding outage probability or BER improves.

Receiver Diversity for Optical Fading Channels

Some of the most popular receiver diversity techniques are Equal-Gain Combining (EGC), Maximal Ratio Combining (MRC), Switch and Combining (SC), Switch and Examine Combining (SEC) etc.

Equal-Gain Combining (EGC)

Equal-Gain Combining (EGC) is a most meaningful and useful receiver diversity technique, at low fading amplitude and less hardware requirement. EGC works better when the system transmits the information using coherent modulation technique. In this scheme, the receiver received the L number of the same information from receiving antennas with the same weight and carrier phase, then adding them up to generate the decision vector. Since the transmitted information bits are equiprobable, the total end-to-end SNR (γ_{EGC}), can be expressed mathematically as

$$\gamma_{EGC} = \frac{\left(\sum_{l=1}^{L} \alpha_l\right)^2 E_s}{\sum_{l=1}^{L} N_l} \tag{40}$$

where E_s is the energy, and N_l is the AWGN power spectral density for the lth path. In case of Rayleigh fading channel, the overall SNR become

$$\gamma_{EGC} = \bar{\gamma}\left[1 + \left(L - 1\right)\frac{\pi}{4}\right] \tag{41}$$

where, $\bar{\gamma}$ is the average SNR.

Maximal-Ratio Combining (MRC)

Maximal-Ratio Combining (MRC) is the most dynamic receiver diversity technique due to its capability of dealing with unequal energy signal. MRC

scheme not only depends on the fading statistics instead it depends on the other channel and fading parameters like fading amplitude and phase in the channel. The MRC diversity scheme also offered better performance for coherent detection. Considering L number of replicas of transmitted information with equal weight received at the receiver antennas, the total end-to-end SNR (γ_{MRC}) can be expressed mathematically as

$$\gamma_{MRC} = \sum_{l=1}^{L} \gamma_l \tag{42}$$

The above equation is useful to calculate the total conditional SNR of any system with MRC diversity technique, like the conditional BER of any system with MRC diversity technique, for the coherent binary signal is $P_b = Q\left(\sqrt{2g\gamma_{MRC}}\right)$ where the range of g is $0.5 \leq g \leq 1$ depend on the different electronic modulation scheme like ASK, BPSK, FSK, PAM, PPM etc., and $Q(\cdot)$ is called the Gaussian Q-function.

Switch-and-Examine Combining (SEC)

Switch-and-Examine Combining (SEC) is the one of the preferred receiver diversity technique in which if the current path is not getting the better response at the receiver terminal then the combiner immediately examine the next available path, and this process continues until combiner does not get the proper path. When diversity paths are independent and identically distributed then the CDF of L-branch SEC at the receiver, of the combined output SNR is (Alouni & Simon, 2005, equation 9.340)

$$F_{\gamma SEC}(\gamma) = \begin{cases} \left[F_\gamma'\left(\gamma_{th}\right)\right]^{L-1} F_\gamma'(\gamma); & \gamma < \gamma_{th} \\ \sum_{j=0}^{L-1}\left[F_\gamma(\gamma) - F_\gamma(\gamma_{th})\right] \times \left[F_\gamma(\gamma_{th})\right]^j + \left[F_\gamma(\gamma_{th})\right]^L; & \gamma \geq \gamma_{th} \end{cases}$$

$$\tag{43}$$

where $F_\gamma(\cdot)$ is the CDF of the SNR for an individual receiver branch, depends on the statistical distribution, and γ_{th} is the constant predetermined switching threshold. The corresponding MGF is given by (Alouni & Simon, 2005), [equation (9.342)] as

$$\mathcal{M}_{\eta SEC}(s) = \left[F_\eta(\gamma_{th})\right]^{L-1} \mathcal{M}_\eta(s) + \sum_{j=0}^{L-2} \left[F_\eta(\gamma_{th})\right]^j \psi(s) \tag{44}$$

where $f_\eta(\gamma)$ and $\mathcal{M}_\eta(\gamma)$ are the PDF and MGF of the individual receiver branch respectively and $\psi(s) = \int_{\gamma_{th}}^{x} \exp(s\gamma) f_\eta(\gamma) d\gamma$.

Transmit Diversity for Optical Fading Channels

Alamouti Space-Time (ST) Scheme

Alamouti coding is a proven technique to achieve the full diversity order at the transmitter section, and therefore it increases the chance to receive multiple copies at the receiver. Now to take out the actual information as much as possible, receiver side diversity techniques can also be implemented. Figure 11 exhibits a $2 \times L$ MIMO FSO communication system, where two T_X apertures transmit 2×1 Alamouti coded symbols to each of the L receiving photo detectors. Let $\{s1, s2\}$ be two successive baseband message symbols that are to be transmitted. According to the 2×1 Alamouti scheme (Alamouti, 1998), during the first time slot, T_{X1} transmits signal s_1 and T_{X2} transmits s_2. During the second time slot, T_{X1} transmits $-s_2{}^*$ whereas T_{X2} transmits $s_1{}^*$, where $(\cdot)^*$ indicates complex conjugate.

Figure 11. A $2 \times L$ MIMO FSO channel employing 2×1 Alamouti coding

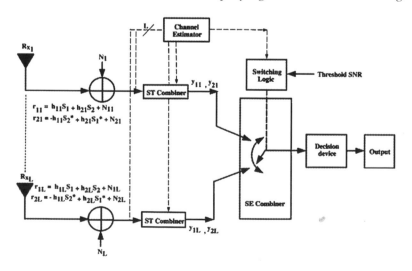

At the receiver side, the signals appearing at R_{Xj} over these two time intervals can be expressed as

$$r_{1j} = h_{1j}s_1 + h_{2j}s_2 + N_{1j} \tag{45a}$$

$$r_{2j} = -h_{1j}s_2^* + h_{2j}s_1^* + N_{2j} \tag{45b}$$

where, h_{ij}; $i \in (1,2)$, $j \in (1,2,....,L)$ is the channel gain between T_{Xi} and R_{Xj}. Each copy of the signal is affected by zero-mean Gaussian noise, N_{ij}, with variance N_0. The noise is assumed to be statistically independent of the channel fading. The received signals are processed by a bank of L space-time (ST) combiners attached to each *RX* antenna branch. The ST combiners attached to the R_{Xj}, act as Alamouti decoders and produces an output pair

$$y_{1j} = \widehat{h}_{1j}^* r_{1j} + \widehat{h}_{2j} r_{2j}^* \tag{46a}$$

$$y_{2j} = -\widehat{h}_{2j} r_{2j}^* + \widehat{h}_{2j}^* r_{1j} \tag{46b}$$

where $\widehat{h}_{ij}$ is an estimate of h_{ij}. As shown in Figure 11, the outputs of ST combiners are fed to a switch-and-examine combiner. The channel estimators help ST combiners in decoding and the SE combiner to choose one of the decoded outputs. In SEC a random branch (say, j) is selected for retrieving the message, and the branch is retained unless average branch signal to noise ratio (SNR) falls below a threshold value γ_t, required to maintain link reliability. Under the scenario $\gamma_j < \gamma_t$, the combiner switches to the next available branch for examining its quality. This iteration process continues until, either a path within tolerable condition is found, or all available diversity paths have been tested (Alouni & Simon, 2005)

Figure 12 (a) shows the average BER performance of OOK modulated SIMO FSO link over gamma-gamma fading channel in the absence of Alamouti coding. For a target BER of 10-3, the diversity gain is about 10 dB when L is increased from 2 to 4. However, when the number of branches are increased to $L = 6$, the diversity gain is about 5 dB. Therefore in this figure,

Figure 12. a) BER for 1 × L SIMO (in absence of Alamouti coding) FSO system (α_t = 2:26; β_t = 0:65) using SEC with fixed threshold (ξ_t = 10 dB). b) BER for 2 × L MIMO FSO system (αt = 2:26; βt = 0:65) using Alamouti code and SEC with fixed threshold (ξ_t = 10 dB).

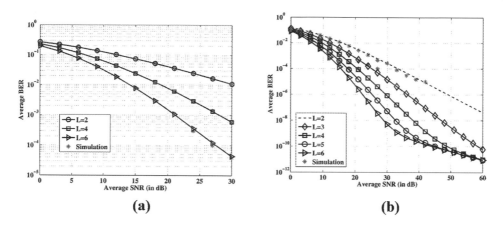

(a)   (b)

the diminishing returns with the added diversity branches are noticeable. Figure 12 (b) depicts that the curvature of BER at fixed switching threshold (ξ_t = 10 dB). All curves converge asymptotically with the increased average SNR, this is because, if the average SNR is either very small or very large then for any predefined switching threshold value, either all branches would be rejected or combiner would choose only one branch frequently. Hence, only the additional number of branches would not be able to improve the performance any further.

COOPERATIVE FSO TRANSMISSION

The technique is one of the emerging and very effective means for combating turbulent weather condition to achieve the significant performance gain in FSO communication technology. Instead of using multiple apertures at the transmitter or receiver end, a single antenna is capable of accomplishing huge diversity gain. In cooperative diversity technique, many nodes within a wireless network form a virtual antenna array to cooperate and get benefit from the underlying spatial diversity (Laneman & G.Wornell, 2004). Due to the broadcast nature of RF transmissions, the cooperative diversity is implemented successfully about a decade back (Laneman & G.Wornell, 2004), but in the context of directive FSO communications, it is a new benchmark. Several

recent researches have been carried out using this cooperative transmission strategy for FSO system considering one or more than one number of relays. Many authors have proposed different cooperation strategy like dual-hop (Alouini, 2004), multi-hop transmission with parallel fashion (i.e., cooperative diversity) or serial, hybrid RF/FSO relaying (Djordjevic, Petkovic, Cvetkovic, & Karagiannidis, 2015) etc., and analyzed their performance in terms of different performance metrics (NasiriKenari, 2009) considering amplify-and-forward (AF) and/or decode-and-forward (DF) relaying techniques.

Indeed, those relay-assisted transmission techniques achieve significant gains over non-cooperative FSO links and improve the performance but still there exist many unsolved issues under adverse weather condition which may cause degrade the FSO link performance and therefore more research in this topic is awaited to make it successful in implementing physically.

Dual-Hop Scenarios

Relay-assisted FSO communications is now a very promising technique to combat the degrading effects of fading under the turbulence-induced fading environment. In relay-assisted FSO transmission, the total distance becomes shorter to individual hop length leads to weakening the distance-dependent degrading effects of the turbulent channel.

The multi-hop FSO transmission can be modelled either using serial relaying or parallel relaying as shown in Figure 14(a) and Figure 14(b) respectively. A serial relaying strategy can significantly outperform the parallel relaying

Figure 13. Dual-hop relay assisted FSO communication.

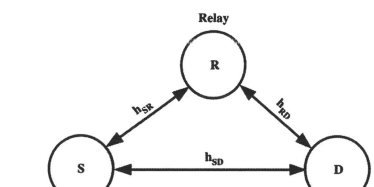

and direct transmission counterparts. It is also observed that parallel relaying takes advantage of the distance-dependency of the fading variance to a lesser extent and is outperformed by serial relaying as the number of relays increases. The authors in (Uysal M. R., 2012) studied on all FSO networks multi-hop relaying.

AF and DF Protocol

In this relay-assisted transmission system, amplify-and-forward (AF) and decode-and-forward (DF) protocols are the most common relaying scheme that can be used. In case of amplify-and-forward (AF), the relay simply amplifies its received signal and retransmit the signal to overcome the fading while maintaining a fixed average transmit power, while a DF protocol decodes the transmitted signal, re-modulates and re-transmit the received signal towards the destination. In the case of amplify-and-forward (AF) the transmitted signal at the relay can be expressed as

$$f_{AF}\left(y_{SR}\right) = \beta y_{SR} \tag{47}$$

where β is the relay transmit average power constraint coefficient that ensures that the average transmit power at the relay is constant.

Figure 14. a) Multi-hop serial relay assisted FSO communication. b) Multi-hop parallel relay assisted FSO communication.

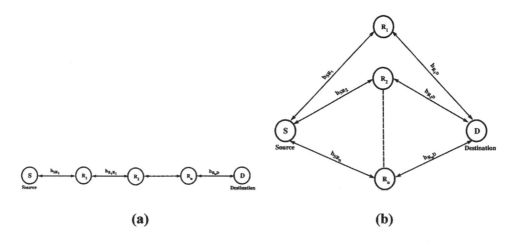

(a) **(b)**

Compared to AF relaying protocol, the DF relaying protocol is much more complicated due to its full processing capability that requires unnecessary access to media control layer. Overall, a DF relay is generally as complex as a base station.

All-Optical Multihop FSO Communication

All-optical multihop FSO communication systems are those systems where each relay signals are processed in an optical domain. This approach has the advantages of allowing efficient high speed implementation without the need for complex optoelectronics and electronic processing at each relay. In this relaying technique, there are two types of forwarding scheme that can be implemented at relay terminals like optical amplify-and-forward (OAF) and optical regenerate-and-forward (ORF). FSO relays with optical amplification have been recently considered for dual-hop transmission (Nasiri-Kenari, 2010; Nasiri-Kenari, 2011). The presented results in the literature show that all-optical relays outperform electrical relays for a limited number of relay terminals, because of the thermal noise that impairs the electrical relays, where the signal-dependent noise dominates the performance of all-optical relaying.

MULTI BEAM FSO SYSTEMS

WDM (Wavelength-division multiplexing) is a technique mainly in fiber optic transmission that enables to transmit several signals into a single optical beam over the same medium by using multiple light beams of different wavelengths. Since WDM allows simultaneous transmission of multiple high-speed signals, it leads to an increase in the capacity and bandwidth of the network without installing more fiber. As both the conventional fiber-optic communication systems and the FSO systems use similar system components, WDM technique can also be applied for FSO system to achieve the higher data transmission rate by allowing the simultaneous transmission of multiple high-speed optical signals. The use of WDM technology in the FSO communication system is a new research field (Ciaramella, 2009, K. Wang, 2012). The performances of various proposed WDM-FSO communication systems for a high-speed and long-distance FSO transmission are satisfactory. The FSO WDM scheme presents promising result for constructing future wireless cellular networks and optical access network extensions. (C.-Y. Lin, 2014, Pavithra, 2016, M. A. Esmail, 2017, Huang, 2018, Shaker, 2019)

Case Study: Hybrid RF/FSO Link

Somewhat with growing interest, the new trend of investigation in this field is the mixed RF/FSO Link, where a dual-hop configuration FSO system is relying on both RF and FSO links (Trigui, Cherif, & Affes, 2017; Ansari, F.Yilmaz, & Alouini, 2016; Dahrouj, Douik, Rayal, Al-Naffouri, & Alouini, 2015; Zedini, Ansari, & Alouin, 2015; Lee, Park, Han, & Yoon, 2011; Bag, Das, Chandra, & Bose, 2017; Samimi & Uysal, 2013; Ansari, Yilmaz, & Alouini, 2013). Some hybrid paradigms incorporating both radio-frequency (RF) and FSO links have been proposed to combine the advantages of both links. In particular, FSO links offer much better data rates than RF links but suffer from atmospheric loss due to fog and scintillation whereas the RF link is a perfect complement to FSO as RF is relatively insensitive to weather and it can penetrate fog easily. There is a strong aggregation between a laser and a radio that increase the availability of the communication link. To address this combined use, mixed RF/FSO systems become increasing attention to the researchers. It is observed that hybrid RF/FSO system provides high link availability even in adverse weather conditions.

In this RF/FSO arrangement, one hop is modelled by RF transmission, and another hop is built for FSO transmission in a dual-hop configuration. Both links within mixed RF/FSO systems are subject to fading where multipath propagation causes fading in the RF link while atmospheric turbulence is the main cause of attenuation in FSO link. The proposed combinations are either serial where the middle node (relay node) of the cascaded link is utilized for RF-optical conversion (Djordjevic, Petkovic, Cvetkovic, & Karagiannidis, 2015) or parallel where a pair of RF and FSO links connects

Figure 15. System model for dual-hop mixed RF/FSO system with S-R (RF) link, relay terminal (R) and R-D (FSO) link

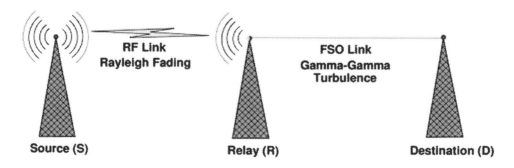

RF Link
Rayleigh Fading

FSO Link
Gamma-Gamma
Turbulence

Source (S)   **Relay (R)**   **Destination (D)**

two network nodes to improve reliability (Dahrouj, Douik, Rayal, Al-Naffouri, & Alouini, 2015). The serial RF-FSO combination has been addressed in (Ansari, Yilmaz, & Alouini, 2013; Zedini, Soury, & Alouini, 2016; Bag, Das, Chandra, & Bose, 2017) where analytical expressions for the amount of fading, outage probability, bit-error-rate, and ergodic capacity have been derived. On the other hand, the parallel RF/FSO combination is considered in (Usman, 2014; Abdulhussein, 2010; Zhang, 2009; B. Bag A. D., 2018) where different coding schemes have been suggested for switching between RF and FSO paths.

A typical dual-hop FSO communication system as shown in Figure 16, consists of a transmitter (S) that transmits the information towards the final destination (D) with the assistance of a relay node (R). The intermediate relay terminal equipped with one receiving antenna and one transmitting antenna is placed between the source (S) and destination (D) equally spaced from a relay node (R) equipped with an RF to FSO converter which converts the incoming RF signal from (S) into an optical signal for (D). At the relay (R), amplify-and-forward (AF) scheme is applied to overcome the fading loss in the S-R link by providing additional gain to the relay. To keep the architecture simple and low budget for relay based applications, average power scaling

Figure 16. Dual-hop configuration for relay assisted FSO communication

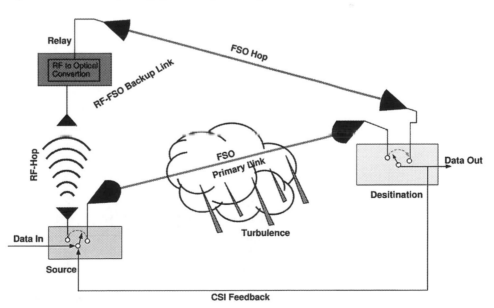

(APS) can be applied which is suitable when channel state information (CSI) is not available (Chandra, Biswas, Ghosh, Biswas, Brante, & Souza, 2013).

Under these constraints, the expression of the received signal at the destination mathematically expressed as, $r_2 = kg_2\left(g_1s + n_1\right) + n_2$ where, $k = 1/\sqrt{\left(1 + 1/N_0\right)}$, is the fixed relay gain under APS scheme, g2 is the random fading amplitude in the R-D link, and $n_2; n_2 \sim \mathcal{N}\left(0, N_0/2\right)$ is the AWGN component. Let us presume that the instantaneous SNR for S-R and R-D links are denoted with γ_1 and γ_2, respectively. The equivalent end-to-end instantaneous SNR is given by $\gamma_{eq} = \gamma_1\gamma_2/\left(g_r + \gamma_2\right)$ (Alouini, 2004), [equation (6)], where $g_r = 1 + 1/N_0$ and $\xi_i = \dfrac{g_i}{N_0}, i \in \{1,2\}$ is the instantaneous SNR of the ith hop. As per our model, the S-R link experiences Rayleigh fading, and the PDF of immediate SNR can be represented as (Alouni & Simon, 2005)

$$f_{\gamma_1}\left(\gamma_1\right) = \frac{1}{\overline{\gamma_1}}\exp\left(-\frac{\gamma_1}{\overline{\gamma_1}}\right); \gamma_1 \geq 0 \qquad (48)$$

where $\overline{\gamma_1}$ is the average SNR. The PDF of instantaneous SNR of the R-D link, on the other hand, follows gamma-gamma distribution (Uysal & T.Li, 2004)

$$f_{\gamma_2}\left(\gamma_2\right) = \frac{\left(\alpha_t\beta_t\right)^{\frac{\left(\alpha_t + \beta_t\right)}{2}}}{\Gamma\left(\alpha_t\right)\Gamma\left(\beta_t\right)\sqrt{\gamma_2\overline{\gamma_2}}}\left(\sqrt{\frac{\gamma_2}{\overline{\gamma_2}}}\right)^{\frac{\left(\alpha_t + \beta_t\right)}{2} - 1} K_{\alpha_t - \beta_t}\left(2\sqrt{\alpha_t\beta_t\sqrt{\frac{\gamma_2}{\overline{\gamma_2}}}}\right); \gamma_2 \geq 0 \qquad (49)$$

where γ is the average SNR. The CDF of end-to-end SNR, $F_{\gamma_{eq}}\left(\gamma\right) = Pr\left(\gamma_{eq} \leq \gamma\right)$ where Pr($\cdot$) denotes probability, may be derived by integrating the conditional probability, $Pr\left(\gamma_{eq} \leq \gamma \mid \gamma_2\right)$ over the whole range of γ_2 and using (Prudnikov, Brychkov, & Marichev, 1990, equation 2.24.3.1), resulting in a closed-form expression

$$F_{\gamma_{eq}}(\gamma) = 1 - \mathcal{A}\exp\left(-\frac{\gamma}{\overline{\gamma_1}}\right)(\gamma)^{\tau_1} G_{05}^{50}\left[\omega\gamma\left|\overline{}_P\right.\right] \tag{50}$$

where,

$$\mathcal{A} = (\alpha_t\beta_t)^{\frac{(\alpha_t+\beta_t)}{2}}\left(g_r/\overline{\gamma_1}\right)^{\tau_1} / \left[4\pi\Gamma(\alpha_t)\Gamma(\beta_t)\left(\overline{\gamma_2}\right)^{\tau_1}\right]$$

$$\omega = \left(\alpha_t^2\beta_t^2 g_r\right)/\left(16\overline{\gamma_1}\,\overline{\gamma_2}\right), \tau_1 = (\alpha_t+\beta_t)/4$$

$$P \in \left\{(\alpha_t-\beta_t)/4, (\alpha_t-\beta_t+2)/4, (\beta_t-\alpha_t)/4, (\beta_t-\alpha_t+2)/4, -\tau_1\right\}$$

and $G_{pq}^{mn}\left[z\left|\begin{matrix}(a_p)\\(b_q)\end{matrix}\right.\right]$ is the Meijer's G-function (Prudnikov, Brychkov, & Marichev, 1990), [equation (8.2.1)].

Now, differentiating (50) using (Prudnikov, Brychkov, & Marichev, 1990, equation 8.2.2.30), the corresponding PDF (γ_{eq}) can be obtained as

$$f_{\gamma_{eq}}(\gamma) = \mathcal{A}\exp\left(-\frac{\gamma}{\overline{\gamma_1}}\right)(\gamma)^{(\tau_1-1)} G_{16}^{60}\left[\omega\gamma\left|\begin{matrix}-\tau_1\\1-\tau_1,P\end{matrix}\right.\right] + \frac{\mathcal{A}}{\overline{\gamma_1}}\exp\left(-\frac{\gamma}{\overline{\gamma_1}}\right)(\gamma)^{\tau_1} G_{05}^{50}\left[\omega\gamma\left|\overline{}_P\right.\right] \tag{51}$$

Finally, using (51) and (Prudnikov, Brychkov, & Marichev, 1990, equation 2.24.3.1), one may get the corresponding MGF $\mathcal{M}_{\gamma_{eq}}(s) = \int_0^\infty \exp(-\gamma s) f_{\gamma_{eq}}(\gamma) d\gamma$ as

$$\mathcal{M}_{\gamma_{eq}}(s) = \mathcal{A}\left(s+\frac{1}{\overline{\gamma_1}}\right)^{-\tau_1} G_{26}^{61}\left[\frac{\omega}{s+\dfrac{1}{\overline{\gamma_1}}}\left|\begin{matrix}1-\tau_1,-\tau_1\\1-\tau_1,P\end{matrix}\right.\right] + \frac{\mathcal{A}}{\overline{\gamma_1}}\left(s+\frac{1}{\overline{\gamma_1}}\right)^{-(\tau_1+1)} G_{15}^{51}\left[\frac{\omega}{s+\dfrac{1}{\overline{\gamma_1}}}\left|\begin{matrix}-\tau_1\\P\end{matrix}\right.\right] \tag{52}$$

Outage Probability

The outage probability (OP) expression can be obtained with a simple substitution in (50). Mathematically speaking,

$$P_{out}\left(\gamma_{th}\right) = Pr\left(\gamma \le \gamma_{th}\right) = F_{\gamma_{eq}}\left(\gamma_{th}\right).$$

i.e.

$$P_{out}\left(\gamma_{th}\right) = 1 - \mathcal{A}\exp\left(-\frac{\gamma_{th}}{\gamma_1}\right)\left(\gamma_{th}\right)^{\tau_1} G_{05}^{50}\left[\omega\gamma_{th}\left|\begin{matrix}-\\P\end{matrix}\right.\right] \qquad (53)$$

The threshold $\left(\gamma_{th}\right)$ acts as a minimum SNR value above which the link can guarantee a specific quality of service. Figure 17 exhibits the end-to-end outage probability of this dual-hop RF-FSO system.

Figure 17. a) Outage Probability for dual-hop RF-FSO system where cutoff SNR (γ_{th}=0.9337 dB) b) BER vs Average SNR (γ) for different values of gamma-gamma fading parameters under strong turbulence when α_t =4.2, 2.73 and 2.26 and corresponding β_t values are 1.71, 1.25 and 0.65.

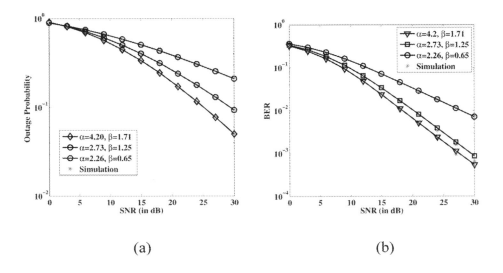

(a)   (b)

Average BER

In fading channels, the average bit error rate (BER) can be found by averaging the instantaneous SNR, which is a function of the RF-FSO link SNR, γ.

$$P_e = \int_0^\infty P_e(\gamma) f_\gamma(\gamma) d\gamma \tag{54}$$

Now, if it is possible to express $P_e(\gamma)$ in the form of $A \exp(-\beta r)$, using MGF method, the BER can be derived easily. The procedure to find the MGF from PDF discussed in (52).

Finally putting the value of $s = -\dfrac{1}{2(\sin\theta)^2}$ in (52) and using (34) we may find the resultant bit error rate (BER) of the system. Figure 17, present the BER graph of a dual-hop system with different fading parameter values under strong atmospheric turbulence condition. It seems that the performance is enhanced when the atmospheric turbulence decline.

Average Channel Capacity

The channel capacity in bits/s/Hz, *Cora*, for this case can be obtained by averaging the instantaneous capacity over the fading SNR PDF (Bag, Das, Chandra, & Bose, 2017), i.e. we need to solve the integral,

$$C_{ora} = \int_0^\infty \log_2(1+\Omega) f_{\gamma_{eq}}(\Omega) d\Omega.$$

The above integral can be solved using the negative exponential integral function, $E_i(\cdot)$ (Stegun & Abramowitz, 1972, equation 5.1.2), as

$$C_{ora} = (1/\ln 2) \int_0^\infty E_i(-\Omega) \mathcal{M}_{\gamma_{eq}}^{(1)}(\Omega) d\Omega \tag{55}$$

where $\mathcal{M}_{\gamma_{eq}}^{(1)}(\cdot)$ represents the first derivative of the MGF, which may be obtained by differentiating (52) using (Prudnikov, Brychkov, & Marichev,

1990, equation 8.2.2.30). The exponential integral can also be expressed in terms of the Meijer's *G* function using the transformation (Prudnikov, Brychkov, & Marichev, 1990, equation 8.4.11.1), as

$$E_i\left(-\Omega\right) = -G_{12}^{20}\left[\Omega\left|\begin{matrix}1\\0,0\end{matrix}\right.\right]$$

(56)

Finally, after some mathematical manipulation the closed-form expression of the average channel capacity for the mixed RF/FSO link become

$$C_{ora} = \frac{A}{\ln\left(2\right)}\left(G_{83}^{18}\left[\frac{1}{\omega}\left|\begin{matrix}A\\B\end{matrix}\right.\right] + \frac{1}{\gamma_1}G_{72}^{17}\left[\frac{1}{\omega}\left|\begin{matrix}C\\D\end{matrix}\right.\right]\right)$$

(57)

where, $\omega = \left(\alpha_t^2\beta_t^2 g_r\right)/\left(16\overline{\gamma_1}\,\overline{\gamma_2}\right)$,

$$A \in \left(a_1,\ldots a_8\right), B \in \left(b_1,b_2,b_3\right), C \in \left(c_1,\ldots c_7\right), D \in \left(d_1,d_2\right)$$

$$\begin{cases} a_1 = 1 - \dfrac{\alpha_t - \beta_t}{4}, a_2 = 1 - \dfrac{2 + \alpha_t - \beta_t}{4}, a_3 = 1 - \dfrac{\beta_t - \alpha_t}{4}, \\ a_4 = 1 - \dfrac{2 + \beta_t - \alpha_t}{4}, a_5 = 1 + \tau_1; \\ a_6 = \tau_1, a_7 = a_8, b_1 = b_2 = a_5, b_3 = \tau_1; \\ c_1 = a_1, c_2 = a_2, c_3 = a_3, c_4 = a_4, c_5 = a_5 \\ c_6 = 2 - a_6, c_7 = c_6; d_1 = 2 + \tau_1, d_2 = 1 + \tau_1 \end{cases}$$

Considering the different atmospheric turbulence conditions ($1\times 10^{-14}\,\text{m}^{-2/3}$, $1 \times 10^{-15}\,\text{m}^{-2/3}$, and $1.9\times 10^{-16}\,\text{m}^{-2/3}$ for strong, moderate, and weak turbulence, respectively), three distinct pairs of turbulence parameters,

$$\left\{\alpha_t,\beta_t\right\} = \left\{\left(5.07,1.53\right)\left(4.10,2.35\right)\left(3.99,3.07\right)\right\}$$

are taken into account. The average SNR per hop is considered to be identical, i.e. $\overline{\gamma_1} = \overline{\gamma_2} = \overline{\gamma}$. The performance in term of average capacity for mixed RF/FSO system is shown in Figure 18.

OPEN CHALLENGES AND SCOPE OF FUTURE RESEARCH

There are several techniques have been proposed from last two decades, and a lot of theoretical studies and research has been carried out to improve the FSO link performance by mitigating the obstacles presents in the atmospheric channel (Khalighi, 2014), but still more research and analysis is required for this technology to be deployed successfully in all weather conditions throughout all types of climate regions. Research is required to reduce the existing demerits of FSO system by introducing any new technique or, by enhancing the existing techniques. In FSO links, the transmitted optical signal is affected by various impairments before arriving at the receiver. Some of the areas of existing and future research are:

Figure 18. Channel capacity as a function of average SNR for different degrees of turbulence.

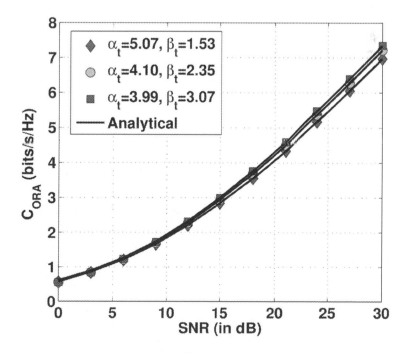

1. The random fluctuation of the received signal results from the atmospheric turbulence that degrades the performance of FSO communication systems. The effect of power loss due to attenuation is medium, but the power level cannot be increased more than a value defined by various organizations that obeys the principle of laser safety. A 10 mW power level for Class 1 M laser in 1550 nm wavelength is permissible as per IEC (International Electro technical Commission) standards (S. Bloom, 2013).

2. To improve the performance of existing FSO system further continuation of research van be carried out in open areas, such as wavelength-diversity, using different wavelength-based concepts. The system BER can be reduced further using wavelength diversity and coding simultaneously with somewhat increased degree of system complexity.

3. To improve BER, coding and diversity techniques can be applied together. Time diversity technique can also be investigated. Spatial diversity and/or relay-assisted FSO nodes can be employed to mitigate such impairments.

4. To establish the satellite-based future optical communications like the ground to satellite communication under all weather-conditions and inter-satellite communication links successfully, further study and research is essential.

5. In future to support high bandwidth based mobile applications, highly efficient tracking system can be developed to utilize the benefit of FSO communication.

6. Rather than mostly used intensity modulation (OOK), other modulation techniques (like PSK, DPSK, OFDM, M-PPM, MFSK etc.) may be implemented for FSO communication which demands a lower power requirement.

7. For a better and efficient FSO link performance under adverse weather conditions for long distances, development of optical source and detection modules for longer wavelength might be an exciting area of research.

8. The optical beam is attenuated mainly due to fog compared to rain and RF links are mostly attenuated by rain but can penetrate fog easily. Therefore, combining the advantages of both, hybrid RF/FSO link can be used to meet the desired performance in all weather conditions. This area of research can be explored more deeply.

CONCLUSION

The FSO communication (FSO) technology has gained a rapid growth in the last few years. FSO technology becomes a promising alternative to the conventional fiber optic cables utilized for backhaul links due to the ease of deployment, rapid setup time, low maintenance cost and free from any licensing issues . The FSO technology is the ultimate solution for providing high capacity last mile connectivity and is expected to play a vital role in 5G wireless networks which allows connectivity to remote places where it is difficult to access 3G or 4G signals.

This technology can be an excellent alternative to underwater wireless communication for short distance which can be applied for various applications like intercommunication between underwater submarines, monitoring undersea explorations or ocean currents and winds for improving weather forecast and tsunami warning etc. This technology can also be implemented with an underwater sensor network for long-term basis which would be used to collect geophysical data.

However, to fully utilize the terabit capacity of FSO system, it has to overcome various challenges offered by the heterogeneous nature of the atmospheric channel. Currently, FSO communication through atmospheric turbulence under adverse weather conditions is an active research topic. The main challenges and objective in this area of research is to minimize the various limitations which are faced during data transmission through the atmospheric channel and improve the performance regarding BER, outage probability and channel capacity etc.

A lot of studies and experiments have been carried out on the effect of attenuation, mainly due to snow and fog on FSO technology deployment in the temperate climates; but still, much more research is necessary for implementing this technology successfully in the tropical climate region where the rain and haze throughout the year are the main obstacles.

However, the FSO technology seems to have a great prospect in future, and bring a revolution in wireless communication technology with the advancement of this technology.

ACKNOWLEDGMENT

This work is a part of research activities within the framework of the National Scholarship Programme of the Slovak Republic conducted by SAIA, Bratislava.

REFERENCES

Abdulhussein, A., Oka, A., Nguycn, T., & Lampe, L. (2010). Rateless coding for hybrid free-space optical and radio-frequency communication. *IEEE Transactions on Wireless Communications*, *9*(3), 907–913. doi:10.1109/TWC.2010.03.090108

Al-Habash, M. A., Andrews, L. C., & Phillips, R. L. (2001). Mathematical model for the irradiance probability density function of a laser. *Optical Engineering (Redondo Beach, Calif.)*, *40*(8), 1554–1562. doi:10.1117/1.1386641

Alamouti, S. M. (1998). A simple transmit diversity technique for wireless communication. *IEEE Journal on Selected Areas in Communications*, *16*(8), 1451–1458. doi:10.1109/49.730453

Ali Shahpari, A. N. (2014). Free space optical communications for ultra high-capacity PON system. *Second International Conference on Applications of Optics and Photonics.* Aveiro, Portugal: SPIE.

Alouini, M. O. (2004). A performance study of dual-hop transmissions with fixed gain relays. *IEEE Transactions on Wireless Communications*, *3*(6), 1963–1968. doi:10.1109/TWC.2004.837470

Alouni, M. S., & Simon, M. K. (2005). *Digital Communication Over Fading Channels* (2nd ed.). New York: John Wiley & Sons.

Amon, D. K. (2004). Urban optical wireless communication networks: The main challenges and possible solutions. *IEEE Opt.Commun.*, *42*(5), 51–57.

Ansari, I. S., Yilmaz, F., & Alouini, M. S. (2013). On the performance of mixed RF/FSO dual-hop transmission system. In *77th IEEE Vehicular Technology Conference (VTC Spring)*, (pp. pp. 1–5.). Dresden, Germany: IEEE. 10.1109/VTCSpring.2013.6692668

Ansari, I. S., Yilmaz, F., & Alouini, M.-S. (2016). Performance Analysis of Free-Space Optical Links Over Ma ´laga (M) Turbulence Channels With Pointing Errors. *IEEE Transactions on Wireless Communications*, *15*(1), 91–102. doi:10.1109/TWC.2015.2467386

Arimoto, Y. (2010). *Developing a new free-space optical communication terminal that realizes high-speed broadband communications. National Institute of Information and Communications Technology.* NICT.

Arnon, S. (2003). Effects of atmospheric turbulence and building sway on optical wireless communication systems. *Optics Letters*, *28*(2), 129–131. doi:10.1364/OL.28.000129 PMID:12656506

Bag, B., Das, A., Ansari, I. S., Prokeš, A., Bose, C., & Chandra, A. (2018). Performance analysis of hybrid fso systems using FSO/RF-FSO link adaptation. *IEEE Photonics Journal*, *10*(3), 1–17. doi:10.1109/JPHOT.2018.2837356

Bag, B., Das, A., & Chandra, A. (2014). Performance analysis of dual-hop af relaying fso system using alamouti scheme over G-G fading. *12th International Conference on Fiber Optics and Photonic*. 10.1364/PHOTONICS.2014. M4A.56

Bag, B., Das, A., Chandra, A., & Bose, C. (2017). Capacity Analysis for Rayleigh/Gamma-Gamma Mixed RF/FSO Link with Fixed-Gain AF Relay. *IEICE Transactions on Communications*, *E100-B*(10), 1747–1757. doi:10.1587/transcom.2017OBP0001

Bayaki, E., Schobe, R., & Mallik, R. K. (2009). Performance analysis of MIMO free-space optical systems in gamma-gamma fading. *IEEE Transactions on Communications*, *57*(11), 3415–3424. doi:10.1109/TCOMM.2009.11.080168

Bloom, E. K. (2013). Understanding the performance of free-space optics. *Journal of Optical Networking*, *2*(6), 178–200.

Chandra, A., Biswas, S., Ghosh, B., Biswas, N., Brante, G., & Souza, R. D. (2013). *Energy Efficient Relay Placement in Dual Hop 802.15.4 Networks.* New York: Springer, Wireless Pers Commun.

Chen, C.-H. Y.-S.-S.-J.-W.-C.-B. (2018). Hybrid free space optical communication system and passive optical network with high splitting ratio for broadcasting data traffic. *Journal of Optics*, *20*(12), 125702. doi:10.1088/2040-8986/aaef29

Ciaramella, E., Arimoto, Y., Contestabile, G., Presi, M., D'Errico, A., Guarino, V., & Matsumoto, M. (2009). 1.28 terabit/s (32×40 Gbit/s) WDM transmission system for free space optical communications. *IEEE Journal on Selected Areas in Communications, 27*(9), 1639–1645. doi:10.1109/JSAC.2009.091213

Dahrouj, H., Douik, A., Rayal, F., Al-Naffouri, T. Y., & Alouini, M. S. (2015). Cost-effective hybrid RF/FSO backhaul solution for next generation wireless systems. *IEEE Wireless Communications, 22*(5), 98–104. doi:10.1109/MWC.2015.7306543

Datsikas, C. K., Peppas, K. P., Sagias, N. C., & Tombras, G. S. (2010). Serial free-space optical relaying communications over gamma-gamma. *Journal of Optical Communications and Networking, 2*(8), 576–586. doi:10.1364/JOCN.2.000576

Davis, S. M. (2005). Aperture averaging for optimizing receiver design and system performance on free space optical. *J. Opt. Netw., 4*(8), 462–475. doi:10.1364/JON.4.000462

Dimitrov, S., Sinanovic, S., & Haas, H. (2012). Signal shaping and modulation for optical wireless communication. *Journal of Lightwave Technology, 30*(9), 1319–1328. doi:10.1109/JLT.2012.2188376

Djordjevic, G. T., Petkovic, M. I., Cvetkovic, A. M., & Karagiannidis, G. K. (2015). Mixed RF/FSO relaying with outdated channel state information. *IEEE Journal on Selected Areas in Communications, 33*(9), 1935–1948. doi:10.1109/JSAC.2015.2433055

Esmail, M. A., Ragheb, A., Fathallah, H., & Alouini, M.-S. (2017). Investigation and Demonstration of High Speed Full-Optical Hybrid FSO/Fiber Communication System Under Light Sand Storm Condition. *IEEE Photonics Journal, 9*(1), 1–12. doi:10.1109/JPHOT.2016.2641741

Farid, A. A., & Hranilovic, S. (2007). Outage capacity optimization for free-space optical links with pointing errors. *IEEE/OSA J. Lightw., 25*(7), 1702–1710. doi:10.1109/JLT.2007.899174

Ghasemi, A. A. (2012). *Propagation Engineering in Wireless Communications*. New York: Springer. doi:10.1007/978-1-4614-1077-5

Goldsmith, A. J., & Alouini, M. S. (1999). Capacity of Rayleigh fading channels under different adaptive transmission and diversity-combining techniques. *IEEE Trans. Veh. Tech.*, *48*(4), 1165–1181. doi:10.1109/25.775366

Hecht, J. (2005). Beam: The race to make the laser. *Optics and Photonics News*, *16*(7), 24. doi:10.1364/OPN.16.7.000024

Huang, X. (2018). WDM Free-Space Optical Communication System of High-Speed Hybrid Signals. *IEEE Photonics Journal*, *10*(6), 1–7.

Jurado-Navas, A., Garrido-Balsells, J. M., Paris, J. F., Vazquez, M. C.-V., & Puerta-Notario, A. (2012). Further insights on Malaga distribution for atmospheric optical communications. In *International Workshop on Optical Wireless Communications (IWOW)* (pp. 1–3.). Pisa, Italy: Academic Press.

Jurado-Navas, A., Garrido-Balsells, J. M., Paris, J. F., & Puerta-Notario, A. (2011, Feb). A Unifying Statistical Model for Atmospheric Optical Scintillation. *ArXiv e-prints*.

Kahn, J. M., & Zhu, X. (2003). Performance bounds for coded free-space optical communications through atmospheric turbulence channels. *IEEE Transactions on Communications*, *51*(8), 1233–1239. doi:10.1109/TCOMM.2003.815052

Kahn, X. Z. (2002). Free-space optical communication through atmospheric turbulence channels. *IEEE Transactions on Communications*, *50*(8), 1293–1300. doi:10.1109/TCOMM.2002.800829

Kahn, X. Z. (2003). Performance bounds for coded free-space optical communications through atmospheric turbulence channels. *IEEE Transactions on Communications*, *51*(8), 1233–1239. doi:10.1109/TCOMM.2003.815052

Khalighi, M.-A. &. (2014). Survey on Free Space Optical Communication: A Communication Theory Perspective. *IEEE Communications Surveys & Tutorials*, 2231-2258.

Laneman, D. T., & Wornell, G. (2004). Cooperative diversity in wireless networks: Efficient protocols and outage behavior. *IEEE Transactions on Information Theory*, *50*(12), 3062–3080. doi:10.1109/TIT.2004.838089

Lee, E., Park, J., Han, D., & Yoon, G. (2011). Performance analysis of the asymmetric dual-hop relay transmission with mixed RF/FSO links. *IEEE Photonics Technology Letters*, *23*(21), 1642–1644. doi:10.1109/LPT.2011.2166063

Lee, E. J., & Chan, V. W. (2004). Part 1: Optical communication over the clear turbulent atmospheric channel using diversity. *IEEE Journal on Selected Areas in Communications, 22*(9), 1896–1906. doi:10.1109/JSAC.2004.835751

Li, R. (2018). *Towards a New Internet for the Year 2030 and Beyond.* Retrieved from https://www.google.com/url?sa=t&rct=j&q=&esrc=s&source=web& cd=3&ved=2ahUKEwiotcvgwabhAhVo4XMBHdUVAaQQFjACegQIAx AC&url=https%3A%2F%2Fwww.itu.int%2Fen%2FITU-T%2FWorkshops- and-Seminars%2F201807%2FDocuments%2F3_Richard%2520Li.pdf&usg =AOvVaw3QSQqAo8WKAHXyxziYp

Lin, C.-Y., Lin, Y.-P., Lu, H.-H., Chen, C.-Y., Jhang, T.-W., & Chen, M.-C. (2014). Optical free-space wavelength-division-multiplexing transport system. *Optics Letters, 39*(2), 315–318. doi:10.1364/OL.39.000315 PMID:24562135

McQuistan, L. D. (1962). *Elements of Infrared Technology: Generation, Transmission and Detection.* Wiley.

Miller, J. M. (2017). Communications expands its space. *Nature Photonics, 11*(1), 5–8. doi:10.1038/nphoton.2016.256

Nadeem, E. L. F, J. T. (2010). Continental fog attenuation empirical relationship from measured visibility. *J. Radioeng, 19*(4), 596–600.

Nadeem, M. S., Kvicera, V., Leitgeb, E., Muhammad, S., & Kandus, G. (2009). Weather effects on hybrid FSO/RF communication link. *IEEE Journal on Selected Areas in Communications, 27*(9), 1687–1697. doi:10.1109/ JSAC.2009.091218

Nasiri-Kenari, M. K. (2009). BER analysis of cooperative systems in free-space optical networks. *Journal of Lightwave Technology, 27*(12), 5639–5647.

Nasiri-Kenari, M. K. (2010). Outage analysis of relay-assisted freespace optical communications. *IET Communications, 4*(12), 1423–1432. doi:10.1049/iet-com.2009.0335

Nasiri-Kenari, M. K. (2011). Free space optical communications via optical amplify-andforward relaying. *IEEE/OSA J. Lightw. Technol., 29*(2), 242–248. doi:10.1109/JLT.2010.2102003

Novak, M. K.-K. (1995). *An introduction to Infrared technology: Applications in the home, classroom, workplace, and.* Madison, WI: Trace R and D Center, University of Wisconsin.

Pavithra, S. R. (2016). Investigation on multi-beam hybrid WDM for free space optical communication system. *Int. J. Photon. Opt. Technol.*, *2*(2), 24–28.

Popoola, Z. G. (2010). Terrestial Free-Space Optical Communications. In Z. G. Popoola (Ed.), *Terrestial Free-Space Optical Communications* (pp. 356–392.). InTech.

Prudnikov, A. P., Brychkov, Y. A., & Marichev, O. I. (1990). *Integrals and Series Volume 3: More Special Functions.* Gordon and Breech Science.

Sandalidis, G. K., Tsiftsis, T., & Uysal, M. (2008). BER performance of FSO links over strong atmospheric turbulence channels with. *IEEE Communications Letters*, *12*(1), 44–46. doi:10.1109/LCOMM.2008.071408

Shaker, F. &. (2019). Multi-Beam Free-Space Optical Link to Mitigation of Rain Attenuation. *Journal of Optical Communications*.

Stegun, I. A., & Abramowitz, M. (1972). *Handbook of Mathematical Functions With Formulas*. Dover, NY: Graphs, and Mathematical Tables.

Trigui, I., Cherif, N., & Affes, S. (2017). Relay-Assisted Mixed FSO/RF Systems over Ma´laga-M and k − μ Shadowed Fading Channels. *IEEE Communications Letters*, *6*(5), 682–685. doi:10.1109/LWC.2017.2730204

Usman, M., Hong-Chuan Yang, & Alouini, M.-S. (2014). Practical switching-based hybrid FSO/RF transmission and its performance analysis. *IEEE Photonics Journal*, *6*(5), 1–13. doi:10.1109/JPHOT.2014.2352629

Uysal, H. S. (2013). End-to-end performance of mixed RF/FSO transmission systems. *Journal of Optical Communications and Networking*, *5*(11), 1139–1144. doi:10.1364/JOCN.5.001139

Uysal, M., & Li, T., J. (2004). Error rate performance of coded free-space optical links over gamma-gamma turbulence channels. *IEEE International Conference on Communications (ICC '04)*, (pp. 3331–3335). IEEE.

Uysal, M. R. (2012). Multi-hop relaying over the atmospheric Poisson channel: Outage analysis and optimization. *IEEE Transactions on Communications*, *60*(3), 817–829. doi:10.1109/TCOMM.2012.010512.100630

Varaiya, A. J. (1997). Capacity of Fading Channels with Channel Side Information. *IEEE Transactions on Information Theory*, *43*(6), 1986–1992. doi:10.1109/18.641562

Wang, A. N. (2012). Impact of crosstalk on indoor WDM optical wireless communication systems. *IEEE Photon. J., 4*(2), 375–386.

Yilmaz, F., Kucur, O., & Alouini, M. S. (2010). Exact capacity analysis of multi-hop transmission over Amplify-and-Forward relay fading channels. In *Proc. 21st International Symposium on Personal Indoor and Mobile Radio Communications (PIMRC)*, (pp. 2293–2298). Academic Press.

Zedini, E., Ansari, I. S., & Alouin, M. (2015). Unified performance analysis of mixed line of sight RF-FSO fixed gain dual-hop transmission systems. In *IEEE Wireless Communications and Networking Conference (WCNC 2015)*, (pp. 46–51.). New Orleans, LA: IEEE. 10.1109/WCNC.2015.7127443

Zedini, E., Ansari, I. S., & Alouini, M. S. (2015). Performance Analysis of Mixed Nakagami-m and Gamma-Gamma Dual-Hop FSO Transmission Systems. *IEEE Photonics Journal, 7*(1), 1–20. doi:10.1109/JPHOT.2014.2381657

Zedini, E., Soury, H., & Alouini, M. (2016). On the performance analysis of dual-hop mixed FSO/RF systems. *IEEE Transactions on Wireless Communications, 15*(5), 3679–3689. doi:10.1109/TWC.2016.2524685

Zhang, W., Hranilovic, S., & Shi, C. (2009). Soft-switching hybrid FSO/RF links using short-length Raptor codes: Design and implementation. *IEEE Journal on Selected Areas in Communications, 27*(9), 1698–1708. doi:10.1109/JSAC.2009.091219

KEY TERMS AND DEFINITIONS

Free Space Optical Communication: This is a wireless data transmission technology in which optical signal has been used to carry the information instead of radio frequency signal for wireless communication.

Jitter: Jitter is simply the difference in packet delay. In other words, jitter is measuring time difference in packet inter-arrival.

Last Mile: The last mile is a phrase widely used in the telecommunications refers to the final leg of the telecommunications networks that deliver telecommunication services to the final destination (end-users).

Orthogonal Frequency-Division Multiplexing (OFDM): Orthogonal frequency-division multiplexing is a method of digital signal modulation in

which a single data stream is divided across several separate narrowband close-spaced subcarriers channels at different frequencies to reduce interference and crosstalk.

Passive Optical Network: A passive optical network (PON) is a data transmission technology in which no active component is used to communicate between fiber to the end user, for both domestic and commercial uses.

Throughput: In the context of communication networks, throughput is the rate of successful message/data delivery through a communication channel.

Wavelength Division Multiplexing (WDM): Wavelength division multiplexing is a technology or technique modulating numerous data streams (i.e., optical carrier signals of varying wavelengths [colors] of laser light) onto a single optical fiber. WDM enables bi-directional communication as well as multiplication of signal capacity.

Chapter 5

Challenges in Future Intra-Data-Center Networks and Possible Solutions

Muhammad Ishaq
Pakistan Institute of Research and Development, Pakistan

Mohammad Kaleem
iD https://orcid.org/0000-0001-5005-3467
COMSATS University – Islamabad, Pakistan

Numan Kifayat
iD https://orcid.org/0000-0002-5172-5787
KAIST, South Korea

ABSTRACT

This chapter briefly introduces the data center network and reviews the challenges for future intra-data-center networks in terms of scalability, cost effectiveness, power efficiency, upgrade cost, and bandwidth utilization. Current data center network architecture is discussed in detail and the drawbacks are pointed out in terms of the above-mentioned parameters. A detailed background is provided that how the technology moved from opaque to transparent optical networks. Additionally, it includes different data center network architectures proposed so far by different researchers/team/ companies in order to address the current problems and meet the demands of future intra-data-center networks.

DOI: 10.4018/978-1-5225-9767-4.ch005

INTRODUCTION

The facility used to house massive amounts of computing, storage and network resources like servers, hard drives and bandwidth is called a Data Center (DC). These resources can either be used by the DC operators to deploy their own services or be rented to their customers. These customers are usually Small and Medium Enterprises (SMEs) which have reduced resource requirements and would find very expensive to deploy and maintain their own infrastructure. Therefore, the DC operators provide Infrastructure as a Service (IaaS) (Buyya et al., 2009) to their customers.

The main issues which DCs address are linked to the fulfillment of the Service Level Agreement (SLA) (Bouillet, Mitra, & Ramakrishnan, 2002) which their operators sign with the customers and the maximization of the profits they obtain. In such a context, the key challenges DCs operators have to face are:

- **Scalability**: The capability of being able to increase the number of housed resources and bandwidth.
- **Fault Tolerance**: The capability of being able to withstand failures without producing an impact on the service.
- **Cost Effectiveness**: The capability of reducing the amount of required resources. This can be achieved through the use of several virtualization technologies, abstracting the physical resources into several virtual (or logical) resources. This allows the DC operators to optimize the resource usage by providing to each customer only what he needs and pays for.
- **Power Efficiency**: The capability of minimizing the power consumption produced by the resources.

By taking a closer look into intra Data Center Networks (DCNs) it can be observed that they intend to follow these same principles. An intra DCN's function is to allow resilient, high bit-rate and low-latency communications between the DC's computing and storage resources.

This is a critical task since a failure (or congestion) in the network would degrade the performance of the connections or directly block them. If this happens, the outcome (from the user's point of view) is the same as if the computing or storage resources were down since his request cannot be attended. An example of this would be the communication between a virtual machine and a storage server (Figure 1).

Figure 1. Virtual machine to storage successful and failed communications
Source: Predieri et al. (2013)

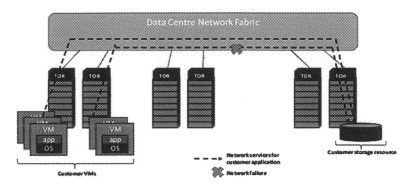

Several forecasts, among them the Cisco GCI 2016 (Figure 2), indicate that the global

DC traffic will grow from about 6.8 Zettabytes/Year on the year 2016 up to approximately 20.6 Zettabytes/Year on the year 2021 experiencing a threefold increase. Moreover, the expected Compound Annual Growth Rate (CAGR) for global DC traffic is around 25%.

Furthermore, in such a period of time, the 73% of the global DC traffic is expected to be intra DC traffic (Figure 3). This forthcoming substantial growth in intra DC traffic will push to the limit the scalability and performance of currently deployed intra DCNs' architecture.

In the next section the currently deployed intra DCNs' architecture is analyzed in order to determine if it will be able to meet the requirements for future intra DCNs.

Figure 2. Global data center IP traffic growth
Source: Cisco GCI (2016)

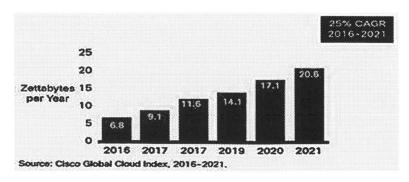

Figure 3. Global data center traffic by destination
Source: Cisco GCI (2019)

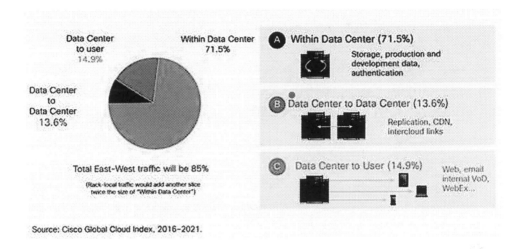

BACKGROUND

Current Architecture

Current DCNs present a Fat Tree (Al-Fares, Loukissas, & Vahdat, 2008) (or hierarchical) architecture (Figure 4) with three distinguished levels: access, aggregation and core.

Figure 4. "Current DCN Architecture"
Source: Predieri et al. (2013)

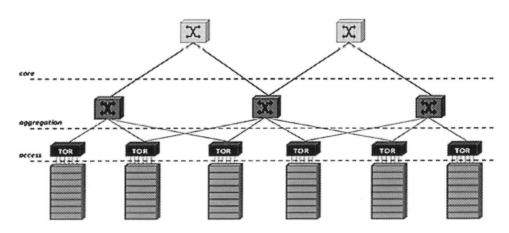

In the next sections, a bottom-up analysis of the architecture will be performed by starting with the access level, then proceeding with the aggregation level and finishing with the core level.

Access Level

In the access level the servers are stacked and placed into racks. Nowadays, each rack usually contains between 20 and 40 servers. Each server can host around 40 virtual machines (depending on the amount of resources each virtual machine requires). Each rack also contains a Remote Direct Memory Access over Converged Ethernet (RoCE) (InfiniBand Trade Association, 2010) or an InfiniBand (IB) (InfiniBand Trade Association, 2007) switch which is also known as top of the rack (ToR) switch.

ToR switches have a high port density (24 or 48 ports) since each server of the rack is connected to a ToR switch by twisted pair or biaxial copper cables. The most used standards for deploying these types of links are shown in the Table 1.

Thanks to the ToR switches any server can exchange traffic with any other server of its same rack.

Aggregation Level

The aggregation level consists on several RoCE or InfiniBand switches which are used to exchange traffic between servers which are located in different racks. The aggregation switches usually have fewer ports than a ToR switch but they can achieve higher bit-rates (10Gbps, 40Gbps or even 100Gbps).

Table 1. Gigabit Ethernet and InfiniBand access level standards

Standard	Bit-Rate	Cable	Maximum Length
1000Base-T	1 Gbps	5e (TIA/EIA-568-B) or higher	100 m
10GBase-T	10 Gbps	6 (TIA/EIA-568-B.2-1)	55 m
10GBase-T	10 Gbps	6a (TIA/EIA-568-B.2-10) or higher	100 m
10GBASE-CX4	10 Gbps	InfiniBand biaxial cable	15m
InfiniBand SDR	2.5 Gbps	InfiniBand biaxial cable	60m
InfiniBand DDR	5 Gbps	InfiniBand biaxial cable	30m
InfiniBand QDR	10 Gbps	InfiniBand biaxial cable	15m

This traffic exchange is performed by connecting the ToR switches to the aggregation switches with these higher bit-rate links (also known as uplinks). In order to provide redundancy, each ToR switch has at least two uplinks (each one connected to a different aggregation switch). When working with RoCE the Spanning Tree Protocol (STP) (IEEE, 2004) or the Provider Backbone Bridge - Traffic Engineering (PBB-TE) (IEEE, 2011) are usually set up to ensure a loop-free topology while also providing fast failure recovery. InfiniBand provides out of the box topology loop control.

The aggregation level can also be used to partition the network into clusters (or sectors). Only the subset of the ToR switches (instead of all of them) is directly connected to each aggregation switch. This may help to improve the scalability of the architecture (primarily due to the reduction in the number of ports which each aggregation switch requires).

The uplinks are usually optical due to the impossibility of achieving such high bit-rates with copper-based links which have a limited bandwidth. The switches which implement this kind of high capacity links typically are equipped with Small Form Pluggable (SFP) or XFI Form Pluggable (XFP) ports which allow different types of transceivers.

Since the distances among the ToR switches and the aggregation switches in a DC environment tend to be short (in the order of few hundreds of meters) there are no significant attenuation or dispersion effects on the optical links. Consequently low power lasers operating at the first and second window (850 nm and 1310 nm respectively) are typically used in conjunction with multi-mode optical fibres. Also, neither amplifiers nor regenerators are needed. The most used standards for deploying these type of links are shown in the table 2.

Core Level

The core level consists on the switches and routers which are responsible for the exchange of the traffic which is headed to (or comes from) outside the DC. This includes communications with other DCs and access to the Internet.

The core switches and routers usually have fewer ports than the aggregation and ToR switches but instead their ports can work at huge bit-rates (100 Gbps or more) and their backplane is designed to support a throughput of several Tbps.

In order to obtain such high degree of connectivity the DC operators usually need to sign several peering agreements with Tier 1 (9) ISPs. This guarantees that enough bandwidth is available for the customers and end-users.

Table 2. Gigabit Ethernet and InfiniBand aggregation level standards

Standard	Bit-Rate	Fibre Type	Band	Maximum Length
10GBASE-USR	10 Gbps	Multi-mode	850 nm	100 m
10GBASE-SR	10 Gbps	Multi-mode	850 nm	400 m
10GBASE-LRM	10 Gbps	Multi-mode	1310 nm	220 m
10GBASE-LR	10 Gbps	Single-mode	1310 nm	10 km
40GBASE-SR4	40 Gbps	Multi-mode	850 nm	400 m
40GBASE-LR4	40 Gbps	Single-mode	1310 nm	10 km
100GBASE-SR4	100 Gbps	Multi-mode	850 nm	100 m
100GBASE-SR10	100 Gbps	Multi-mode	850 nm	400 m
100GBASE-LR4	100 Gbps	Single-mode	1310 nm	10 km
InfiniBand QDR	10 Gbps	-	-	-
InfiniBand 4X QDR	40 Gbps	-	-	-
InfiniBand 12X QDR	120 Gbps	-	-	-

MAIN FOCUS OF THE CHAPTER

Drawbacks of Current DCNs' Architecture

To conclude this analysis, several drawbacks of the current intra DCNs' architecture and some possible solutions for overcoming them are discussed.

Scalability

The most critical drawback of the current intra DCNs' architecture is the existence of a bottleneck in the core level due to its hierarchical structure. The traffic headed to (or coming from) outside the DC goes all through a single node or very few nodes. This concentration of the traffic in such few nodes constitutes a critical failure point and also requires those nodes to be able to manage an extremely high throughput (which is very expensive).

Also, due to the forthcoming increase in global DC traffic the number of servers per rack is expected to increase. Since the number of ports in the ToR switches is limited the current architecture will not be able to withstand such growth.

A possible solution for this limitation would be to switch to a non-hierarchical architecture (also known as flat architecture) which balances

the traffic among more nodes. Also, the need to process the packet headers could be avoided by switching to a transparent optical network architecture (further explained in the upcoming topics).

Power Consumption

The high power consumption of the network equipment is another drawback of the current architecture. All the network equipment need to process the headers of the Ethernet or InfiniBand frames in order to successfully determine the output port they should be sent to. This process implies several calculations. Even though most of them are quite simple (like searching in a look-up table or performing a binary AND operation with a mask) they still constitute a complex computational issue when dealing with high throughputs and require power-hungry hardware.

Moreover, this power consumption problem is aggravated since the network equipment consume almost the same amount of power when they are idle as when they are working at full load (Chabarek et al., 2008).

Therefore it is clear that the only method to decrease the consumption of power is by shutting down as many idle network equipment as possible or by not having electrical network equipment at all. A way to do this is by switching to a transparent optical network architecture (further explained in the upcoming sections).

Heat Dissipation

As a consequence of this high-power consumption a lot of heat is dissipated. In order for the network equipment to work properly and to avoid physical damages due to over-heating it is necessary to deploy a cooling system.

Furthermore, it needs to be taken into account that cooling systems do have a pretty high power consumption too. Several studies indicate that in command to estimate real power consumption of a DC network, the power consumption of the network equipment should be considered as double because of the consequence of the cooling costs (Tzanakaki et al., 2011).

Upgrade Cost

When a network is built some extra capacity is provisioned in order to withstand future traffic increases. But in the long term some old equipment

of the network have to be replaced by newer ones in order to increase the available bandwidth.

Subsequently all the optical links of the network are point-to-point so the traffic undergoes several optical-to-electrical and electrical-to-optical conversion stages along the path between the source and the destination servers. It implies that enough bandwidth must be available on the path to carry the traffic. Also, traffic grooming is performed (at the electrical level) at each one of the intermediate nodes. This electrical processing of the traffic requires the network equipment to have a powerful enough backplane. Therefore an increase in the available bandwidth between two servers may require the replacement of several transponders and/or network equipment along the path by newer ones which offer a higher capacity.

The device which allows the transmission and reception of optical signals is an optical transponder. The Light Emitting Diode (LED) (12) is used for achieving the optical transmission or a Light Amplification by Stimulated Emission of Radiation (LASER) (Ramaswami, Sivarajan, & Saski, 2009) device. The optical reception is achieved through the use of a Photodiode (Ramaswami, Sivarajan, & Saski, 2009).

The cost of a transponder highly depends on several parameters. For the transmitter: Its maximum optical power at the output and the spectral width of the optical signal at the output. For the receiver: Its sensitivity, its noise figure and its bandwidth. Each optical link of the network needs two transponders: One at the head node and another at the tail node.

A possible solution to reduce the upgrade cost of the network would be to decrease the number of transponders (by avoiding point-to-point links) and electrical network equipment (by avoiding the need to process the frame headers) by switching to a transparent optical network architecture.

Quality of Service

In any packet switched network, the frames received by an input interface of a network equipment are processed by inspecting their headers and then transmitted by the selected output interface.

But when the rate of the input traffic destined to a certain output interface is higher than its available bandwidth not all the frames can be processed and transmitted at once. Then, the frames which have not been able to be transmitted will be stored in a queue in the same order they reached the input interface.

If the queue is full and more frames arrive they will be dropped. A scheduler will then decide in which order the frames of the queue will be processed and transmitted once there is enough bandwidth available. Usually, schedulers apply a First in First out (FIFO) policy which consists on attending the frames in the same order they reached the queue.

Therefore, a frame will need to wait in the queue until the scheduler decides it is time for it to be processed and transmitted. The amount of time a frame stays in a queue waiting for its turn its named queuing delay.

The queuing delay and the frame loss ratio increase with the network load because the queues are more populated. The queuing delay and frame loss are inherent to all frame switched networks even though different scheduler policies can be applied to favor certain types of frames (and reduce their queuing delay). Nevertheless, this comes at the cost of increasing the queuing delay of the rest of frames (the mean queuing delay always remains constant).

Moreover, the queuing delay and frame loss ratio between two servers not only depends on the traffic they are exchanging but also on the traffic other servers are exchanging between them. This is so because frames from different sources and destinations may share the same queue in a certain network equipment.

Also, bandwidth intensive applications which work with TCP/IP may experience delay and jitter due to the processing of the segments through systems calls to the kernel of the operating system. Furthermore, due to the behavior of TCP when a segment loss is detected then the bandwidth is dramatically reduced during several Round Trip Times (RTT) (Allman, Paxson, & Blanton, 2009).

Several DC applications like Fibre Channel over Ethernet (FCoE) (American National Standards Institute, 2010) are extremely sensitive to queuing delay and frame loss. RoCE and InfiniBand solve these issues by implementing several flow control and Quality of Service mechanisms which reduce the congestion on the network. Also, Remote Direct Memory Access (RDMA) (Cohen et al., 2009) is implemented to allow data transfers to directly access the hardware (bypassing the kernel system calls).

Despite these improvements introduced by RoCE and InfiniBand, the only way to completely avoid that an increase in the load produced by one customer affects the queuing delay which the rest of customers experience is by switching to a circuit-switched architecture which provides dedicated resources for each customer.

Traffic Isolation

In order to block unauthorized communications between servers rented by different customers and to prevent the broadcast and multicast traffic to spread through the entire network, the current architecture relies on the RoCE Virtual LANs (IEEE, 2011) and the InfiniBand Subnets.

A VLAN is a virtual slice of a LAN which is constituted by a subset of the LAN's resources (links, equipment, servers, etc). The servers which are assigned to a VLAN can only establish layer 2 communications between them. Several VLANs can coexist over the same LAN sharing its physical resources.

There is a limit of VLANs which RoCE LAN can support. This has to do with the 12 bit VLAN ID (VID) header field which the 802.1Q (IEEE, 2011) frame (Table 3) uses to indicate the VLAN number. If there are 12 available bits and each bit can take a 0 or a 1 value then there are $2^{12} = 4,096$ possible VLANs.

The only way to overcome this limitation is by using double-tagged frames (802.1AD or 802.1QinQ) which provide $2^{24} = 16,777,216$ possible values (more than enough for today's requirements).

An InfiniBand subnet is the InfiniBand counterpart of a RoCE VLAN. InfiniBand Subnets are set up by using the InfiniBand Subnet Manager.

This segmentation of the network is useful to implement security and traffic control functionalities but a proper configuration is required in all the involved network equipment and servers. This can be an important issue in big networks, where a lot of network equipment and servers may have to be reconfigured quite often either manually or by an automated process (running scripts).

A way to avoid the need for the configuration of traffic isolation is by switching to a circuit switched architecture.

Table 3. 802.1Q frame

16 Bits	3 Bits	1 Bit	12 Bits
TPID		TCI	
	PCP	DEI	VID

CONCLUSION

To conclude this analysis, the scalability drawbacks of the current architecture and the proposed potential solutions are provided in table 4.

After a brief inspection of the table it is clear that all of the current architecture drawbacks could be avoided by switching to a circuit-switched transparent optical architecture. In the next sections several optical architectures for intra DCNs are discussed.

SOLUTIONS AND RECOMMENDATIONS

An optical network is used to transport signals in an optical form between a source and one or more destinations by using optical fiber as a medium. Optical networks are preferred for transporting high bit-rate signals over several kilometers as it provides a very high bandwidth-distance product.

In order to understand the advantages which optical networks offer the concept of transparency needs to be introduced.

From Opaque to Transparent Optical Networks

The first optical networks which appeared were used to provide higher capacity and lower bit error rate than their contemporary copper-based networks. All the switching and intelligent network functions in this type of networks are handled electronically. All the links of the network were point to point and all the traffic needed to be electronically processed in all of the intermediate nodes. As bandwidth requirements began to increase, this type of networks required expensive and power hungry network equipment.

Table 4. Current architecture drawbacks and solutions summary

Drawbacks	Potential Solutions
Scalability	Flat Architecture, Transparent Optical Architecture
Power Consumption	Transparent Optical Architecture
Upgrade Cost	Transparent Optical Architecture
Quality of Service	Circuit-Switched Architecture
Traffic Isolation	Circuit-Switched Architecture

An optical-to-electrical and electrical-to-optical conversion in all the intermediate nodes is performed in this type of network. Therefore, the wavelength used to carry an optical signal can be different in each one of the links of the path between the source and the destination nodes.

The signal undergoes these optical-to-electrical and electrical-to-optical conversions along its path, so this type of networks require proper transponder upgrading in order to support different bit-rates and protocols. This is why they are known as opaque networks.

Opaque networks present a low blocking probability because any available wavelength in a link can be used to establish a connection. On the other hand, this type of networks require a high number of transponders per demand (2 per each link) and also produce a high power consumption.

An example of this type of optical networks are Synchronous Digital Hierarchy (SDH) (Ramaswami, Sivarajan, & Sasaki, 2009). By using Add and Drop Multiplexers (ADMs) and Digital Cross Connects (DXCs) the traffic is multiplexed electrically in the SDH networks. ADMs allow multiplexing and de-multiplexing of several Virtual Containers (VCs) inside a Synchronous Transport Module (STM) signal. DXCs allow the rearrangement of VCs among several STMs.

When optical technology reached matureness, optical networks began to offer more advantages than just a high bandwidth-distance product. Several functionalities which were previously handled electronically were moved to the optical layer in order to remove the need for electrical processing at each node. Also, point-to-point links were substituted by end-to-end optical connections which go through several intermediate nodes without any need for electrical processing. This significantly reduced the load of the nodes which now only have to process the traffic intended to them.

Since the signal is carried in an optical form all the way between the source and the destination, the network is clear to the data that is being sent over the optical signal. This means the network is compatible with any bit-rate and protocol, even with analogue data.

Any optical-to-electrical or electrical-to-optical conversion is not performed in transparent optical networks at any of the intermediate nodes. Therefore, the wavelength used to carry an optical signal is always the same along all the links of the path between the source and the destination nodes.

This type of networks present a higher blocking probability than opaque networks because no node is able to perform a wavelength conversion. Hence to establish a connection between the source and destination nodes more restrictions are to be faced. Additionally, this type of networks require a

lower number of transponders than opaque networks (2 per each connection) and also produce a lower power consumption. However, in order to provide higher bandwidth than opaque networks, transparent networks require all the transponders to be able to work at very high speeds (100 Gbps or more) resulting in a substantial increase in the transponder cost.

An example of this type of optical networks are Optical Transport Networks (OTNs) (12). In OTN networks the traffic is multiplexed (being the smallest multiplexing unit an entire wavelength) by using Optical Add and Drop Multiplexers (OADMs) and Optical Cross Connects (OXCs). OADMs (Figure 5) allow to insert or extract optical signals inside an optical fibre. OXCs allow to rearrange optical signals between two or more optical fibres.

Due to the promising features of transparent optical networks, they have been thoroughly studied (and still are) by the research community and have arisen the industry's interest on them. As a result several switching technologies have been proposed, among them Optical Circuit Switching (OCS) and Optical Packet Switching (OPS). At the time being, OCS technology is mature enough and already being deployed in a wide number of optical networks while OPS is still in an early development stage.

In the next sections both OCS and OPS technologies are discussed.

Optical Circuit Switching

An optical end-to-end circuit (light-path) to each connection is provided by OCS networks. Each light-path is carried over the same wavelength on each

Figure 5. Fully Tunable OADM
Source: Ramaswami, Sivarajan, & Sasaki (2009)

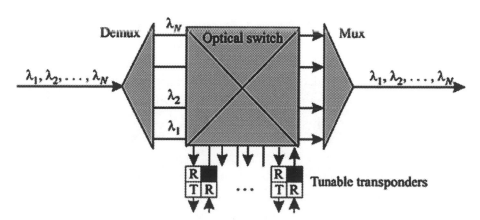

one of the links of the path between the source and destination nodes. Several wavelengths are available for each of the link because of the Dense Wavelength Division Multiplexing (DWDM) technology. As long as they do not share any common links then different light-paths can use the same wavelength. So a wavelength is allowed to be used simultaneously in several light-paths.

These circuits provide a certain amount of bandwidth which is allotted for the exclusive use of the connection during all the time it is active. As a consequence, Quality of Service is guaranteed because different connections never share their bandwidth.

However, in OCS networks the bandwidth allocated for a connection is always a full wavelength. This means that connections which require a bandwidth which is close to the bandwidth of a wavelength will make an efficient use of the spectrum while connections which require a low amount of bandwidth will waste a lot of spectrum. For this same reason the OCS technology also presents a poor spectral efficiency when dealing with burst traffic.

The channel spacing between wavelengths in a DWDM link can be set to 100, 50, 25 or 12.5 GHz according to the DWDM frequency grid (International Telecommunication Union, 2012) defined by the International Telecommunication Union (ITU). Such wavelengths have a center frequency which can be obtained from the Table 5 according to the selected channel spacing. (where $n \in Z$ and it represents the number of wavelength channels)

The lower the channel spacing, the higher will be the number of wavelengths which the DWDM link can contain. Nevertheless, this comes at the cost of also reducing the available bandwidth for each wavelength. The use of spectral efficient modulations is required to achieve high bit-rate transmissions over a reduced bandwidth. Figure 6 shows an example of a 50GHz channel spacing frequency grid.

Table 5. DWDM frequency grid

Bandwidth	Center Frequency (THz)
100 GHz	$193.1 + n \cdot 0.1$
50 GHz	$193.1 + n \cdot 0.05$
25 GHz	$193.1 + n \cdot 0.025$
12.5 GHz	$193.1 + n \cdot 0.0125$

Source: International Telecommunication Union (2012)

Figure 6. 50 GHZ channel spacing example
Source: International Telecommunication Union (2012)

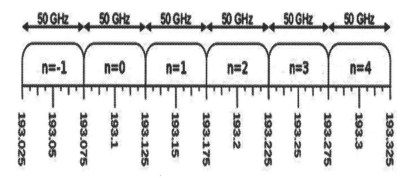

A possible way to increase the spectral efficiency of OCS networks would be to assign to each wavelength the channel spacing which best fits its bandwidth requirements. In Mixed Line-Rate (MLR) DWDM links, wavelengths with different channel spacing can coexist as long as there is no spectrum overlapping. Despite of this, the rigidity of the frequency grid may lead to spectrum gaps. In order to avoid such situations the ITU has also defined a flexible frequency grid (International Telecommunication Union, 2012).

This flexible grid defines a set of frequency slots which have a central frequency and a width. The central frequency of a slot (in THz) is calculated by using the Equation 1 (where $n \in Z$). The slot width (in THz) is calculated by using the Equation 2 (where $m \in N$, it represents the number of frequency slots and 12.5 is the slot granularity in THz).

$$s_f = 193.1 + n\left(0.00625\right) \tag{1}$$

$$s_w = 12.5m \tag{2}$$

As long as no two frequency slots overlap then any combination of frequency slots is allowed. An example of a flexible frequency grid is shown in Figure 7.

However, the flexible grid technology is still at an early development stage and has not been yet implemented in commercial equipment.

Furthermore, when a new circuit is established a suitable combination of path and wavelength needs to be found. This requires to maintain an

Figure 7. Flexible grid example
Source: International Telecommunication Union (2012)

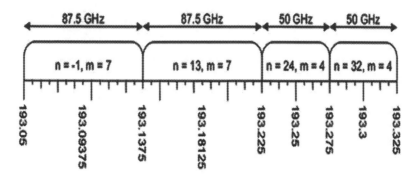

updated database with the current status of all the links and wavelengths of the network and to perform several computations with this data in order to determine a feasible solution.

Similarly, once a path and a wavelength have been selected, some signal processing is required between the Reconfigurable Optical Add and Drop Multiplexers (ROADMs) of the network in order to establish the circuit. ROADMs are devices which can dynamically modify their switching behavior, enabling the network to provide on-demand end-to-end optical circuits (light-paths).

These functionalities are provided by the Generic Multi-Protocol Label Switching (GMPLS) protocol in currently deployed Automatically Switched Optical Networks (ASONs). This process significantly increases the required time to establish a connection insomuch that short-lived connections experience high delays.

These two drawbacks of the OCS technology (spectral efficiency and connection establishment delay) have motivated the appearance of the OPS technology. In the following section the details of such technology are discussed.

Optical Packet Switching

OPS networks provide a virtual optical end-to-end circuit to each connection. This virtual circuit emulates the behavior of a light-path with the difference that connections can allocate a bandwidth smaller than a full wavelength.

This is achieved by breaking the connection's data streams into optical packets and adding them a new header which identifies the optical destination node. Optical packets from different connections are multiplexed in the time

domain by using Optical Time Division Multiplexing (OTDM) and sent over a wavelength. By doing so, each connection has available the entire bandwidth of a wavelength during a certain period of time. This type of multiplexing is also known as sub-wavelength switching because streams with bandwidths smaller than a full wavelength are switched (unlike OCS).

By performing the multiplexing process directly in the optical domain OPS switches can easily manage high bit-rate streams. The OPS switches of the network read the header of the incoming optical packets and then send them to the appropriate output port. By doing this, the OPS switches are sending optical packets over OCS circuits which are established between them. Figure 8 shows the architecture of an OPS based switch.

OPS nodes also need to handle contention at their output ports. When two or more optical packets from different input ports wants to access the same output port at the same time so then contention occurs. Since the optical signals would collide in this scenario so only one of them can be sent at the same time and the rest are dropped or sent through another output port. Due to the higher probability of collision the packet losses are increased exponentially with the traffic load.

This is due to the current non-existence of optical buffers (the optical counterpart of electronic buffers) which would be required to store optical packets. The research community is currently studying the use of delay lines (very long optical fibres) as a way to temporarily store optical packets. However, delay lines introduce attenuation and dispersion effects to the optical signals and therefore should be used carefully. Moreover, since electromagnetic waves propagate through optical fibers at a speed of ($\frac{2}{3} * c$) (where the speed of light in vacuum is denoted by c), the required length for a delay line in order to obtain a significant delay would be in the order of thousands of kilometers.

Existing Architectures

Future intra DCNs are expected to provide higher bandwidth, scalability, flexibility, power efficiency and cost effectiveness and lower end-to-end latencies. In order to achieve these goals, several optical architectures have been proposed. Over the next sections the technical details of such architectures and their scalability drawbacks are discussed.

Figure 8. OPS switch architecture
Source: Ramaswami, Sivarajan, and Sasaki (2009)

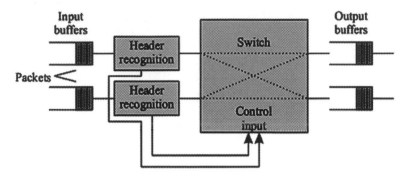

C-Through and Helios

C-Though (Edmonds, 1965) and Helios (Kachris & Tomkos, 2012) are two hybrid optical/electrical architectures designed to enhance currently deployed intra DCNs.

The C-Through architecture is an evolution of the Fat Tree architecture where the ToR switches are connected to both an OCS network and an electrical packet-switched network (Ethernet or InfiniBand). The low bandwidth demands are handled by the electrical- packet switched network while the pairs of ToR switches with high bandwidth demands can be connected through optical circuits by configuring the OCS network. So, there is a need of a traffic monitoring system which is placed in the hosts and it is used to measure the bandwidth requirements with the other hosts. This data is collected by an optical configuration manager (OCM) and based on the traffic requirements it decides the configuration of the optical switch. The traffic demand along with the connected links are articulated as a maximum weight perfect matching problem. The Edmond's algorithm is mainly used by the c-Through architecture in order to get the result of perfect matching algorithm (Edmonds, 1965). When the optical circuit switch is configured then the OCM communicates with the ToR switches for the purpose of routing the packets accordingly. VLAN-based routing is used to de-multiplex the traffic in the ToR switches. So, optical packet and circuit based networks utilize two different VLANs respectively. If the packets have to reach a ToR switch and it's connected to the source ToR via the optical circuit then the second VLAN will handle/receive these packets and vice versa. The simulation of a packet switch network was performed for the evaluation of the system. Both

micro-benchmarks and real applications were also used for the evaluation of the proposed scheme. During the evaluation it was demonstrated that in applications where the demand of traffic between some hosts changes slowly, then this architecture can perform well with reduced latency by using the optical circuit.

The Helios architecture (Kachris & Tomkos, 2012) is basically a 2 tier design which contains hybrid optical/electrical ToR switches (named as pod switches). The connection of the above mentioned hybrid ToR switches are established to an OCS switches (via DWDM optical transceivers) and electrical packet switches are connected through a colorless optical transceivers. Similar to C-through, the electrical packet switched network is utilized to tackle the low bandwidth requirements while the high bandwidth demands are handled through OCS network while connecting pairs of ToR switches. It is comprised of ToR switches (named as pod switches) and core switches. The common electrical packet switches are called the Pod switches, while the core switches can either be electrical packet switches or optical circuit switches. So, this architecture attempts to combine the benefits of optical and the electrical networks. Figure 9 demonstrates the high level architecture of the Helios. The pod switches are connected with the core electrical packet switches through the colorless optical transceivers (e.g. 10G SFP+ modules).A passive optical multiplexer is utilized to multiplex the WDM optical transceivers making *super-links* and are connected to the optical circuit switches. These *super-links* can support up to w x 10 Gbps (where w represents the number of wavelengths; ranging from 1 to 32). So, the proposed design is capable of delivering full bisection bandwidth. If the number of colorless transceivers equal the WDM then half of the bandwidth is shared between pods and the remaining half is assigned to specific routes based on the need of traffic. The three main modules: the topology Manager (TM), the circuit switch Manager (CSM) and the Pod Switch Manager (PSM) are associated with the Helios control scheme. The topology manager is utilized to monitor the traffic of the data center in terms of traffic requirements (i-e. traffic-demand, number of active connections, etc.) in order to find the best configuration for the optical circuit switch network. The demand of traffic relies on the traffic that each server shares with the other servers, however the number of active flows is the maximum number of connections that can all be active at the same time. The CSM receives the graph of the connections and then configures the Glimmerglass MEMS switch. The Pod Switches host the PSM and is used as an interface with the TM. When the TM receives the configuration results then the pod-manager routes the packet either to the packet switch via the colorless transceivers or

to the optical circuit switch through the WDM transceivers. The circuit switch is configured on a simple demand matrix where the "bipartite graph" has to be calculated. The key benefit of the Helios architecture is that it relies on already available optical modules and transceivers that are extensively used in optical telecommunication networks. The optical circuit switch uses the commercially available Glimmerglass switch while the WDMSFP+ optical transceivers are used by the pod switches. The WDM transceivers can either be utilized as a Coarse WDM (CWDM) or Dense WDM (DWDM).The CWDM modules are comparatively less expensive to DWDM modules but it supports a limited number of wavelengths. However DWDM can support higher number of wavelengths (e.g. 40) as they use narrower channel spacing. The readily available Glimmer-glass crossbar optical circuit switch was used for performance evaluation and up to 64 ports (Glimmerglass, n.d.) are supported by this switch. The key disadvantage of this scheme is that it relies on MEMS switches and any reconfiguration of the circuit switch requires several milli-seconds. The reconfiguration time was 25 ms for the Glimmerglass switch. Hence, this design is best for applications where the connections between some nodes last more than a couple of seconds in order to overcome the reconfiguration overhead. During the process of evaluation it was demonstrated that when the stability parameter was changed from 0.5 to 16 seconds so it resulted in a significant increase of throughput.

Though, both the designs face scalability problems because of the inherent limitations of electronics. The c-Through (left) and the Helios (right) architectures are depicted in Figure 9.

Figure 9. C-Through Architecture (left) and Helios Architecture (right)
Source: Kachris and Tomkos (2012)

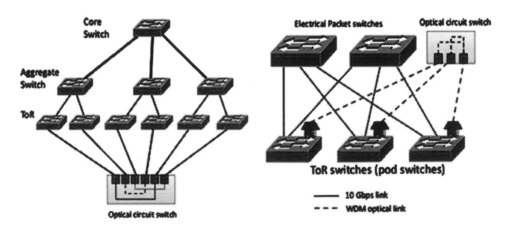

Proteus

This is an all-optical OCS architecture (Kachris & Tomkos, 2012) based on Wavelength Selective Switches (WSSs) (Ramaswami, Sivarajan, & Sasaki, 2009) and an optical switching matrix (OSM). OSM relies on Micro-Electro-Mechanical Switches (MEMSs) (Ramaswami, Sivarajan, & Sasaki, 2009). Several optical transceivers operating at different wavelengths are associated with each ToR switch in the Proteus architecture. Multiplexer is utilized to combine optical wavelengths and they are then routed to a WSS. So, connection of each group of wavelengths is established to a port in the MEMS optical switch to make a point-to-point connections between the ToR switches. The Proteus architecture is shown in Figure 10. All of the wavelengths are de-multiplexed on the receiver's path and then they are routed to the optical transceiver. MEMS decides that which set of ToRs will be connected directly. When ToR has to communicate with other ToR and it's not directly connected then hop-by-hop communication is adopted. On the other hand when MEMS is doing reconfiguration then Proteus has to ensure that the complete ToR graph is connected. To utilize direct optical connections between ToR switch for high-volume traffic and use multi-hop connections in case of low volume traffic was actually the main objective of this design. The achievement of coarse-grain flexible bandwidth is actually the main benefit of Proteus. Basically, n-optical transceivers are associated to each ToR. If in case there is increase in traffic between two switches then extra connections can be made (up to n, whether directly or indirectly) which increases the optical bandwidth up to n times the bandwidth of one optical transceiver. In order to locate the optimum configuration for the MEMS switch for each traffic pattern is actually the main issue in this architecture. In order to find the optimum configuration, an Integer Linear Programming scheme is utilized based on the traffic requirements in (Singla et al., 2010). The important benefit of this project is that it relies on already available off-the-shelf optical modules (WSS such as the Finisar WSS (Strasser & Wagener, 2010), and optical multiplexers) that are extensively utilized in optical networks so minimizing the entire cost when compared with ad-hoc solutions. The key disadvantage associated with the Proteus design is the reconfiguration time of the MEMS switch which is in the order of a few milli-seconds. Normally, the traffic flow lasts a few millisecond in majority. So, the Proteus architecture cannot follow the traffic fluctuations where the traffic flow changes quickly and the connection of each server to another

Figure 10. Proteus architecture
Source: Kachris and Tomkos (2012)

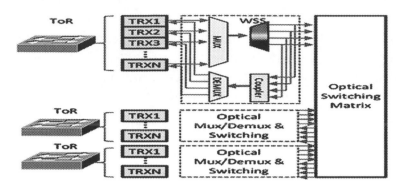

server lasts only a few milliseconds. Therefore, in several cases by the time the MEMS switch is reconfigured, a new reconfiguration has to take place to meet the new traffic demands. Though, the aggregated traffic between the ToR switches may change slowly. So, in the case of aggregated traffic the Proteus scheme can show high performance and reduced latency. The key drawback noticed so far is the elevated circuit reconfiguration time because of the utilization of the MEMSs in this architecture.

Data Center Optical Switch (DOS)

Datacenter Optical Switch (DOS) (Kachris & Tomkos, 2012) is all-optical OPS architecture that mainly utilizes Arrayed Waveguide Grating Routers (AWGRs) (Ramaswami, Sivarajan, & Sasaki, 2009) and Tunable Wavelength Converters (TWCs) (Ramaswami, Sivarajan, & Sasaki, 2009).

The optical switch fabric of the DOS architecture consists of an array of TWCs (one TWC for each node), an AWGR and a loop-back shared buffer. Configuration of the transmitting wavelength of TWC enables each node to access any other node through AWGR. The control plane configures the switch fabric and it in turn then controls the TWC and label extractors (LEs). Contention resolution and TWC tuning is done by the control plane. The purpose of LEs is to separate he label from the optical payload when a node transmits a packet to the switch. The Optical to Electrical (O/E) converter module in the control plane converts the optical label from optical to electrical signal as it contains the packet length and destination information. This is then forwarded to the arbitration unit. The label processor stores this label

and it sends a request to the arbitration unit for solving the contention. The arbitration unit decides the output port and then the control plane configures the TWC and AWGR routing characteristics enable the packet to reach to its decided output. When the number of output receivers is less than the transmitting nodes then in this case contention happens because any of the two transmitting packets may reach the same output port. A shared SDRAM buffer is utilized to temporarily store and control the transmitted packets. O/E converter routes the contending wavelengths to the SDRAM buffer. The controller in the buffer is used to handle these packets. The controller in the SDRAM buffer sends request to the control plane for the buffered packets and waits for the grant. The packet is retrieved from the SDRAM when the grant is received. Afterwards, this packet is converted back to optical from electrical by an electrical to optical (E/O) converter and it's sent to the destined output port by configuring the TWC and using AWGR. The arbitration of requests in the control plane is one of the key challenge in the deployment of the DOS switch. As virtual output ques (VOQ) are not used so every input issues a request to the arbiter and waits for a grant. So, a 2-phase arbiter can be utilized for scheduling of packets (McKeown, 1999). In the first phase, there will be arbitration of requests and the second phase will include grants for the arbitrations. The scalability of the AWGR and the tuning range of the TWC determines the scalability of the DOS architecture. An AWGR that supports up to 400 ports have been demonstrated by some research centers (Hida et al., 2001). So, up to 512 nodes (or 512 racks assuming that each node is used as a ToR switch) can be connected through the DOS architecture. The important benefit associated with DOS is that its latency is independent of the number of input ports and it remains low even when there is high input loads. The latency is low because the packet only travels through an optical switch and the delay of electrical switch's buffer is avoided. Though, the main flaw of the DOS design is that it uses electrical buffers for congestion management and electrical buffer is composed of power hungry hardware as it includes O/E and E/O converters. Thus, results in an increase of overall power consumption and packet latency. Additionally, it uses tunable wavelength transceivers that are quite expensive compared to commodity optical transceivers used in current switches. Though, DOS is still an attractive candidate for DCNs when the traffic pattern is like a burst with high temporary peaks. The switching time of TWCs is in the order of a few ns. So, DOS can be reconfigured to meet the traffic fluctuations

compared to the slow switching time of MEMS optical switches. UCD and NPRC (Proietti et al, 2011) has already presented a 40 Gbps 8x8 prototype of the DOS architecture. The prototype relies on an 8x8 200 GHz spacing AWGR and it's associated with four wavelength converters (WC) built on cross-phase modulation (XPM) in a semiconductor optical amplifier Mach-Zehnder interferometer (SOA-MZI). The latency of the DOS prototype was measured to be only 118.2 ns which is comparatively lower to the latency of legacy data centers (i.e. in the order of few microseconds). Figure 11 shows the DOS architecture.

OSMOSIS

OSMOSIS (Kachris & Tomkos, 2012) is basically an all-optical packet switched based broadcast-and-select (B&S) architecture and it utilizes couplers, splitters and SOA broadband optical gates.

The OSMOSIS consists of two stages. Multiple wavelengths are multiplexed to a common WDM line in the first stage. Then, by using coupler the wavelengths are broadcasted to all the modules of the second stage. In the second stage, the potential output wavelength is selected by SOA. This architecture works on a demux-SOA and select mux instead of utilizing tunable filters. Though, the key drawback of this architecture is that it relies on power hungry SOA devices and it results in a significant increase of overall power consumption. Figure 12 shows the OSMOSIS architecture.

Figure 11. DOS architecture
Source: Kachris and Tomkos (2012).

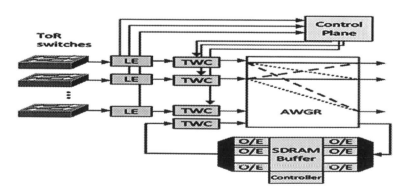

Figure 12. OSMOSIS architecture
Source: Ramaswami, Sivarajan, and Sasaki (2009)

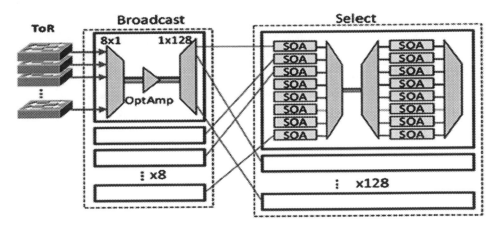

The TONAK-LION Switch With Limited Number of Wavelengths

TONAK (Proietti et al., 2013) works on All-Optical Physical Layer Negative Acknowledgement (AO-NACK) and TOKEN (AO-TOKEN) techniques. The requirement for electrical buffers at the input/output ports of the switch is removed by AO-NACK, and a distributed all-optical arbiter is enabled by the TOKEN technique to handle packet contention.

The architecture of TONAK LION switch is shown in figure 13 One Tunable Laser (TL) that is part of the optical transmitter is used to generate both packets and corresponding token requests (TRs) as shown in figure 13, in set *ii*. As compared to packets the TRs are usually generated earlier. The RTT time from the TONAK line-card to the reflective semi-conductor optical amplifier (RSOA) is set to the offset time among these two. Each AWGR input port faces a line card as shown in Inset *i*). The key component i.e., the line-card combines both the AO-NACK and AO-TOKEN procedures. The following tasks such as generating TR signals and the transmission/reflection of the data packet after its token is allowed/rejected are performed by the line card. The working principle of TONAK is now explained, with the help of timing diagram in figure14.

The fast TL of H1 is first tuned to λ_{1N} (i.e., the wavelength that will reach the output port numbered N from input 1 according to the routing table of AWGR) when the host (H_1) wants to send a packet to host (H_N). It is for this purpose that a TR A is generated and it reaches the control plane (CP) of

Figure 13. Distributed TONAK architecture

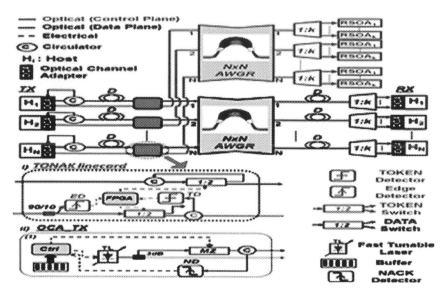

Figure 14. Timing diagram for all-optical control plane detecting contention

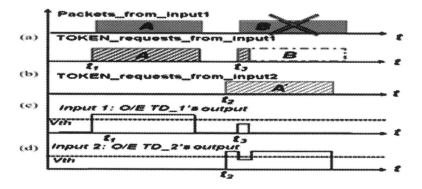

AWGR input port one at a time, $t = t_1$. TR A should enter into an RSOA through output port N in order to request for a token A after passing through a 1: k optical de-multiplexer. In order to achieve wavelength parallelism and reduce the probability of contention (Clos, 1952) different K RSOAs are placed at each of the CP AWGR output port. It should be noted that every nodc has k RXs and is able to receive k concurrent packets. If we are receiving requests from a different contention group and the requests are not greater than k simultaneous requests, there is no chance of contention as each request is going to a different RSOA. Although, if more than one request arrives from

the identical contention group, more than one request will go to the same RSOA and contention will occur.

The RSOA amplifies TR A and it is reflected back to the AWGR input port, where an optical channel (OC) that is placed on the token path (inset *i*)) extracts the TR A and it is converted in the electrical domain through a token detector (TD). The TD performs the job as an O/E converter and is followed by a threshold comparator. An electrical signal having a voltage V_{p1} is generated and it's proportional to the optical power (P_{TO1}) of the reflected TR. The output *N* is available when V_{p1} is greater than V_{th}. Then the 1:2 LiNbO$_3$ switch whose switching time is <1 ns is set in the data path to the cross state by the controller (FPGA or ASIC) so that packet *A* can be switched on-the-fly to the desired output port of the data-plane AWGR. It should be noted that during the entire packet transmission time the TR stays active in order to get the token and avoid collision. When the edge detector (ED) intellects an arriving TR the 1:2 LiNbO$_3$ switch in the token path is raised to the cross state.

The previous scenario is the case with no packet contention. H$_2$ is used to generate a TR and packet *A*, that is sent to the identical output *N* as depicted in figure 13. This request is received at the CP AWGR input port one at $t = t_2$. Formerly at $t = t_3$, when the transmission of packet *A* is yet to be completed, a new TR from H$_1$ that is sent to output N arrives. The RSOA at output *N* at this instant is already saturated with the TR *A* at λ_{2N}. So, the new TR B at λ_{1N} is amplified and reflected by the RSOA with a lower power. When the TD receives the TR B with optical power P_{TO3}, then an electrical signal with

Figure 15. Flow diagram of the TONAK architecture

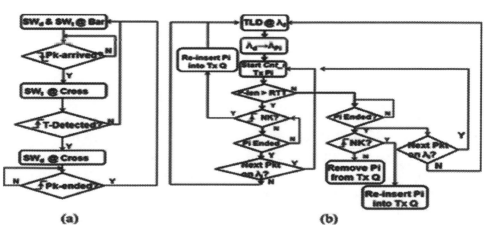

(a)   (b)

V_{p3} is generated by TD. The power, P_{TO3} will be $\approx$ Psat/2 and V_{p3} will be $\approx$ $V_{p1}/2$ due to the gain saturation effect (29), where the saturated output power of the RSOA is Psat. When the V_{th} is set between V_{p1} and $V_{p1}/2$, then the token for output N is not available as recognized by the controller. The 1:2 switch in the data path is set to the *bar* state by the controller when the token application gets failed. So, in this scenario the arriving packet B is obstructed and directed back to the Tx, and OC extracts it and this procedure acts as "AO-NACK". This rejected packet is then re-transmitted.

Figure 15 shows the complete workflow of an optical channel adapter (OCA) Tx and a TONAK line card in the flow chart. It should be noted that based on the ratio of RTT time and the packet length (Proietti et al., 2012) the flow is divided into two sub flows at the transmitters. A centralized CP is not required for TONAK as in AO-TOKEN and the attainment of the token is controlled in a completely distributed way. Though, the key differences amongst "TONAK-LIONS and TOKEN-LIONS" are that (a) the TD in TONAK is placed at the input port of the switch, as previously it was placed on the distant Tx side; (b) The AO-NACK technique is used by TONAK in order to inform the senders of any packets that are facing contention, as previously the packet was being hold at the Tx side until it wins the contention.

After providing sufficient background in terms of DCN architectures and switches, now in the upcoming sections some of the top most recent intra DCN architectures will be discussed.

Hybrid Electro-Optical Intra-Data Center Networks Tailored for Different Traffic Classes

A large Fat-Tree-based DCN architecture is considered that consists of 32 thousand servers, each server contains thousand racks with a distribution of 32 servers/rack (Figure 16a). These racks are further classified into 5 clusters, each hosting a specific application, like Facebook's DCN (Roy et al., 2015). Neighboring racks organized in clusters, hosting similar services is one of the key feature of traffic modeling and network optimization. Additionally, the servers that support the same application communicate within their cluster only. The traffic that originates from each rack is aggregated by the corresponding ToR switch, which owns an oversubscription ratio (northbound to southbound throughputs ratio) OR $=2\times100$Gb/s/32×10Gb/s $= 1:1.6$. For the purpose of traffic balancing and reliability, every ToR is further linked to two aggregation switches. In the direction of southbound, the aggregation

Figure 16a. Electrical Fat-Tree intra-data center network before optimization
Source: Balanici and Pachnicke (2018)

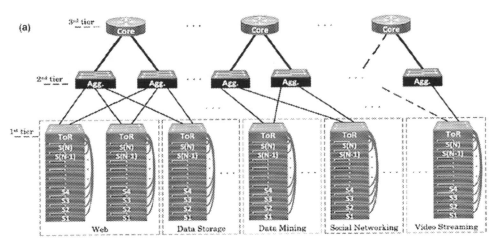

switch possesses 32×100 Gb/s interfaces and 5×400 Gb/s in the direction of northbound, likewise resulting in an OR $=5 \times 400$ Gb/s/32×100 Gb/s $= 1 : 1.6$. The components of Electrical packet switch (EPS) grid were chosen according to the equivalent hardware recently available on the market for DCN applications. The traffic from the aggregation layer is further aggregated at the core switches when it's the next tier level. A comprehensive summary of all DCN parameters is provided in table 6. The EPS grid is partially replaced by an eight hundred port MEMS based OCS unit from the second and third tier in order to optimize the network (Figure 16b). The main concept is to reduce the heavy-tailed traffic from EPS grid and transfer it to the OCS unit,

Table 6. DCN architecture before (e) and after (h) optimization

Device	Interface/Throughput	$\sum E / H$
Server	SFP + 10Gb/s	32000
ToR	SB: SFP + 32 x 10Gb/s NB: QSFP 28/2 x 100Gb/s (E) NB: QSFP 28/3 x 100Gb/s (H)	1000
Aggregation	NB: QSFP 28/32 x 100Gb/s NB: CFP8/5 x 400Gb/s	63/38
Core	SB: CFP8/15 x 400Gb/s	21/13
OCS	800 ports	0/1

Source: Balanici and Pachnicke (2018)

Figure 16b. Electrical Fat-Tree intra-data center network after optimization
Source: Balanici and Pachnicke (2018)

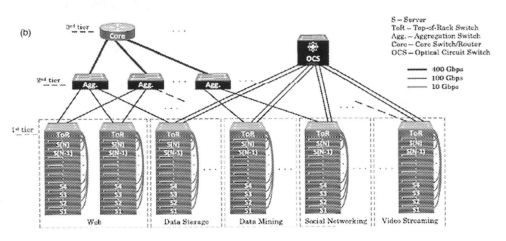

and to reduce its payload only to self-similar, bursty traffic (mice).As the MEMS provides high port density, so the complexity of network is noticeably reduced by an OCS, and this results in significant gain with respect to capital investment and operational costs. Additionally, high speed data transmission capacity is provided by optical switching because of its agnostic nature with respect to data rates. Moreover, it's transparent to modulation formats and communication protocols and this feature results in throughput capacities ranging from 100–400 Gb/s and beyond, without the need of upgrading or replacing the underlying switching fabric (35). The low power consumption as compared to EPS and the insignificant insertion loss (Calient Technologies, 2013; Polatis, 2016) of OCS makes it a perfect solution for DCN optimization and scalability upgrades.

The parameters provided in table 6, which includes the number of switches in the aggregation and core layers, have been calculated based on their interface number characteristics. That is, when a DCN is equipped with thousand ToRs and with two northbound interfaces then each needs ($2 \times 1000/32$) ≈ 63 aggregation switches with 32 southbound interfaces to house them all. After optimization and OCS deployment, EPS grid is connected to eight hundred racks through one link and two WDM links are connected to OCS unit. However, 200 ToRs will maintain their initial configuration i-e two links to the aggregation layer. This results in ($2 \times 200 + 800$) $/32 \approx 38$ aggregation switches. Clearly, the similar method has been repeated for

the core layer as well, which gives twenty-one versus thirteen required core switches. So, this results in the simplification and further relaxation of both electrical switching top tiers (Balanici & Pachnicke, 2018)

NEPHELE: AN END-TO-END SCALABLE AND DYNAMICALLY RECONFIGURABLE OPTICAL ARCHITECTURE FOR APPLICATION-AWARE SOFTWARE DEFINED NETWORK (SDN) CLOUD DATA CENTERS

Overview of NEPHELE Data Plane Architecture

The design of NEPHELE (Bakopoulos et al., 2018) network is shown in Figure 17(a). The key building block is the pod, which hosts a number of racks and accommodates a few thousand disaggregated resources (e.g., storage, compute) called the innovation zones; so, the pod can be called as a small-scale data center. The top-of-rack (ToR) switch is used to manage each rack and all the ToR switches are interlinked to the pod in a star topology, utilizing one port per ToR. A tunable laser and a burst mode receiver is associated with each ToR. The traffic that has to be communicated within the pod (intra-pod), then the passive switching is done by the use of optical filtering elements (Bakopoulos). To scale the network further, multiple pods are interconnected

Figure 17a. The NEPHELE optical data center network architecture

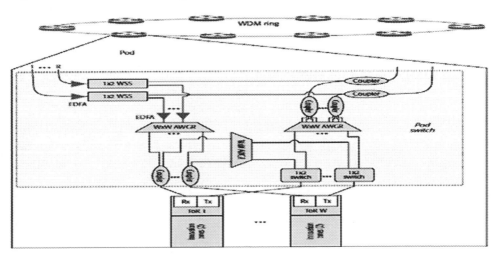

into a ring topology, which provides the facility of using small-port count optical switches. Each NEPHELE ring is associated with WDM traffic and the necessary capacity between pods is supplied by using multiple fibers (which are also the part of NEPHELE ring). Communication between servers of different pods (inter-pod) is established by using the wavelength and space switching and it allows the reuse of wavelengths among pods. So, this results in the scalability of network beyond the typical wavelength count of DWDM systems. The process of adding and dropping of multiplexed wavelengths to and from the NEPHELE ring is done on a per-wavelength basis; so, despite its ring physical topology, the network makes a basic topology of a mesh. The combination of a NEPHELE ring, corresponding pod switches and the ToR ports make a NEPHELE optical plane. To increase the capacity of network, additional and independent optical planes are installed. This includes the process of installing additional NEPHELE pod switches and connecting them through new rings, as well as increasing the ports in the ToR switches that can be connected to the newly added pod switches, as shown in Figure 17(b). The existing optical planes are not affected by the addition of new optical planes. However, it ensures the scalability of design and allowing pay-as you- go deployment. The reference parameter values of the NEPHELE design (used for scalability and techno-economic studies (Bakopoulos et al., 2018) throughout this article) are summed up in table 7. The NEPHELE data plane works in a slotted Time division multiple access (TDMA) manner, where slots represents the time segments that can be accessed by a single rack-

Figure 17b. Scaling the NEPHELE network with the addition of optical planes

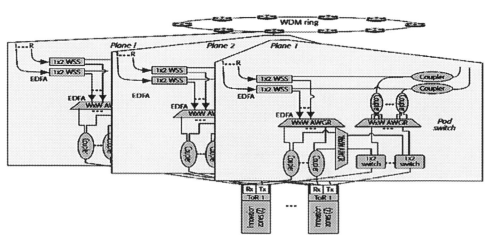

Table 7. Dimensions of the NEPHELE reference network data plane architecture

Parameter	Meaning	Typical Value
Z	Number of innovation zones per ToR switch	4
S	Number of innovation zones' ports per ToR switch	20
W	Number of racks and ToRs per pod; also number of wavelengths in the system	80
R	Number of fiber rings per optical plane	20
P	Number of pods	20
I	Number of NEPHELE optical planes	20

Source: Bakopoulos et al. (2018)

to-rack communication. Slots (and therefore the network resources) can be allocated dynamically to communicating racks, and the design can get close to full utilization of the network capacity, thus resulting in the savings of both energy and cost. The use of slotted operation by NEPHELE and its scalability utilizing optical planes significantly grow on current demonstrations of optical data centers, while depending on mature photonic components (Liu et al., 2013; Wang, McArdle, & Barry, 2015). Compared to the methods based on the elastic spectrum allocation (Saridis et al., 2015), dynamic assignment of network capacity is provisioned by the NEPHELE's TDMA approach without the use of complex flex-grid hardware that would considerably increase the deployment cost. When considering dynamic traffic that is dominated by mice flows, then a hybrid electronic- optical implementation is chosen, with the two networks interfacing at the ToR level. The NEPHELE topology is based on a two level (tier) network: the first level contains the ToR switches, and above them, there is a single level of pod switches. To facilitate more servers, the network grows in the east-west direction, comparatively much better to the east-west type of traffic that flows in current data centers. So, the NEPHELE's network is flat and it doesn't traverse traffic through different tree levels which is done in traditional DCNs. The number of levels in fat tree network depends on the servers available in this network. It should be noted that in the NEPHELE architecture, the required network equipment scales linearly. Whereas the fat tree network needs the addition of switches at all levels, and after a point when a new level has to be added then it also yields the direct scaling of the number of servers.

NEPHELE CONTROL PLANE INFRASTRUCTURE

Software Defined Networking (SDN) is getting attention by providing the resource programmability for the management of operations in DC, as the quality control needed to manage the resources of DC lies at the control and orchestration level (Peng et al., 2015)

The NEPHELE control plane infrastructure is associated with the following components (Figure 18): A *cloud orchestration framework* and a *network control framework*.

The DC resources such as computing, memory, network and storage is managed by the cloud orchestration framework within the Innovation Zones. This is executed by using a cloud management platform such as OpenStack. The key function is to provide the right and on demand delivery of different virtual resources that includes: deployment, provisioning, and configuration. This job is done by OpenStack's Heat component.

The NEPHELE control framework relies on the SDN controller and it's associated with SDN applications which implements the algorithms and logic of the NEPHELE data center network. The SDN is a centralized controller used to configure the optical data plane for the deployment of virtual networks, as requested by the cloud orchestration framework. In fact, the NEPHELE scheduling algorithms driving resource allocation described above take as input the connection requirements of the cloud applications, as declared in

Figure 18. NEPHELE data center control infrastructure

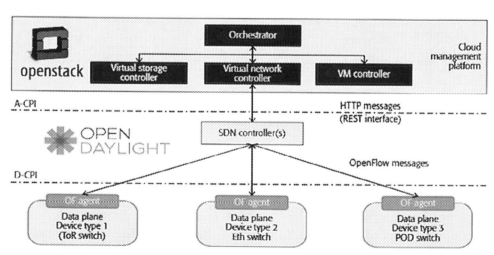

the requests issued by the cloud orchestrator in order to continuously update the traffic matrix and compute the network allocation solution. Afterwards, it is automatically translated into a set of OpenFlow-based commands sent to the agents of the data plane devices and configured on their FPGAs. The protocol of OpenFlow is adopted by NEPHELE in order to establish the interaction between the SDN controller and the data plane. Three types of interaction are defined:

- Advertisement of the data plane devices capabilities (e.g., active ports, switching capabilities, available wavelengths and time slots)
- Operational configuration of the devices (e.g., adding a flow entry, creating a cross-connection with time slots and wavelength specification)
- Data plane monitoring, including asynchronous notifications from the data plane to the controller and retrieval of traffic counters from the controller to the data plane

The extensions mentioned above are realized by using an SDN agent. Its key job is to receive the OpenFlow command from the controller, translate them, and forward them to the devices of data plane. The prototype SDN agent acts as a proxy for both the legacy Ethernet and novel optical switching devices. Because of this, it implements the parsing mechanism for both standardized and extended (NEPHELE-specific optical extensions) OpenFlow 1.3 commands. Moreover, it's capable of detecting the out-of-order arrival of control plane commands, and re-order them in a specific schedule before sending the flows to the device FPGA.

The NEPHELE project has received funding from the European Union's Horizon 2020 research and innovation program under the grant agreement No. 645212 (NEPHELE) (NEPHELE, n.d.)

CONCLUSION

To conclude this analysis, all the scalability drawbacks of the non-recommended architectures are summarized in the table 8. According to the details of all the architectures and the data provided in table: 8, TONAK LION Switch is the best amongst the existing DCNs optical switches presented previously. The authors recommend TONAK LION Switch as an intra-DCN optical switch because of the following major reasons:

Table 8. Summary of existing solutions

Architecture	University Company	Year	Technology	Connection	WDM	Cap. Lim	Scalability	Prototype
C Through(17)	RiceU,CMU,Intel	2010	Hybrid	Circuit		Trasnc.	low	✓
Helios(17)	UC San Diego	2010	Hybrid	Circuit	✓	Transc.	low	✓
Proteus(17)	Illinois, NEC	2010	All optical	Circuit	✓	Transc.	medium	✓
DOS(17)	UC Davis	2010	All optical	Packet		TWC, Electrical loop back buffers	medium	✓
OSMOSIS(17)	IBM	2004	All optical	Packet	✓	SOA	medium	
TONAK LION Switch	University of California,USA	2013	All optical	Packet			high	

1. It avoids electronic buffering (one of the major issue that limits the high bandwidth produced by the optical transmitters and electronic buffering also uses a power hungry hardware as well) by using re-transmission at the site of host. (Yin et al., 2012; Ye et al., 2011)
2. It's highly scalable and is a low latency switch.

Additionally, as an intra DCN architecture the authors will go with the NEPHELE (NEPHELE, n.d.) architecture as it's a flat network architecture and it also meets the requirement of future intra DCNs.

CONCLUSION

Due to the increasing network load/traffic, future intra-DCNs must provide ultra-high capacity. Additionally, DCNs architectures have to be scalable, cost and power efficient along with maintaining lower end-to-end latencies. Moreover, a detail background is provided that how technology evolved in the area of optical communication/optical networks. The problems of current DCNs were discussed in detail along with the possible solutions presented so far. The TONAK LION Switch (Proietti et al., 2013) is recommended as an intra-DCN optical switch and the NEPHELE (Bakopoulos et al., 2018) is recommended as an intra DCN architecture. Additionally, the details of existing DCN architectures were provided in order to further investigate their problems, improve them by addressing the problems or presenting a new DCN architecture that meets all the demands of future intra DCNs.

REFERENCES

Agrawal, G. (2002). *Fiber-optic communication systems.* Wiley-Interscience.

Al-Fares, M., Loukissas, A., & Vahdat, A. (2008). A scalable, commodity data center network architecture. In *Proceedings of the ACM SIGCOMM 2008 Conference on Data Communication, SIGCOMM '08*, (pp. 63–74). New York: ACM. 10.1145/1402958.1402967

Allman, M., Paxson, V., & Blanton, E. (2009). *TCP Congestion Control.* RFC 5681 (Draft Standard), Retrieved from https://tools.ietf.org/html/rfc5681

American National Standards Institute. (2010). *Fibre channel backbone 5* (FC-BB-5). Retrieved from https://www.techstreet.com/standards/incits-462-2010?product_id=1724386

Bakopoulos, P., Christodoulopoulos, K., Landi, G., Aziz, M., Zahavi, E., Gallico, D., ... Avramopoulos, H. (2018). NEPHELE: An End-to-End Scalable and Dynamically Reconfigurable Optical Architecture for Application-Aware SDN Cloud Data Centers. *IEEE Communications Magazine, 56*(2), 178–188. doi:10.1109/MCOM.2018.1600804

Balanici, M., & Pachnicke, S. (2018). Hybrid electro-optical intra-data center networks tailored for different traffic classes. *IEEE/OSA Journal of Optical Communications and Networking, 10*(11), 889–901. doi:10.1364/JOCN.10.000889

Barry, L. P., Wang, J., McArdle, C., & Kilper, D. (2017). *Optical switching in datacenters: architectures based on optical circuit switching. In Optical Switching in Next Generation Data Centers* (pp. 23–44). Springer.

Bouillet, E., Mitra, D., & Ramakrishnan, K. G. (2002). The structure and management of service level agreements in networks. *IEEE Journal on Selected Areas in Communications, 20*(4), 691–699. doi:10.1109/JSAC.2002.1003036

Buyya, R., Yeo, C. S., Venugopal, S., Broberg, J., & Brandic, I. (2009). Cloud computing and emerging IT platforms: Vision, hype, and reality for delivering computing as the 5th utility. *Future Generation Computer Systems, 25*(6), 599–616. doi:10.1016/j.future.2008.12.001

Chabarek, J., Sommers, J., Barford, P., Estan, C., Tsiang, D., & Wright, S. (2008). Power awareness in network design and routing. In *INFOCOM 2008. The 27th Conference on Computer Communications*. IEEE. 10.1109/INFOCOM.2008.93

Clos, C. (1952). A study of non-blocking switching networks. *The Bell System Technical Journal, 32*(2), 406–424. doi:10.1002/j.1538-7305.1953.tb01433.x

Cohen, D., Talpey, T., Kanevsky, A., Cummings, U., Krause, M., Recio, R., . . . Grun, P. (2009). Remote direct memory access over the converged enhanced ethernet fabric: Evaluating the options. In *High Performance Interconnects, 2009. HOTI 2009. 17th IEEE Symposium on*, (pp. 123–130). IEEE.

Dhamdhere, A., Dovrolis, C., & Francois, P. (2010). A value-based framework for internet peering agreements. *Tele-traffic Congress (ITC), 2010 22nd International*, 1–8. 10.1109/ITC.2010.5608736

Edmonds, J. (1965). Paths, trees, and flowers. *Canadian Journal on Mathematics, 17*, 449–467. doi:10.4153/CJM-1965-045-4

Eramo, V., & Listanti, M. (2009). Power Consumption in Bufferless Optical Packet Switches in SOA Technology. *Journal of Optical Communications and Networking, 1*(3), B15–B29. doi:10.1364/JOCN.1.000B15

Glimmerglass. (n.d.). *Glimmerglass Intelligent Optical System*. Retrieved from www.glimmerglass.com

Hida, Y., Hibino, Y., Kitoh, T., Inoue, Y., Itoh, M., Shibata, T., . . . Himeno, A. (2001). 400-channel 25-GHz spacing arrayed-waveguide grating covering a full range of C- and L-bands. Optical Fiber Communication Conference and Exhibit.

IEEE. (2004). *IEEE standard for local and metropolitan area networks: Media access control (MAC) bridges* (802.1D-2004). Retrieved from https://ieeexplore.ieee.org/servlet/opac?punumber=9155

IEEE. (2011). *IEEE Standard for Local and metropolitan area networks--Media Access Control (MAC) Bridges and Virtual Bridged Local Area Networks* (802.1Q-2011). Retrieved from https://ieeexplore.ieee.org/document/6009146

InfiniBand Trade Association. (2007). *InfiniBand Architecture Specification Volume 1: Release 1.2.1*. Retrieved from http://www.afs.enea.it/asantoro/V1r1_2_1.Release_12062007.pdf

InfiniBand Trade Association. (2010). *Annex A16: RDMA Over Converged Ethernet (RoCE).* Retrieved from https://cw.infinibandta.org/document/dl/7148

International Telecommunication Union. (2012). *Series G Transmission Systems and Media, Digital Systems, and Networks.* Retrieved from https://www.itu.int/rec/dologin_pub.asp?lang=e&id=T-REC-G.694.1-201202-I!!PDF-E&type=items

Kachris, C., & Tomkos, I. (2012). A survey on optical interconnects for data centers. *Communications Surveys Tutorials, IEEE, 14*(4), 1021–1036.

Liu, H., Lu, F., Kapoor, R., Forencich, A., Voelker, G. M., & Papen, G., ... Porter, G. (2013). *2013 IEEE Photonics Society Summer Topical Meeting Series.* IEEE.

McKeown, N. (1999, April). The islip scheduling algorithm for input-queued switches. *IEEE/ACM Transactions on Networking, 7*(2), 188–201. doi:10.1109/90.769767

NEPHELE. (n.d.). *About NEPHELE.* Retrieved from www.nepheleproject.eu

Peng, S., Guo, B., Jackson, C., Nejabati, R., Agraz, F., & Spadaro, S. (2015).…. Simeonidou, D. (2015). Multi-Tenant Software-Defined Hybrid Optical Switched Data Centre. *Journal of Lightwave Technology, 33*(15), 3224–3233. doi:10.1109/JLT.2015.2438398

Pina, J. F., da Silva, H. J. A., Monteiro, P. N., Wang, J., Freude, W., & Leuthold, J. (2007). Performance Evaluation of Wavelength Conversion at 160Gbit/s using XGM in Quantum- Dot Semiconductor Optical Amplifiers in MZI configuration. Photonics Switching.

Polatis. (2016). *Series 7000n Network Optical Matrix Switch.* Retrieved from https://www.phoenixdatacom.com/wp-content/uploads/2017/02/Polatis_384x384_7000n_Network_Optical_Switch_pdl.pdf

Predieri, Biancani, Spadaro, Bernini, Cruschelli, Ciulli, ... Hussain. (2013). *Deliverable 2.2 - architecture design.* Technical report, The Lightness project.

Proietti, R., Ye, X., Yin, Y., Potter, A., Yu, R., Kurumida, J., ... Yoo, S. J. B. (2011). 40 Gb/s 8x8 Low-latency Optical Switch for Data Centers. *Optical Fiber Communication Conference (OFC/NFOEC).* 10.1364/OFC.2011.OMV4

Proietti, R., Yin, C. J. N. Y., Yu, R., Yoo, S. J. B., & Akella, V. (2012). Scalable and distributed contention resolution in AWGR-based data center switches using RSOA-based optical mutual exclusion. *IEEE Journal of Selected Topics in Quantum Electronics, 19*(2). doi:10.1109/JSTQE.2012.2209113

Proietti, R., Yin, Y., Yu, R., Nitta, C. J., Akella, V., Mineo, C., & Yoo, J. B. (2013). Scalable Optical Interconnect Architecture using AWGR-Based TONAK LION Switch with Limited Number of Wavelengths. *Journal of Lightwave Technology, 31*(24), 4087–4097. doi:10.1109/JLT.2013.2285883

Proietti, R., Yin, Y., Yu, R., Ye, X., Nitta, C., Akella, V., & Yoo, S. J. B. (2012). All-Optical Physical Layer NACK in AWGR-Based Optical Interconnects. *IEEE Photonics Technology Letters, 24*(5), 410–412. doi:10.1109/LPT.2011.2179923

Ramaswami, R., Sivarajan, K., & Sasaki, G. (2009). *Optical Networks: A Practical Perspective. Morgan Kaufmann series in networking*. Elsevier Science.

Roy, Zeng, Bagga, Porter, & Snoeren. (2015). Inside the social network's (datacenter) network. *ACM SIGCOMM*, 123–137.

Saridis, G. M., Peng, S., Yan, Y., Aguado, A., Guo, B., Arslan, M., ... Simeoni. dou, D. (2015). Lightne.ss: A Function-Virtualizable Software Defined Data Center Network With All-Optical Circuit/Packet Switching. *Journal of Lightwave Technology, 34*(7), 1618–1627. doi:10.1109/JLT.2015.2509476

Singla, A., Singh, A., Ramachandran, K., Xu, L., & Zhang, Y. (2010). Proteus: a topology malleable data center network. In *Proc. Ninth ACM SIGCOMM Workshop on Hot Topics in Networks*. ACM. Retrieved from http://conferences.sigcomm.org/hotnets/2010/papers/a8-singla.pdf

Strasser, T. A., & Wagener, J. L. (2010). Wavelength-Selective Switches for ROADM Applications. *IEEE Journal of Selected Topics in Quantum Electronics, 16*(5), 1150–1157. doi:10.1109/JSTQE.2010.2049345

Technologies, C. (2013). *S320 Photonic Switch*. Retrieved from https://whitepapers.em360tech.com/wp-content/files_mf/1377248645CalientS320DataSheetMarch12013.pdf

Tzanakaki, A., Anastasopoulos, M., Georgakilas, K., Buysse, J., De Leenheer, M., Develder, C., . . . Jimenez, J. (2011). Energy efficiency in integrated it and optical network infrastructures: The geysers approach. In *Computer Communications Workshops (INFOCOM WKSHPS), 2011 IEEE Conference on*, (pp. 343–348). IEEE.

Wang, J., McArdle, C., & Barry, L. P. (2015). Energy-Efficient Optical HPC and Datacenter Networks Using Optimized Wavelength Channel Allocation. *Proceedings of 2015 International Symposium on Performance Evaluation of Computer and Telecommunication Systems (SPECTS)*. 10.1109/SPECTS.2015.7285286

Yates, J. M., Rumsewicz, M. P., & Lacey, J. P. R. (1999). Wavelength converters in dynamically-reconfigurable WDM networks. *IEEE Communications Surveys and Tutorials*, 2(2), 2–15. doi:10.1109/COMST.1999.5340515

Ye, X., Proietti, R., Yin, Y., Yoo, S. J. B., & Akella, V. (2011, August). Buffering and flow control in optical switches for high performance computing. *Journal of Optical Communications and Networking*, 3(8), A59–A72. doi:10.1364/JOCN.3.000A59

Yin, Y., Proietti, R., Ye, X., Nitta, C., Akella, V., & Yoo, S. (2012). LIONS: An AWGR-based low-latency optical switch for high performance computing and data centers. *IEEE Journal of Selected Topics in Quantum Electronics*, 19(2), 3600409. doi:10.1109/JSTQE.2012.2209174

KEY TERMS AND DEFINITIONS

Arrayed-Waveguide Grating (AWG): AWGs are passive optical devices that are not dependent on data-rate and are used to route each wavelength of an input to a different output (wavelength w of input i is routed to output $[(i + w - 2) \bmod N]+1$, $1 \leq i \leq N$, $1 \leq w \leq W$, where N represents the number of ports and W *is* the total number of wavelengths). AWGs are used as de-multiplexers to separate the individual wavelengths or as multiplexers to combine them in WDM communication systems.

Coupler: Coupler is a passive optical device that is utilized to aggregate and distribute signals in an optical network, but it can support multiple inputs

and outputs. For example, a 2x2 coupler gets a fraction of the power from the first input and gives it on output 1 and the remaining fraction on output 2 (similar goes for the second input).

Micro-Electro-Mechanical Systems Switches (MEMS Switches): MEMS optical switches are mechanical devices that are used to physically rotate the mirror arrays and redirecting the laser beam to make a connection between the input and the output. As they rely on mechanical systems, so the reconfiguration time is a few milliseconds. Currently, the commercial available MEMS optical switches can support up to 32 input/output ports.

Splitter and Combiner: Splitter is a passive optical device that is used to split the optical signal from one fiber to two or more fibers. On the other hand, combiner is utilized to combine optical signals from two or more fibers into a single fiber.

Related Readings

To continue IGI Global's long-standing tradition of advancing innovation through emerging research, please find below a compiled list of recommended IGI Global book chapters and journal articles in the areas of next generation optical networks, wireless communications, and wireless technologies. These related readings will provide additional information and guidance to further enrich your knowledge and assist you with your own research.

Abdullah, H. M., & Kumar, A. S. (2019). Selective Cooperative Jamming Based Relay Selection and Blowfish Encryption for Enhancing Channel and Data Security in CRAHN Routing. In M. Elkhodr (Ed.), *Enabling Technologies and Architectures for Next-Generation Networking Capabilities* (pp. 105–124). Hershey, PA: IGI Global. doi:10.4018/978-1-5225-6023-4.ch005

Aboshosha, A., El-Mashade, M. B., & Hegazy, E. A. (2019). Design and Analysis of Rectangular Microstrip Patch Array Antenna on 28 GHz Band for Future of 5G. In M. Elkhodr (Ed.), *Enabling Technologies and Architectures for Next-Generation Networking Capabilities* (pp. 71–89). Hershey, PA: IGI Global. doi:10.4018/978-1-5225-6023-4.ch003

Abu-Ella, O. A., & Elmusrati, M. S. (2016). Recent Trends for Interference Mitigation in Multi-Antenna Wireless Systems. In A. Panagopoulos (Ed.), *Handbook of Research on Next Generation Mobile Communication Systems* (pp. 66–84). Hershey, PA: IGI Global. doi:10.4018/978-1-4666-8732-5.ch004

Alavi, S. M., & Zhou, C. (2016). Auction-Based Resource Management in Multi-Cell OFDMA Networks. In C. Yang & J. Li (Eds.), *Game Theory Framework Applied to Wireless Communication Networks* (pp. 273–295). Hershey, PA: IGI Global. doi:10.4018/978-1-4666-8642-7.ch011

Anadiotis, A., Gkonis, P., Kaklamani, D. I., & Venieris, I. S. (2016). Bandwidth Efficient Relay Transmission Strategy for MIMO-OFDMA Multicellular Networks: Relay Transmission in OFDMA Networks. In A. Panagopoulos (Ed.), Handbook of Research on Next Generation Mobile Communication Systems (pp. 31-48). Hershey, PA: IGI Global. doi:10.4018/978-1-4666-8732-5.ch002

Anaissi, A., & Goyal, M. (2019). Blending Association Rules for Knowledge Discovery in Big Data. In M. Elkhodr (Ed.), *Enabling Technologies and Architectures for Next-Generation Networking Capabilities* (pp. 254–271). Hershey, PA: IGI Global. doi:10.4018/978-1-5225-6023-4.ch012

Anandkumar, R., & Kalpana, R. (2019). A Survey on Chaos Based Encryption Technique. In M. Elkhodr (Ed.), *Enabling Technologies and Architectures for Next-Generation Networking Capabilities* (pp. 147–165). Hershey, PA: IGI Global. doi:10.4018/978-1-5225-6023-4.ch007

Araniti, G., Condoluci, M., Pizzi, S., & Molinaro, A. (2019). Resource Management of Mixed Unicast and Multicast Services Over LTE. In R. Trestian & G. Muntean (Eds.), *Paving the Way for 5G Through the Convergence of Wireless Systems* (pp. 84–99). Hershey, PA: IGI Global. doi:10.4018/978-1-5225-7570-2.ch004

Arbi, A., O'Farrell, T., Zheng, F., & Fletcher, S. C. (2017). Toward Green Evolution of Cellular Networks by High Order Sectorisation and Small Cell Densification. In C. Yang & J. Li (Eds.), *Interference Mitigation and Energy Management in 5G Heterogeneous Cellular Networks* (pp. 1–28). Hershey, PA: IGI Global. doi:10.4018/978-1-5225-1712-2.ch001

Arya, K. V., & Gore, R. (2019). Internet of Things Using Software-Defined Network and Cognitive Radio Network. In A. Bagwari, J. Bagwari, & G. Tomar (Eds.), *Sensing Techniques for Next Generation Cognitive Radio Networks* (pp. 312–328). Hershey, PA: IGI Global. doi:10.4018/978-1-5225-5354-0.ch017

Bagwari, A., Kanti, J., & Tomar, G. S. (2019). Multiple Antennas-Based Improved Sensing Detector. In A. Bagwari, J. Bagwari, & G. Tomar (Eds.), *Sensing Techniques for Next Generation Cognitive Radio Networks* (pp. 143–163). Hershey, PA: IGI Global. doi:10.4018/978-1-5225-5354-0.ch009

Bhowmick, A., Roy, S. D., & Kundu, S. (2019). Cooperative Spectrum Sensing Under Double Threshold With Censoring and Hybrid Spectrum Access Schemes in Cognitive Radio Network. In A. Bagwari, J. Bagwari, & G. Tomar (Eds.), *Sensing Techniques for Next Generation Cognitive Radio Networks* (pp. 164–188). Hershey, PA: IGI Global. doi:10.4018/978-1-5225-5354-0.ch010

Bhuvaneswari, P. T. V., & Bino, J. (2019). Basic Spectrum Sensing Techniques. In A. Bagwari, J. Bagwari, & G. Tomar (Eds.), *Sensing Techniques for Next Generation Cognitive Radio Networks* (pp. 70–84). Hershey, PA: IGI Global. doi:10.4018/978-1-5225-5354-0.ch004

Bishnu, A., & Bhatia, V. (2019). Cognitive Radio Networks: IEEE 802.22 Standards. In A. Bagwari, J. Bagwari, & G. Tomar (Eds.), *Sensing Techniques for Next Generation Cognitive Radio Networks* (pp. 27–50). Hershey, PA: IGI Global. doi:10.4018/978-1-5225-5354-0.ch002

Bisio, I., Delucchi, S., Lavagetto, F., Marchese, M., Portomauro, G., & Zappatore, S. (2016). Hybrid Simulated-Emulated Platform – HySEP. In A. Panagopoulos (Ed.), *Handbook of Research on Next Generation Mobile Communication Systems* (pp. 380–409). Hershey, PA: IGI Global. doi:10.4018/978-1-4666-8732-5.ch015

Biswas, R. (2019). Spectrum Sensing Techniques: An Overview. In A. Bagwari, J. Bagwari, & G. Tomar (Eds.), *Sensing Techniques for Next Generation Cognitive Radio Networks* (pp. 125–132). Hershey, PA: IGI Global. doi:10.4018/978-1-5225-5354-0.ch007

Bojkovic, Z., Bakmaz, B., & Bakmaz, M. (2019). Principles and Enabling Technologies of 5G Network Slicing. In R. Trestian & G. Muntean (Eds.), *Paving the Way for 5G Through the Convergence of Wireless Systems* (pp. 271–284). Hershey, PA: IGI Global. doi:10.4018/978-1-5225-7570-2.ch011

Bousia, A. (2017). Energy Efficient Resource Allocation Scheme via Auction-Based Offloading in Next-Generation Heterogeneous Networks. In C. Singhal & S. De (Eds.), *Resource Allocation in Next-Generation Broadband Wireless Access Networks* (pp. 167–189). Hershey, PA: IGI Global. doi:10.4018/978-1-5225-2023-8.ch008

Bousia, A., Kartsakli, E., Antonopoulos, A., Alonso, L., & Verikoukis, C. (2016). Game Theoretic Infrastructure Sharing in Wireless Cellular Networks. In C. Yang & J. Li (Eds.), *Game Theory Framework Applied to Wireless Communication Networks* (pp. 368–398). Hershey, PA: IGI Global. doi:10.4018/978-1-4666-8642-7.ch014

Brito, J. M. (2018). Technological Trends for 5G Networks Influence of E-Health and IoT Applications. *International Journal of E-Health and Medical Communications*, 9(1), 1–22. doi:10.4018/IJEHMC.2018010101

Chaitanya, T. V., Le-Ngoc, T., & Larsson, E. G. (2016). Energy-Efficient Power Allocation for HARQ Systems. In A. Panagopoulos (Ed.), *Handbook of Research on Next Generation Mobile Communication Systems* (pp. 179–198). Hershey, PA: IGI Global. doi:10.4018/978-1-4666-8732-5.ch008

Chana, I., Benkhouya, R., Rhattoy, A., & Hadi, Y. (2019). Improved Spectrum Sensing Based on Polar Codes for Cognitive Radio Networks. In A. Bagwari, J. Bagwari, & G. Tomar (Eds.), *Sensing Techniques for Next Generation Cognitive Radio Networks* (pp. 229–256). Hershey, PA: IGI Global. doi:10.4018/978-1-5225-5354-0.ch013

Chen, X., & Huang, J. (2016). Self-Organizing Spectrum Access with Geo-Location Database. In C. Yang & J. Li (Eds.), *Game Theory Framework Applied to Wireless Communication Networks* (pp. 254–272). Hershey, PA: IGI Global. doi:10.4018/978-1-4666-8642-7.ch010

Chourasia, S., & Sivalingam, K. M. (2017). Experimental Study of SDN-Based Evolved Packet Core Architecture for Efficient User Mobility Support. In C. Singhal & S. De (Eds.), *Resource Allocation in Next-Generation Broadband Wireless Access Networks* (pp. 273–298). Hershey, PA: IGI Global. doi:10.4018/978-1-5225-2023-8.ch012

Cortés-Polo, D., González-Sánchez, J., Rodríguez-Pérez, F. J., & Carmona-Murillo, J. (2016). Mobile-Fixed Integration for Next-Generation Mobile Network: Classification and Evaluation. In A. Panagopoulos (Ed.), *Handbook of Research on Next Generation Mobile Communication Systems* (pp. 466–484). Hershey, PA: IGI Global. doi:10.4018/978-1-4666-8732-5.ch018

Curiel, H. M. J. (2016). Wireless Grids: Recent Advances in Resource and Job Management. In A. Panagopoulos (Ed.), *Handbook of Research on Next Generation Mobile Communication Systems* (pp. 293–320). Hershey, PA: IGI Global. doi:10.4018/978-1-4666-8732-5.ch012

Debroy, S., & Chatterjee, M. (2017). Radio Environment Maps and Its Utility in Resource Management for Dynamic Spectrum Access Networks. In C. Singhal & S. De (Eds.), *Resource Allocation in Next-Generation Broadband Wireless Access Networks* (pp. 32–54). Hershey, PA: IGI Global. doi:10.4018/978-1-5225-2023-8.ch002

Demirpolat, A., Ergenç, D., Ozturk, E., Ayar, Y., & Onur, E. (2019). Software-Defined Network Security. In M. Elkhodr (Ed.), *Enabling Technologies and Architectures for Next-Generation Networking Capabilities* (pp. 232–253). Hershey, PA: IGI Global. doi:10.4018/978-1-5225-6023-4.ch011

Dey, P. (2019). Characterization of Online Social Network: A Case Study on Twitter Data. In M. Elkhodr (Ed.), *Enabling Technologies and Architectures for Next-Generation Networking Capabilities* (pp. 272–299). Hershey, PA: IGI Global. doi:10.4018/978-1-5225-6023-4.ch013

Dhaya, R., Rajeswari, A., & Kanthavel, R. (2019). Sensing Techniques for Next Generation Cognitive Radio Networks: Spectrum Sensing in Cognitive Radio Networks. In A. Bagwari, J. Bagwari, & G. Tomar (Eds.), *Sensing Techniques for Next Generation Cognitive Radio Networks* (pp. 108–124). Hershey, PA: IGI Global. doi:10.4018/978-1-5225-5354-0.ch006

Diab, A., & Mitschele-Thiel, A. (2016). Self-Organized Future Mobile Communication Networks: Vision and Key Challenges. In A. Panagopoulos (Ed.), *Handbook of Research on Next Generation Mobile Communication Systems* (pp. 321–359). Hershey, PA: IGI Global. doi:10.4018/978-1-4666-8732-5.ch013

Donelli, M. (2016). Applications of Advanced Reconfigurable Antenna for the Next Generation 4G Communication Devices. In A. Panagopoulos (Ed.), *Handbook of Research on Next Generation Mobile Communication Systems* (pp. 49–65). Hershey, PA: IGI Global. doi:10.4018/978-1-4666-8732-5.ch003

Donelli, M. (2017). Reconfigurable Antenna Systems for the Next Generation Devices Based on 4G/5G Standard. *International Journal of Interactive Communication Systems and Technologies*, 7(2), 53–71. doi:10.4018/IJICST.2017070103

El-Khamy, S. E., el-Malek, M. B., & Kamel, S. H. (2019). Compressive Spectrum Sensing: Wavelet-Based Compressive Spectrum Sensing in Cognitive Radio. In A. Bagwari, J. Bagwari, & G. Tomar (Eds.), *Sensing Techniques for Next Generation Cognitive Radio Networks* (pp. 203–228). Hershey, PA: IGI Global. doi:10.4018/978-1-5225-5354-0.ch012

Giannoulakis, I., Kafetzakis, E., & Kourtis, A. (2016). Device-to-Device Communications. In A. Panagopoulos (Ed.), *Handbook of Research on Next Generation Mobile Communication Systems* (pp. 234–255). Hershey, PA: IGI Global. doi:10.4018/978-1-4666-8732-5.ch010

Grigoriou, E. (2019). A Survey of Quality of Service in Long Term Evolution (LTE) Networks. In M. Elkhodr (Ed.), *Enabling Technologies and Architectures for Next-Generation Networking Capabilities* (pp. 125–146). Hershey, PA: IGI Global. doi:10.4018/978-1-5225-6023-4.ch006

Gupta, N., Bohara, V. A., & Singh, V. K. (2017). Design and Measurement Results for Cooperative Device to Device Communication. In C. Singhal & S. De (Eds.), *Resource Allocation in Next-Generation Broadband Wireless Access Networks* (pp. 81–97). Hershey, PA: IGI Global. doi:10.4018/978-1-5225-2023-8.ch004

Gupta, S., Singhal, S., & Sinha, A. (2019). Cognitive Radio Network for E-Health Systems. In A. Bagwari, J. Bagwari, & G. Tomar (Eds.), *Sensing Techniques for Next Generation Cognitive Radio Networks* (pp. 281–298). Hershey, PA: IGI Global. doi:10.4018/978-1-5225-5354-0.ch015

Gurjar, D. S., & Upadhyay, P. K. (2019). Spectrum Sharing for D2D Communications in Fifth-Generation Wireless Networks. In M. Elkhodr (Ed.), *Enabling Technologies and Architectures for Next-Generation Networking Capabilities* (pp. 166–196). Hershey, PA: IGI Global. doi:10.4018/978-1-5225-6023-4.ch008

Gürsel, G. (2016). Mobility in Healthcare: M-Health. In A. Panagopoulos (Ed.), *Handbook of Research on Next Generation Mobile Communication Systems* (pp. 485–511). Hershey, PA: IGI Global. doi:10.4018/978-1-4666-8732-5.ch019

Hayes, T., & Ali, F. (2016). Mobile Wireless Sensor Networks: Applications and Routing Protocols. In A. Panagopoulos (Ed.), *Handbook of Research on Next Generation Mobile Communication Systems* (pp. 256–292). Hershey, PA: IGI Global. doi:10.4018/978-1-4666-8732-5.ch011

Huang, K., Li, M., Zhong, Z., & Zhao, H. (2016). Applications of Game Theory for Physical Layer Security. In C. Yang & J. Li (Eds.), *Game Theory Framework Applied to Wireless Communication Networks* (pp. 297–332). Hershey, PA: IGI Global. doi:10.4018/978-1-4666-8642-7.ch012

Hussain, S., & Ginige, A. (2019). Extending a Conventional Chatbot Knowledge Base to External Knowledge Source and Introducing User-Based Sessions for Diabetes Education. In M. Elkhodr (Ed.), *Enabling Technologies and Architectures for Next-Generation Networking Capabilities* (pp. 333–343). Hershey, PA: IGI Global. doi:10.4018/978-1-5225-6023-4.ch015

Islam, N., & Wahab, A. W. (2019). 5G Networks: A Holistic View of Enabling Technologies and Research Challenges. In M. Elkhodr (Ed.), *Enabling Technologies and Architectures for Next-Generation Networking Capabilities* (pp. 37–70). Hershey, PA: IGI Global. doi:10.4018/978-1-5225-6023-4.ch002

Janczukowicz, E., Bouabdallah, A., Braud, A., Tuffin, S., & Bonnin, J. (2016). Firefox OS Ecosystem: Ambitions and Limits of an Open Source Operating System for Mobile Devices. In A. Panagopoulos (Ed.), *Handbook of Research on Next Generation Mobile Communication Systems* (pp. 440–465). Hershey, PA: IGI Global. doi:10.4018/978-1-4666-8732-5.ch017

Jayakody, N. D., & Nguyen, D. K. (2017). Green Cognitive Relay Communications with Hardware Impairments for Future Wireless Networks. In C. Singhal & S. De (Eds.), *Resource Allocation in Next-Generation Broadband Wireless Access Networks* (pp. 98–128). Hershey, PA: IGI Global. doi:10.4018/978-1-5225-2023-8.ch005

Ji, W., Chen, B., Chen, Y., Kang, S., & Zhang, S. (2016). Game Theoretic Analysis for Cooperative Video Transmission over Heterogeneous Devices: Mobile Communication Networks and Wireless Local Area Networks as a Case Study. In C. Yang & J. Li (Eds.), *Game Theory Framework Applied to Wireless Communication Networks* (pp. 427–456). Hershey, PA: IGI Global. doi:10.4018/978-1-4666-8642-7.ch016

Joshi, P., & Bagwari, A. (2019). An Overview of Cognitive Radio Networks: A Future Wireless Technology. In A. Bagwari, J. Bagwari, & G. Tomar (Eds.), *Sensing Techniques for Next Generation Cognitive Radio Networks* (pp. 1–26). Hershey, PA: IGI Global. doi:10.4018/978-1-5225-5354-0.ch001

Joshi, P., Bagwari, A., & Negi, A. (2019). A Quick Overview of Different Spectrum Sensing Techniques. In A. Bagwari, J. Bagwari, & G. Tomar (Eds.), *Sensing Techniques for Next Generation Cognitive Radio Networks* (pp. 52–69). Hershey, PA: IGI Global. doi:10.4018/978-1-5225-5354-0.ch003

Khang, A. W., Elobaid, M. E., Ramli, A., Zulkifli, N., & Idrus, S. M. (2019). Routing Optimization for Integrated Optical and Mobile Ad hoc Networks. In M. Elkhodr (Ed.), *Enabling Technologies and Architectures for Next-Generation Networking Capabilities* (pp. 90–104). Hershey, PA: IGI Global. doi:10.4018/978-1-5225-6023-4.ch004

Kitanov, S., Popovski, B., & Janevski, T. (2019). Quality Evaluation of Cloud and Fog Computing Services in 5G Networks. In M. Elkhodr (Ed.), *Enabling Technologies and Architectures for Next-Generation Networking Capabilities* (pp. 1–36). Hershey, PA: IGI Global. doi:10.4018/978-1-5225-6023-4.ch001

Kittali, R. M., & Sutagundar, A. V. (2019). Spectrum Sensing and Identification Techniques of Cognitive Radio Networks. In A. Bagwari, J. Bagwari, & G. Tomar (Eds.), *Sensing Techniques for Next Generation Cognitive Radio Networks* (pp. 189–202). Hershey, PA: IGI Global. doi:10.4018/978-1-5225-5354-0.ch011

Kotzanikolaou, P. (2016). Security and Privacy in Next Generation Networks and Services. In A. Panagopoulos (Ed.), *Handbook of Research on Next Generation Mobile Communication Systems* (pp. 361–379). Hershey, PA: IGI Global. doi:10.4018/978-1-4666-8732-5.ch014

Kourogiorgas, C., Moraitis, N., & Panagopoulos, A. D. (2016). Radio Channel Modeling and Propagation Prediction for 5G Mobile Communication Systems. In A. Panagopoulos (Ed.), *Handbook of Research on Next Generation Mobile Communication Systems* (pp. 1–30). Hershey, PA: IGI Global. doi:10.4018/978-1-4666-8732-5.ch001

Lahby, M., Essouiri, A., & Sekkaki, A. (2019). An Improved Modeling for Network Selection Based on Graph Theory and Cost Function in Heterogeneous Wireless Systems. In R. Trestian & G. Muntean (Eds.), *Paving the Way for 5G Through the Convergence of Wireless Systems* (pp. 285–304). Hershey, PA: IGI Global. doi:10.4018/978-1-5225-7570-2.ch012

Lai, W., Chang, T., & Lee, T. (2016). Distributed Dynamic Resource Allocation for OFDMA-Based Cognitive Small Cell Networks Using a Regret-Matching Game Approach. In C. Yang & J. Li (Eds.), *Game Theory Framework Applied to Wireless Communication Networks* (pp. 230–253). Hershey, PA: IGI Global. doi:10.4018/978-1-4666-8642-7.ch009

Liampotis, N., Papadopoulou, E., Kalatzis, N., Roussaki, I. G., Kosmides, P., Sykas, E. D., ... Taylor, N. K. (2016). Tailoring Privacy-Aware Trustworthy Cooperating Smart Spaces for University Environments. In A. Panagopoulos (Ed.), *Handbook of Research on Next Generation Mobile Communication Systems* (pp. 410–439). Hershey, PA: IGI Global. doi:10.4018/978-1-4666-8732-5.ch016

Liang, Y. (2017). Interference Management in Heterogeneous Networks. In C. Yang & J. Li (Eds.), *Interference Mitigation and Energy Management in 5G Heterogeneous Cellular Networks* (pp. 190–226). Hershey, PA: IGI Global. doi:10.4018/978-1-5225-1712-2.ch008

Liao, Y., Li, Y., Zhang, S., Zhao, M., Zhou, X., Chen, L., ... Hu, Y. (2017). Interference Mitigation for Satellite: Terrestrial Heterogeneous Coexistence Cognitive MIMO System Based on Digital Beamforming. In C. Yang & J. Li (Eds.), *Interference Mitigation and Energy Management in 5G Heterogeneous Cellular Networks* (pp. 123–138). Hershey, PA: IGI Global. doi:10.4018/978-1-5225-1712-2.ch005

Liu, Z., Dong, M., Zhou, H., Wang, X., Ji, Y., & Tanaka, Y. (2017). User-Oriented Intercell Interference Coordination in Heterogeneous Networks (HetNets). In C. Singhal & S. De (Eds.), *Resource Allocation in Next-Generation Broadband Wireless Access Networks* (pp. 145–166). Hershey, PA: IGI Global. doi:10.4018/978-1-5225-2023-8.ch007

Magalhães, J. M., Henrique da Mata, S., & Guardieiro, P. R. (2016). Downlink and Uplink Resource Allocation in LTE Networks. In A. Panagopoulos (Ed.), *Handbook of Research on Next Generation Mobile Communication Systems* (pp. 199–233). Hershey, PA: IGI Global. doi:10.4018/978-1-4666-8732-5.ch009

Mahmoodi, T., Johnson, S. H., Condoluci, M., Ayadurai, V., Cuevas, M. A., & Dohler, M. (2019). Managing 5G Converged Core With Access Traffic Steering, Switching, and Splitting: From Hybrid Access to Converged Core. In R. Trestian & G. Muntean (Eds.), *Paving the Way for 5G Through the Convergence of Wireless Systems* (pp. 209–226). Hershey, PA: IGI Global. doi:10.4018/978-1-5225-7570-2.ch008

Majumder, A., & Nath, S. (2019). Classification of Handoff Schemes in a Wi-Fi-Based Network. In M. Elkhodr (Ed.), *Enabling Technologies and Architectures for Next-Generation Networking Capabilities* (pp. 300–332). Hershey, PA: IGI Global. doi:10.4018/978-1-5225-6023-4.ch014

Meng, Y., Dong, Y., & Shi, S. (2017). The Combination of Resource Allocation and Interference Alignment for Ultra-Dense Heterogeneous Cellular Networks. In C. Yang & J. Li (Eds.), *Interference Mitigation and Energy Management in 5G Heterogeneous Cellular Networks* (pp. 139–161). Hershey, PA: IGI Global. doi:10.4018/978-1-5225-1712-2.ch006

Militano, L., Iera, A., Scarcello, F., Molinaro, A., & Araniti, G. (2016). Game Theoretic Approaches for Wireless Cooperative Content-Sharing. In C. Yang & J. Li (Eds.), *Game Theory Framework Applied to Wireless Communication Networks* (pp. 399–426). Hershey, PA: IGI Global. doi:10.4018/978-1-4666-8642-7.ch015

Misra, A., & Sarma, K. K. (2017). Self-Organization and Optimization in Heterogenous Networks. In C. Yang & J. Li (Eds.), *Interference Mitigation and Energy Management in 5G Heterogeneous Cellular Networks* (pp. 246–268). Hershey, PA: IGI Global. doi:10.4018/978-1-5225-1712-2.ch010

Mohan, P. T., & Stephen, B. J. (2019). Advanced Spectrum Sensing Techniques. In A. Bagwari, J. Bagwari, & G. Tomar (Eds.), *Sensing Techniques for Next Generation Cognitive Radio Networks* (pp. 133–141). Hershey, PA: IGI Global. doi:10.4018/978-1-5225-5354-0.ch008

Molnar, A., & Muntean, C. H. (2019). User-Based Adaptive Multimedia Delivery Over 5G Network. In R. Trestian & G. Muntean (Eds.), *Paving the Way for 5G Through the Convergence of Wireless Systems* (pp. 1–17). Hershey, PA: IGI Global. doi:10.4018/978-1-5225-7570-2.ch001

Moura, J., Marinheiro, R. N., & Silva, J. C. (2019). Game Theory for Cooperation in Multi-Access Edge Computing. In R. Trestian & G. Muntean (Eds.), *Paving the Way for 5G Through the Convergence of Wireless Systems* (pp. 100–149). Hershey, PA: IGI Global. doi:10.4018/978-1-5225-7570-2. ch005

Mukherjee, A., Saeed, R. A., Dutta, S., & Naskar, M. K. (2017). Fault Tracking Framework for Software-Defined Networking (SDN). In C. Singhal & S. De (Eds.), *Resource Allocation in Next-Generation Broadband Wireless Access Networks* (pp. 247–272). Hershey, PA: IGI Global. doi:10.4018/978-1-5225-2023-8.ch011

Mustafa, M. F., Ahmad, A., & Ahmed, R. (2019). Handoff Management in Macro-Femto Cellular Networks. In R. Trestian & G. Muntean (Eds.), *Paving the Way for 5G Through the Convergence of Wireless Systems* (pp. 227–249). Hershey, PA: IGI Global. doi:10.4018/978-1-5225-7570-2.ch009

Nagarajan, G., Minu, R. I., & Jayanthiladevi, A. (2019). Cognitive Internet of Things (C-IOT). In A. Bagwari, J. Bagwari, & G. Tomar (Eds.), *Sensing Techniques for Next Generation Cognitive Radio Networks* (pp. 299–311). Hershey, PA: IGI Global. doi:10.4018/978-1-5225-5354-0.ch016

Nomikos, N., & Vouyioukas, D. (2016). Spectral Efficient Opportunistic Relay Selection Policies for Next Generation Mobile Systems. In A. Panagopoulos (Ed.), *Handbook of Research on Next Generation Mobile Communication Systems* (pp. 85–111). Hershey, PA: IGI Global. doi:10.4018/978-1-4666-8732-5.ch005

Omer, A. E. (2019). Review of Spectrum Sensing Techniques in Cognitive Radio Networks. In A. Bagwari, J. Bagwari, & G. Tomar (Eds.), *Sensing Techniques for Next Generation Cognitive Radio Networks* (pp. 85–107). Hershey, PA: IGI Global. doi:10.4018/978-1-5225-5354-0.ch005

Panigrahi, B., Rath, H. K., Jagyasi, B., & Simha, A. (2017). D2D- and DTN-Based Efficient Data Offloading Techniques for 5G Networks. In C. Singhal & S. De (Eds.), *Resource Allocation in Next-Generation Broadband Wireless Access Networks* (pp. 190–209). Hershey, PA: IGI Global. doi:10.4018/978-1-5225-2023-8.ch009

Peng, M., Sun, Y., Sun, C., & Ahmed, M. (2016). Game Theory-Based Radio Resource Optimization in Heterogeneous Small Cell Networks (HSCNs). In C. Yang & J. Li (Eds.), *Game Theory Framework Applied to Wireless Communication Networks* (pp. 137–183). Hershey, PA: IGI Global. doi:10.4018/978-1-4666-8642-7.ch006

Pitas, C. N., Fertis, A. G., Charilas, D. E., & Panagopoulos, A. D. (2016). Advances in QoS/E Characterization and Prediction for Next Generation Mobile Communication Systems. In A. Panagopoulos (Ed.), *Handbook of Research on Next Generation Mobile Communication Systems* (pp. 512–535). Hershey, PA: IGI Global. doi:10.4018/978-1-4666-8732-5.ch020

Plazas, J. E., Bimonte, S., De Sousa, G., & Corrales, J. C. (2019). Data-Centric UML Profile for Wireless Sensors: Application to Smart Farming. *International Journal of Agricultural and Environmental Information Systems*, *10*(2), 21–48. doi:10.4018/IJAEIS.2019040102

Prasad, G., Mishra, D., & Hossain, A. (2019). QoS-Aware Green Communication Strategies for Optimal Utilization of Resources in 5G Networks. In R. Trestian & G. Muntean (Eds.), *Paving the Way for 5G Through the Convergence of Wireless Systems* (pp. 186–208). Hershey, PA: IGI Global. doi:10.4018/978-1-5225-7570-2.ch007

Reshmi, T. R. (2019). Survey on Autoconfiguration Schemes in IPV6 Based Manets. In M. Elkhodr (Ed.), *Enabling Technologies and Architectures for Next-Generation Networking Capabilities* (pp. 214–231). Hershey, PA: IGI Global. doi:10.4018/978-1-5225-6023-4.ch010

Róka, R. (2019). Converged Fi-Wi Passive Optical Networks and Their Designing Using the HPON Network Configurator. In R. Trestian & G. Muntean (Eds.), *Paving the Way for 5G Through the Convergence of Wireless Systems* (pp. 150–184). Hershey, PA: IGI Global. doi:10.4018/978-1-5225-7570-2.ch006

Rossi, F. D., Severo de Souza, P. S., Marques, W. D., Calheiros, R. N., & Rodrigues, G. D. (2019). Network Support for IoT Ecosystems. In M. Elkhodr (Ed.), *Enabling Technologies and Architectures for Next-Generation Networking Capabilities* (pp. 197–213). Hershey, PA: IGI Global. doi:10.4018/978-1-5225-6023-4.ch009

Sahoo, S. K., & Choudhury, B. B. (2018). An Artificial Intelligent Centered Object Inspection System Using Crucial Images. *International Journal of Rough Sets and Data Analysis, 5*(1), 44–57. doi:10.4018/IJRSDA.2018010104

Saini, R., & De, S. (2017). Fulfilling the Rate Demands: Subcarrier-Based Shared Resource Allocation. In C. Singhal & S. De (Eds.), *Resource Allocation in Next-Generation Broadband Wireless Access Networks* (pp. 55–80). Hershey, PA: IGI Global. doi:10.4018/978-1-5225-2023-8.ch003

Selvaraj, P., & Nagarajan, V. (2018). Need of Algorithm Selection in Next Generation Optical Networks. *International Journal of Business Data Communications and Networking, 14*(1), 81–92. doi:10.4018/IJBDCN.2018010105

Shah, S. D., Kim, D., Khan, P., Kim, H., & Han, S. (2018). A Two Step Multi-Carrier Proportional Fair Scheduling Scheme for Cloud Radio Access Networks. *International Journal of Interdisciplinary Telecommunications and Networking, 10*(1), 49–62. doi:10.4018/IJITN.2018010104

Singh, M., Kaur, N., Kaur, A., & Pushkarna, G. (2017). A Comparative Evaluation of Mining Techniques to Detect Malicious Node in Wireless Sensor Networks. *International Journal of Cyber Warfare & Terrorism, 7*(2), 42–53. doi:10.4018/IJCWT.2017040103

Singhal, C., & Barik, P. K. (2017). Adaptive Multimedia Services in Next-Generation Broadband Wireless Access Network. In C. Singhal & S. De (Eds.), *Resource Allocation in Next-Generation Broadband Wireless Access Networks* (pp. 1–31). Hershey, PA: IGI Global. doi:10.4018/978-1-5225-2023-8.ch001

Singhal, C., & De, S. (2019). Resource Allocation in Heterogeneous Wireless Networks. In R. Trestian & G. Muntean (Eds.), *Paving the Way for 5G Through the Convergence of Wireless Systems* (pp. 56–83). Hershey, PA: IGI Global. doi:10.4018/978-1-5225-7570-2.ch003

Singhal, S., Gupta, S., & Sinha, A. (2019). Role of Artificial Intelligence in Cognitive Radio Networks. In A. Bagwari, J. Bagwari, & G. Tomar (Eds.), *Sensing Techniques for Next Generation Cognitive Radio Networks* (pp. 258–279). Hershey, PA: IGI Global. doi:10.4018/978-1-5225-5354-0.ch014

Tal, I., & Muntean, G. (2019). Clustering and 5G-Enabled Smart Cities: A Survey of Clustering Schemes in VANETs. In R. Trestian & G. Muntean (Eds.), *Paving the Way for 5G Through the Convergence of Wireless Systems* (pp. 18–55). Hershey, PA: IGI Global. doi:10.4018/978-1-5225-7570-2.ch002

Tsiropoulou, E. E., Vamvakas, P., & Papavassiliou, S. (2017). Resource Allocation in Multi-Tier Femtocell and Visible-Light Heterogeneous Wireless Networks. In C. Singhal & S. De (Eds.), *Resource Allocation in Next-Generation Broadband Wireless Access Networks* (pp. 210–246). Hershey, PA: IGI Global. doi:10.4018/978-1-5225-2023-8.ch010

Uriarte-Ramírez, I., Barboza-Tello, N. A., & Medina-Castro, P. (2017). Challenges in Energy-Efficient Communications as Enablers for Green Solutions on the 5G Heterogeneous Networks. In C. Yang & J. Li (Eds.), *Interference Mitigation and Energy Management in 5G Heterogeneous Cellular Networks* (pp. 58–76). Hershey, PA: IGI Global. doi:10.4018/978-1-5225-1712-2.ch003

Vassaki, S., Pitsiladis, G., Sagkriotis, S. E., & Panagopoulos, A. D. (2016). Future M2M Communication Networks: Spectrum Sharing, Random Access and Connectivity. In A. Panagopoulos (Ed.), *Handbook of Research on Next Generation Mobile Communication Systems* (pp. 149–178). Hershey, PA: IGI Global. doi:10.4018/978-1-4666-8732-5.ch007

Wali, P. K. N, A. A., & Das, D. (2017). Link Level Resource Allocation Strategies for Green Communications in LTE-Advanced. In C. Singhal, & S. De (Eds.), Resource Allocation in Next-Generation Broadband Wireless Access Networks (pp. 129-144). Hershey, PA: IGI Global. doi:10.4018/978-1-5225-2023-8.ch006

Wang, C., Wei, H., Bennis, M., & Vasilakos, A. V. (2016). Game-Theoretic Approaches in Heterogeneous Networks. In C. Yang & J. Li (Eds.), *Game Theory Framework Applied to Wireless Communication Networks* (pp. 88–102). Hershey, PA: IGI Global. doi:10.4018/978-1-4666-8642-7.ch004

Wu, D., & Cai, Y. (2016). Coalition Formation Game for Wireless Communications. In C. Yang & J. Li (Eds.), *Game Theory Framework Applied to Wireless Communication Networks* (pp. 28–62). Hershey, PA: IGI Global. doi:10.4018/978-1-4666-8642-7.ch002

Wu, D., Wu, Q., & Xu, Y. (2017). Game Theory for Co-Tiered Interference Mitigation in 5G Small-Cell Networks. In C. Yang & J. Li (Eds.), *Interference Mitigation and Energy Management in 5G Heterogeneous Cellular Networks* (pp. 162–189). Hershey, PA: IGI Global. doi:10.4018/978-1-5225-1712-2.ch007

Xu, K., Xia, X., Xu, Y., & Zhang, D. (2017). Interference Management for Full-Duplex Massive MIMO Relaying System with Hardware Impairments. In C. Yang & J. Li (Eds.), *Interference Mitigation and Energy Management in 5G Heterogeneous Cellular Networks* (pp. 78–122). Hershey, PA: IGI Global. doi:10.4018/978-1-5225-1712-2.ch004

Xu, S., & Fu, T. (2017). Geometric Programming Based Resource Allocation for 5G High-Speed Mobile Networks. In C. Yang & J. Li (Eds.), *Interference Mitigation and Energy Management in 5G Heterogeneous Cellular Networks* (pp. 228–245). Hershey, PA: IGI Global. doi:10.4018/978-1-5225-1712-2.ch009

Xu, S., & Xia, C. (2016). Resource Allocation for Device-to-Device Communications in LTE-A Network: A Stackelberg Game Theory Approach. In C. Yang & J. Li (Eds.), *Game Theory Framework Applied to Wireless Communication Networks* (pp. 212–229). Hershey, PA: IGI Global. doi:10.4018/978-1-4666-8642-7.ch008

Xu, X., Gao, R., Li, M., & Wang, Y. (2016). Interference Mitigation with Power Control and Allocation in the Heterogeneous Small Cell Networks. In C. Yang & J. Li (Eds.), *Game Theory Framework Applied to Wireless Communication Networks* (pp. 103–136). Hershey, PA: IGI Global. doi:10.4018/978-1-4666-8642-7.ch005

Xu, Y., Wang, J., & Wu, Q. (2016). Distributed Learning of Equilibria with Incomplete, Dynamic, and Uncertain Information in Wireless Communication Networks. In C. Yang & J. Li (Eds.), *Game Theory Framework Applied to Wireless Communication Networks* (pp. 63–86). Hershey, PA: IGI Global. doi:10.4018/978-1-4666-8642-7.ch003

Yaacoub, E., Ghazzai, H., & Alouini, M. (2016). A Game Theoretic Framework for Green HetNets Using D2D Traffic Offload and Renewable Energy Powered Base Stations. In C. Yang & J. Li (Eds.), *Game Theory Framework Applied to Wireless Communication Networks* (pp. 333–367). Hershey, PA: IGI Global. doi:10.4018/978-1-4666-8642-7.ch013

Yang, C., Huang, P., Xiao, J., Wang, L., & Li, J. (2017). Stackelberg Game Theoretic Framework in Cognitive Green Heterogeneous Networks. In C. Yang & J. Li (Eds.), *Interference Mitigation and Energy Management in 5G Heterogeneous Cellular Networks* (pp. 269–286). Hershey, PA: IGI Global. doi:10.4018/978-1-5225-1712-2.ch011

Yang, C., Xiao, J., Wang, L., Huang, P., & Li, J. (2017). Pricing Methodology and Its Applications in Cognitive Radio and Multi-Tier Heterogeneous Cellular Networks. In C. Yang & J. Li (Eds.), *Interference Mitigation and Energy Management in 5G Heterogeneous Cellular Networks* (pp. 287–317). Hershey, PA: IGI Global. doi:10.4018/978-1-5225-1712-2.ch012

Zhang, X., Cao, Y., Peng, L., & Li, J. (2019). Enhancing Mobile Data Offloading With In-Network Caching. In R. Trestian & G. Muntean (Eds.), *Paving the Way for 5G Through the Convergence of Wireless Systems* (pp. 250–270). Hershey, PA: IGI Global. doi:10.4018/978-1-5225-7570-2.ch010

Zhong, W., Wang, J., & Tao, M. (2016). Potential Games and Its Applications to Wireless Networks. In C. Yang & J. Li (Eds.), *Game Theory Framework Applied to Wireless Communication Networks* (pp. 1–27). Hershey, PA: IGI Global. doi:10.4018/978-1-4666-8642-7.ch001

Zhou, Y., Huang, L., Tian, L., & Shi, J. (2016). Game Theory-Based Coverage Optimization for Small Cell Networks. In C. Yang & J. Li (Eds.), *Game Theory Framework Applied to Wireless Communication Networks* (pp. 184–211). Hershey, PA: IGI Global. doi:10.4018/978-1-4666-8642-7.ch007

Zhou, Z., Chang, Z., Xu, C., & Ristaniemi, T. (2017). Stable-Matching-Based Energy-Efficient Context-Aware Resource Allocation for Ultra-Dense Small Cells. In C. Yang & J. Li (Eds.), *Interference Mitigation and Energy Management in 5G Heterogeneous Cellular Networks* (pp. 29–57). Hershey, PA: IGI Global. doi:10.4018/978-1-5225-1712-2.ch002

Zompakis, N., Catthoor, F., & Soudris, D. (2016). Efficient Configurations for Dynamic Applications in Next Generation Mobile Systems. In A. Panagopoulos (Ed.), *Handbook of Research on Next Generation Mobile Communication Systems* (pp. 112–147). Hershey, PA: IGI Global. doi:10.4018/978-1-4666-8732-5.ch006

About the Contributors

Rastislav Róka (Assoc. Prof.) was born in Šaľa, Slovakia on January 27, 1972. He received his MSc. and PhD. degrees in Telecommunications from the Slovak University of Technology, Bratislava, in 1995 and 2002. Since 1997, he has been working as a senior lecturer at the Institute of MICT, FEI STU, Bratislava. Since 2009, he is working as an associated professor at this institute. His teaching and educational activities are realized in areas of fixed transmission media, digital and optocommunication transmission systems and network. At present, his research activity is focused on the signal transmission through optical transport, metropolitan and access networks by means of new WDM and TDM technologies using advanced optical signal processing included various modulation and coding techniques. His main effort is dedicated to the effective utilization of the optical fiber's transmission capacity of the broadband passive optical networks by means of DBA and DWA algorithms applied in various advanced hybrid network infrastructures. Assoc. Prof. Róka is the IEEE Senior Member since 2016.

* * *

Banibrata Bag received a B.E. degree from Burdwan University in 2004 and M.Tech. degree from the West Bengal University of Technology in 2009. He has worked as a software developer from 2005 to 2007. Since February 2010, he is working as an Assistant Professor in the Department of Electronic and Communication Engineering, Haldia Institute of Technology, Haldia, India. His primary area of research is free space optical (FSO) communication or optical wireless communication.

Aniruddha Chandra received BE, ME, and PhD degrees from Jadavpur University, Kolkata, India in 2003, 2005, and 2011 respectively. He joined Electronics and Communication Engineering Department, National Institute of Technology, Durgapur, India in 2005. He is currently serving as an Associate Professor there. In 2011, he was a Visiting Lecturer at Asian Institute of Technology, Bangkok. From 2014 to 2016, he worked as a Marie Curie fellow at Brno University of Technology, Czech Republic. Dr. Chandra has published about 80 research papers in refereed journals and peer-reviewed conferences. He is a co-recipient of best short paper award at IEEE VNC 2014 held in Paderborn, Germany and delivered a keynote lecture in IEEE MNCApps 2012 held in Bangalore, India. His primary area of research is physical layer issues in wireless communication.

Akinchan Das received his M.Sc. degree from Vidyasagar University, West Bengal in the year 2007 and M.Tech. degree from West Bengal University of Technology in the year 2009. He is currently working as an Assistant Professor in the department of Electronic and Communication Engineering, Haldia Institute of Technology, Haldia, India. His research interests include optical wireless communication, different types of fading and networking.

Amin Ebrahimzadeh received his B.Sc. and M.Sc. degrees in Electrical Engineering from the University of Tabriz in 2009 and 2011, respectively. From 2011 to 2015, he was with the Sahand University of Technology (SUT), Iran. He is currently pursuing his Ph.D. in the Optical Zeitgeist Laboratory at the Institut National de la Recherche Scientifique (INRS), Montreal, QC, Canada. His research interests include fiber-wireless networks, Tactile Internet, teleoperation, artificial intelligence enhanced mobile edge-computing, and multi-robot task allocation. He is a recipient of the Doctoral Research Scholarship from the B2X Program for foreign students of Fonds de Recherche du Qubec-Nature et Technologies (FRQNT).

Muhammad Ishaq is a post graduate in Electrical Engineering from COMSATS University, Islamabad-Pakistan.He has two journal publication to his name. During his undergraduate study he worked on one of the nationally funded project named "Component wise design of C-Band Dual Polarized Doppler Radar Receiver. He has worked as a research assistant

217

at OPTO-Electronics and Photonics Research group (OERG),COMSATS University-Islamabad from Aug 2015 to Sep 2016.Currently, he is working as a Technical Manager at Pakistan Institute of Research and Development. His research interests preferably include Integrated Optics, Optical Electronics and communication, Optical network on chip.

Mohammad Kaleem completed Bachelor of Science in Electrical and Electronics Engineering from London South Bank University, UK, in 1997. He also got his MSEng in Telecommunication and Computer Networks Engineering from London South Bank University UK, in 1999. He has also worked as an IT consultant in British Telecommunications (BT) (Adastral park- Research Labs) on different projects, Voice /Multimedia over IP, DCU (Data collection unit), Colossus and DLE (digital local Exchange) Grooming. He completed his PhD in Optical Engineering, Hangzhou, China, in 2013. He served at National University of Sciences and Technology (College of E&ME), Rawalpindi, as an Assistant Professor (2002-14). Since 2014, he has been affiliated with the Department of Electrical Engineering, COMSATS, CIIT (Islamabad), where he is serving as an Asstt. Professor. His research interests are in Optoelectronics, Optical communications, Integrated photonics, Bio-sensors, Solar cells, Nano-photonics, Nonlinear optics, Biomedical sensing and environmental monitoring, wireless communication systems, DWDM Systems, cellular networks-/3G/4G/5G, LTE, SDH, SONET, WiMax, MANETs, WSN, simulation and performance analysis, network protocols and architecture.

Faisal Khaskheli is currently a PhD scholar at the institute of Information and Communication Technology, MUET, Jamshoro. he did his BE in telecommunication engineering in 2009 and ME in Electronic System Engineering in 2016 from Mehran University and has been teaching at the Dawood University of Engineering and Technology since September 2012 as a lecturer in the department of Telecommunication Engineering, having taught subjects including Digital Signal Processing, Digital Communication, Radio Frequencies and Mobile Networks, and Laser and Fiber Optic Communication. His areas of interest include Optical Wireless Communication and Electromagnetics.

Numan Kifayat is a graduate in Electrical Engineering(Electronics) from NUCES-FAST, Peshawar. During his coarse of under graduate study, he worked on a Nationally funded project in his final year named "Component wise design of C-Band Dual Polarized Doppler Radar Receiver." After his graduation, he pursued and completed Masters in Electrical Engineering(Electronic System) from COMSATS University, Islamabad-Pakistan. He has published two journal papers . His research interests include Electronic systems, Integrated Optics, Optical Electronics and communication..Currently, he is working as a PhD Fellow at KAIST, South Korea.

Martin Maier is a full professor with the Institut National de la Recherche Scientifique (INRS), Montréal, Canada. He was educated at the Technical University of Berlin, Germany, and received M.Sc. and Ph.D. degrees (both with distinctions) in 1998 and 2003, respectively. In the summer of 2003 he was a postdoc fellow at the Massachusetts Institute of Technology (MIT), Cambridge. He was a visiting professor at Stanford University, Stanford, from October 2006 through March 2007. Further, he was a co-recipient of the 2009 IEEE Communications Society Best Tutorial Paper Award. He was a Marie Curie IIF Fellow of the European Commission from March 2014 through February 2015. In March 2017, he received the Friedrich Wilhelm Bessel Research Award from the Alexander von Humboldt (AvH) Foundation in recognition of his accomplishments in research on FiWi enhanced networks. In May 2017, he was named as one of the three most promising scientists in the category "Contribution to a better society" of the Marie Skłodowska-Curie Actions (MSCA) 2017 Prize Award of the European Commission. He is the founder and creative director of the Optical Zeitgeist Laboratory (www.zeitgeistlab.ca).

220

Index

Ensure Quality Research is Introduced to the Academic Community

Become an IGI Global Reviewer for Authored Book Projects

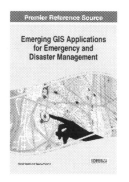

The overall success of an authored book project is dependent on quality and timely reviews.

In this competitive age of scholarly publishing, constructive and timely feedback significantly expedites the turnaround time of manuscripts from submission to acceptance, allowing the publication and discovery of forward-thinking research at a much more expeditious rate. Several IGI Global authored book projects are currently seeking highly qualified experts in the field to fill vacancies on their respective editorial review boards:

Applications may be sent to:
development@igi-global.com

Applicants must have a doctorate (or an equivalent degree) as well as publishing and reviewing experience. Reviewers are asked to write reviews in a timely, collegial, and constructive manner. All reviewers will begin their role on an ad-hoc basis for a period of one year, and upon successful completion of this term can be considered for full editorial review board status, with the potential for a subsequent promotion to Associate Editor.

If you have a colleague that may be interested in this opportunity, we encourage you to share this information with them.

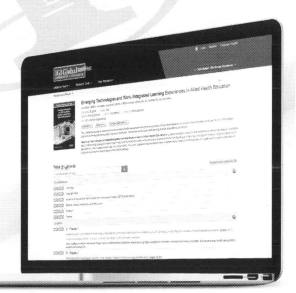

Printed in the United States
By Bookmasters